# HENRY VIII AND
# THE ENGLISH REFORMATION

# British History in Perspective
## General Editor: Jeremy Black

PUBLISHED TITLES

C. J. Bartlett  *British Foreign Policy in the Twentieth Century*
Jeremy Black  *Robert Walpole and the Nature of Politics in Early Eighteenth-Century Britain*
D. G. Boyce  *The Irish Question and British Politics, 1868–1986*
Keith M. Brown  *Kingdom or Province? Scotland and the Regal Union, 1603–1715*
John W. Derry  *British Politics in the Age of Fox, Pitt and Liverpool*
Ann Hughes  *The Causes of the English Civil War*
Ronald Hutton  *The British Republic, 1649–1660*
David Loades  *The Mid-Tudor Crisis, 1545–1565*
Diarmaid MacCulloch  *The Later Reformation in England, 1547–1603*
Keith Perry  *British Politics and the American Revolution*
A. J. Pollard  *The Wars of the Roses*
David Powell  *British Politics and the Labour Question, 1868–1990*
Michael Prestwich  *English Politics in the Thirteenth Century*
G. R. Searle  *The Liberal Party: Triumph and Disintegration, 1886–1929*
Paul Seaward  *The Restoration, 1660–1688*
Robert Stewart  *Party and Politics, 1830–1852*

FORTHCOMING TITLES

Ian Archer  *Rebellion and Riot in England, 1360–1660*
Rodney Barker  *Politics, Peoples and Government*
Jonathan Barry  *Religion and Society in England, 1603–1760*
A. L. Beier  *Early Modern London*
John Belchem  *Nineteenth-Century Radicalism*
A. D. Carr  *Medieval Wales*
Peter Catterall  *The Labour Party, 1918–1940*
David Childs  *Britain since 1939*
Eveline Cruickshanks  *The Glorious Revolution*
Anne Curry  *The Hundred Years' War*
John Davis  *British Politics, 1885–1931*
David Dean  *Parliament and Politics in Elizabethan and Jacobean England, 1558–1614*
Susan Doran  *English Foreign Policy in the Sixteenth Century*
David Eastwood  *England, 1750–1850: Government and Community in the Provinces*
Brian Golding  *The Normans in England 1066–1100: Conquest and Colonisation*
S. J. D. Green  *Religion and the Decline of Christianity in Modern Britain, 1880–1980*
Steven Gunn  *Early Tudor Government, 1485–1558*
Angus Hawkins  *British Party Politics, 1852–1886*
Alan Heesom  *The Anglo-Irish Union, 1800–1922*
Kevin Jefferys  *The Labour Party since 1945*
Hugh McLeod  *Religion and Society in England, 1850–1914*
Hiram Morgan  *Ireland in the Early Modern Periphery, 1534–1690*
Bruce Webster  *Scotland in the Middle Ages*
Ann Williams  *Kingship and Government in pre-Conquest England*
John Young  *Britain and European Unity since 1945*

# HENRY VIII
## AND THE
# ENGLISH REFORMATION

## RICHARD REX

MACMILLAN

First published 1993 by
THE MACMILLAN PRESS LTD
Houndmills, Basingstoke, Hampshire RG21 2XS
and London
Companies and representatives
throughout the world

ISBN 0–333–56748–X hardcover
ISBN 0–333–56749–8 paperback

A catalogue record for this book is available
from the British Library

Copy-edited and typeset by Cairns Craig Editorial, Edinburgh

Printed in Hong Kong

**Series Standing Order**

If you would like to receive future titles in this series as they are
published, you can make use of our standing order facility. To
place a standing order please contact your bookseller or, in case
of difficulty, write to us at the address below with your name
and address and the name of the series. Please state with which
title you wish to begin your standing order. (If you live outside
the United Kingdom we may not have the rights in your area, in
which case we will forward your order to the publisher concerned.)

Customer Services Department, Macmillan Distribution Ltd.
Houndmills, Basingstoke, Hampshire, RG21 2XS, England.

To Bettina

Se quanto infino a qui di lei si dice
fosse conchiuso tutto in una loda,
poca sarebbe a fornir questa vice.

(Dante, *Paradiso* xxx, ll. 16–18)

# CONTENTS

# PREFACE

The debts that authors incur in writing a short survey of this kind are if anything more extensive than those incurred in writing a lengthy monograph. For they must plunder shamelessly from the publications of rivals, colleagues, and predecessors in an attempt to paint a picture which is complete in outline, though not exhaustive in detail; careful in judgement, though not cautious to the point of triviality; and thought-provoking, though not thoughtlessly provocative. Within the inevitable constraints of space I have endeavoured to acknowledge my debts in the notes, but this is a suitable place to emphasise that anything which may be found of value in this study should be attributed not so much to the author as to that community of scholars whose collective researches over the past forty years have cast so much new light on the events here described. It is to the works of these scholars, listed in the bibliography, that readers should go for a fuller understanding of the Henrician Reformation and for other perspectives on it. I should however like to acknowledge a particular debt to those who have generously given time and thought to reading and commenting on drafts of this book: my wife Bettina, who has helped me stick at the task through a difficult year, and to whom the book is gratefully dedicated; my former research supervisor, Brendan Bradshaw, whose contribution can only be appreciated by those who, like me, have experience of the acute and perceptive eye he brings to any text; to the anonymous reader appointed by the publisher to go over the typescript, who will I hope appreciate from the changes made how helpful I found his or her comments; and to Colin Armstrong, Richard Beadle, Peter Cunich, Eamon Duffy, Nicholas Rogers, and my father Peter Rex, with whom I have discussed many aspects of this work, and who have saved me from many blunders and infelicities. A work of this length inevitably leaves out more than it can put in, and its errors are therefore likely to be sins of omission as often as sins of commission. However classified, they remain mine. I have greatly enjoyed writing this book. If readers enjoy it half as much, I will consider my time doubly well spent.

RICHARD REX
St John's College, Cambridge

# INTRODUCTION

'Of all the miracles and wonders of our time, I take the change of our sovereign lord's opinion on matters concerning religion to be even the greatest'.[1] So wrote Richard Morison in 1539, and that contemporary judgement has been echoed in varying terms by historians ever since. This book is a response to the challenge of explanation. However, as the salient events of Henry's Reformation are so well known through narratives of the English Reformation, histories of Tudor England, and biographies of the leading actors, it would be difficult to justify merely recapitulating them in a plain narrative.[2] This short survey therefore hopes to justify itself by adopting a different approach. It seeks to present Henry's Reformation in an analytical fashion, presenting in a logical order its leading ideas and its main features. There is an inherent risk in such an approach, namely that of confusing the reader's sense of chronology by hopping backwards and forwards in time. But the events are so compressed in time, and take place in such various yet interconnected fields, that the more natural choice of a narrative would confuse the reader at least as much by hopping from topic to topic, especially in the busy years of Thomas Cromwell. Before I begin, though, the claim that ideas and events are presented here in a logical order calls for some justification.

The single determining event of Henry VIII's Reformation was the establishment of the royal supremacy over the Church of England. Without this, the changes which ensued would hardly have been possible and, if possible, would certainly have been different. The royal supremacy is therefore the obvious place to start. Its introduction was merely one expression, although arguably the most dramatic, of the main political development of the early Tudor period. This was the expansion of royal authority and power. The reigns of the first two Tudors witnessed a significant increase in the scope and effectiveness of royal government, and a concomitant reduction of political counterweights to the monarchy. The role of the nobility was decisively changed, and Henry VIII reduced the church too to political subservience. The constitutional revolution of the 1530s finally reversed the victory which the church had achieved over the monarchy in the middle ages. The effective negation of the first clause of Magna Carta was underwritten by the anathematisation in 1538 of the medieval clerical hero St Thomas Becket, to whom the church had owed her victory. The new supremacy was justified in terms of divine law as revealed in the word of God, which was identified ever more precisely after the break with Rome as the written word of scripture. The 'word of God' became the basis not only for the supremacy itself, but also for the paramount duty of obedience which subjects owed to their king.

Henry's Reformation, then, was in a very real sense what Maurice Powicke called it – an act of State.[3] Almost all its further aims and achievements are integrally related to the extension of royal power on which they were based. This, surely, is the perception behind the highly charged claim of Reginald Pole that Thomas Cromwell won Henry's favour by proposing a legislative scheme which would not only secure the divorce he so desperately required but also make him the most powerful king England had ever known. The second chapter of this study will examine how the supreme head exercised his new power over his church: over its personnel, administration, and endowments. Having first of all outlined what the structure of that church was, it will argue that every change, from the dissolution of the monasteries to the massive extension of royal patronage, added to the wealth or influence of the crown.

But Henry's Reformation was not merely an act of State. It went beyond issues of jurisdiction and administration. The royal supremacy gave the king not only the power but the duty before God to advance true religion within his realm. This was a duty which Henry took seriously, and official interest soon turned to the question of popular religion. Much of the late medieval cult of the saints, which constituted a major part of the popular religion of the time, came to be redefined in the later 1530s as superstition and even idolatry. It was condemned in terms of the 'word of God' rhetoric adopted with the supremacy, and was systematically suppressed. The third chapter of this survey looks in some detail at this aspect of the Henrician Reformation. It proposes that the attack on the cult of the saints was not only made possible by the royal supremacy, but was also made imaginable and almost necessary by the very rhetoric with which the supremacy was justified.

The fourth chapter considers what was in many respects the natural corollary of the attack on traditional piety: the attempt to reshape English society on the basis of the 'word of God', that is, to promote a more uniform and literate religious culture in place of the oral and visual culture of the past. The centrepiece of this effort was the promulgation of an officially sanctioned English translation of the Bible which was, along with the royal supremacy, Henry's most enduring contribution to English religious history. The rhetoric of the 'word of God' almost dictated the policy. If the people were to live by the word of God, they had to know what it was. The provision of the Bible in the vernacular was designed to ensure that this essential knowledge was available. But there was more to it than the Bible alone. Educational theory and practice, the spread of literacy, vernacular devotional and liturgical publications, and the explosion of printed propaganda all played a part. But if the pen was mightier than the sword, it was an equally double-edged weapon. Henry's latter years are marked by an awareness that seditious forces could pervert the word of God. Censorship and a drive for uniformity mark the regime's determination to control the forces it had unleashed. Much of the success of the Henrician Reformation lay in its hijacking of the vernacular religious culture for its own political ends. Henry had no wish to sit back while others hijacked it for ends more radical still.

The fifth chapter examines the implications for religious belief, both official and popular, of the changes brought about by the Henrician Reformation. The desirability of religious uniformity was a commonplace of early modern political theory, although the tensions of Reformation and Counter-Reformation were to make limited toleration a practical necessity in many countries. Henry VIII never wavered in his determination to secure and enforce uniformity within his domains. His success, however, was far from total. When he ascended the throne England already had its small minority of religious dissidents, the Lollards. From the 1520s, England felt the effect of the new Protestant doctrines emanating from Germany and Switzerland. As long as Henry remained committed to Rome and Catholicism, the impact of these doctrines was limited. But once he departed from Rome, the innovators were encouraged to hope that he might go further, and gave enthusiastic support to his policies. His need for support over the divorce and the supremacy led him to turn a blind eye to some kinds of doctrinal tendentiousness. And the official adoption of Protestant or evangelical rhetoric to bolster the case against the papacy and the attack on popular religion gave the evangelical Reformers more than a foot in the door of the English Church. With the sympathies of such prominent figures as Anne Boleyn and Thomas Cromwell, these Reformers had an effect out of all proportion to their numbers. By the end of the 1530s, Henry had taken fright at the spread of heresy. Yet the conservative reaction of his last years, strong though it was, faced an uphill task. The attack on popular religion had undermined much of the commitment to traditional religious practice, and the new vernacular religious culture was, thanks to Cromwell and Cranmer, strongly tainted with Protestantism.[4]

In conclusion, although England still looked like a Catholic country when Henry VIII died in January 1547, its Catholicism had been compromised by schism and iconoclasm, the conservative clergy had been demoralised, and a committed Protestant minority was firmly established, with members and sympathisers in strategic places. The apparatus of monarchy, immeasurably strengthened over the previous twenty years, lay at the disposal of a Reformist faction which had captured the dying king. The Henrician Reformation had been a curious hybrid, driven by and riven with contradictory impulses. The Edwardian regimes of Somerset and Northumberland resolved those contradictions in the direction of revolution rather than of reaction. Henry's Reformation was thus the beginning of a far longer story. Yet it is as a story in itself that it shall be told in the following pages. I hope that the reader will find that this account makes some sense of those decisive yet often impermanent changes.

# 1

## DIVORCE AND SUPREMACY

Sixteenth-century Catholic historians of the English Reformation were convinced that its cause was Henry VIII's decision to divorce Catherine of Aragon and marry Anne Boleyn. Their Protestant opponents were happy to acclaim Henry's decision as the instrument of divine providence, resulting as it did not only in the abrogation of papal jurisdiction but also in the birth of the Protestant heroine and deliverer of the Anglican Church, Queen Elizabeth. More recent historians, preferring to 'assign deep causes for great events', have been reluctant to attach such importance to Henry's attempt to resolve the problem of the succession. Yet it can scarcely be denied that had Pope Clement VII agreed to annul the king's marriage to Catherine (or had the crisis been resolved in some uncontroversial way), the Act of Supremacy would not have been needed and there would have been no subsequent royal toleration of evangelical clergy (in the interests of supporting the divorce and the supremacy) to foster new doctrines at the highest levels in both the English church and the royal court. The divorce alone does not account for the ultimate triumph of Protestantism over Catholicism in England. But it was of the utmost importance in securing a foothold for evangelical preachers and their doctrines, and the idiosyncratic Reformation of Henry's reign is inconceivable without it. It is therefore essential to gain a clear idea of how personal and political relationships combined to induce the 'Defender of the Faith' to overthrow the authority which had granted him his title, and to transform himself into the 'Supreme Head of the Church'.

The primary motivation for the divorce lay not, as the Catholic polemicists would have had it, in Henry's wanton lust, nor purely, as he himself maintained, in scruples of conscience. The problem was the lack of a legitimate male heir to inherit the crown. Fifteen years of marriage to Catherine of Aragon had left Henry with only one surviving legitimate child, Princess Mary, born in 1516. Besides her he had acknowledged one bastard, Henry Fitzroy, son of Elizabeth Blount. English history offered no successful precedent for a regnant Queen, nor had a royal bastard ever succeeded his father. In the light of the Wars of the Roses, the dynasty looked insecure. Until 1525 a Yorkist pretender remained at large: Richard de la Pole, the 'White Rose' who died in the service of the French King at the Battle of Pavia, has seemed a marginal figure to historians, but when news of his death reached England an order was given for the bells to be rung in every church in London, and a State religious procession was held through the city. Only after de la Pole's death does Henry seem to have given consideration to any way of resolving the dynastic problem other than trusting to providence. His first thought was perhaps to prepare for the succession of his son. For in 1525 Fitzroy was plucked from relative obscurity to become, as Duke of Richmond, the premier nobleman of the realm. The title hints at the king's plans, for Richmond had been the title of his grandmother, Lady Margaret Beaufort, through whom the Tudors derived their claim to the throne. However, it was not long afterwards that Anne Boleyn first came to Henry's attention.[1] Her sister Mary had already been his mistress, but from the start Anne seems to have aimed higher. Precisely when Henry first gave serious thought to disencumbering himself of his barren wife will probably never be known. But the idea was hardly surprising. Throughout the middle ages kings with dynastic problems had resorted to such solutions, formerly at pleasure, but latterly by means of annulments and dispensations from the pope. Henry's own marriage had only been possible by virtue of a papal dispensation. On this turns the whole problem of Henry's conscience and divorce.

Catherine of Aragon had previously, though briefly, been married to Henry's elder brother, Arthur, Prince of Wales. After Arthur's death in 1502, Henry VII hoped to perpetuate the dynastic alliance with the ruling house of Spain by remarrying Catherine to his second son. But marriage to the wife of a deceased brother had been forbidden in the Catholic Church since earliest times, and a papal dispensation was therefore necessary. This was easily obtained from Pope Julius II, although the king then kept Catherine a virtual hostage for the remainder of his reign, leaving his options open to seek a better match for his son elsewhere. Once Henry VIII succeeded to the throne in 1509, though, he rushed through the solemnisation of his marriage to Catherine. When in the mid-1520s he began to reconsider his position, he examined the basis of the Church's prohibition of such marriages as his. It was founded upon two biblical texts, Leviticus 18:16 and 20:21, which stated respectively: 'Thou shalt not uncover the nakedness of thy brother's wife: it is thy brother's nakedness' and 'If a man shall take his brother's wife, it is an unclean thing: he hath uncovered his brother's nakedness: and they shall be childless'. The second text especially worried the king, for in it he could find an explanation of his own predicament: his lack of a male heir was a divine judgement. But despite the apparent clarity of the biblical texts, there was an obvious problem – the papal dispensation. If Henry was to free himself from his wife, this had to be impugned. Two routes were available. One was the legalistic route: to go through the dispensation with a fine-toothed comb and tease out some verbal or technical defect by which it could be invalidated. The radical route was to deny the validity of the dispensation in principle, that is, to argue that the biblical prohibition was of such authority that no pope could legitimately issue a dispensation from it.

From the start, Henry preferred the radical alternative. Although an initial consideration of his case by canon lawyers in May 1527 concentrated on the technical route, it is clear that as early as June Henry himself was more interested in the biblical texts. Cardinal Wolsey asked England's leading theologian, John Fisher (Bishop of Rochester and Chancellor of Cambridge University), for an opinion on whether or not the Levitical prohibition was a matter of 'natural law'. The point of the query was that according to scholastic theory 'natural law' was the highest type of law. It was the immutable ordinance of God by which creation was governed. While other kinds of law could justifiably be broken under certain circumstances – in dire need or by papal dispensation – a breach of natural law was always wrong and could not be permitted even by a pope. It must be emphasised that even the strongest supporters of papal authority agreed that the pope could not lawfully issue dispensations from natural law. So in pursuing the radical route to a divorce, Henry was in no sense impugning papal authority. Fisher's first response to the royal query was to report, truly enough, that theologians disagreed over the question. However, a few days later he produced a fuller account arguing that the reasons for seeing the Levitical prohibition as part of natural law were not compelling. By this time he had come across what was to remain throughout the ensuing controversy the main objection to the royal position: a biblical text (Deuteronomy 25:5) which, far from prohibiting marriage to a deceased brother's wife, actually commanded it under certain circumstances – circumstances which exactly fitted Henry's own case, namely that of a married brother dying without children. The argument Fisher adumbrated here and expanded subsequently was that God could not have commanded an act which he had banned under natural law and which was therefore intrinsically immoral. His fallback position, which also recurred throughout his writings on the divorce, was that since the interpretation of the texts in question was undeniably a matter of controversy, the final judgement must reside with the pope – who had *de facto* decided the matter by issuing the dispensation in the first place. This was the major obstacle to the royal case. In terms of the theology and canon law accepted by both parties, it was irrefutable. However, a way out had to be found. It was provided by a skilled but slightly unscrupulous scholar, a former protégé of Fisher called Robert Wakefield. Wakefield, the leading teacher of Hebrew in England, produced a novel interpretation of the relevant texts. According to him, the commandment in Deuteronomy to marry the wife of a childless deceased brother could apply only when the original marriage had not been consummated. For the Hebrew idiom used in the Levitical prohibitions to denote marriage, 'to uncover the nakedness' of a person, manifestly implied a sexual relationship. Only if the original marriage had been unconsummated could a brother who married his deceased brother's wife be deemed not to have uncovered the nakedness of his brother, and thus not to have transgressed against Leviticus. This interpretation offered the only escape from the dilemma, and it stayed at the centre of the royal case throughout the controversy. Although immense quantities of paper were over the next six years to be covered with further arguments, these arguments of Fisher and Wakefield were the crux. The issue was whether to qualify Leviticus in the light of Deuteronomy (Fisher's position) or Deuteronomy in the light of Leviticus (Wakefield's position).[2]

The diplomatic manoeuvres in pursuit of the divorce are too complex to be fully narrated here. But some account is essential. Cardinal Wolsey, faithful servant as ever, threw himself into the project. Hoping to exploit the divorce in order to secure a marriage alliance with France, he broached the matter on his embassy to François I in 1527. In the meantime, Henry was widening the scope of his search for academic support, recruiting those scholars who, as his 'spiritual learned counsel', were to produce reams of canonistic and theological argumentation on his behalf.[3] The most significant early moves were the negotiations with Rome that culminated in the dispatch in 1528 of two special ambassadors, Stephen Gardiner and Edward Foxe. Unfortunately for the king, the unfavourable political situation of the Pope left the chances of an easy resolution slim. For in 1527 troops of the Holy Roman Emperor Charles V had stormed Rome and rendered Clement VII a virtual prisoner within his fortress of Castel Sant' Angelo. This gave Charles considerable influence over papal policy. As Catherine of Aragon was the emperor's aunt, the pope was understandably reluctant to court his displeasure by inflicting on his family the dishonour of a divorce. Moreover, the objective of the divorce was still believed to be marriage to some French princess. Such an alliance would clearly be against the emperor's interests. Faced with the choice of offending one or other of Europe's most powerful monarchs, Clement took the only possible course: he played for time.

The royal ambassadors were to seek papal permission to have the case tried and judged by Wolsey in England. This was not unprecedented. The previous king of France, Louis XII, had rid himself of an unwanted wife in this way a mere thirty years before. After protracted negotiations, Gardiner obtained the concession – though not in such generous terms as had been hoped. Clement sent to England a papal legate, Cardinal Campeggio, with power to annul the old marriage and issue any necessary dispensations for a new one. He was to preside over the hearing with Wolsey. But Clement was still playing for time. Campeggio arrived in October and at once began to seek a settlement out of court. His idea was that Catherine should become a nun and thus by 'spiritual death' leave her husband free to marry again. The theological and legal viability of this solution was at best dubious, but it was never put to the test. Catherine refused on the grounds that her vocation was to marriage. Procrastination was therefore Campeggio's only option, and he managed to delay judicial proceedings until June 1529. Once they were under way, Catherine again wrecked his plans. Rejecting the authority of the tribunal on the grounds that she could not expect a fair trial in England, she refused to attend, and appealed to Rome. Despite this, the trial proceeded in desultory fashion for a few weeks until Campeggio – playing for time as ever – adjourned the court on 31 July 1529, arguing that it should follow the legal calendar of the Roman courts. Before the court could reconvene, letters came from Rome accepting Catherine's appeal and revoking the case.[4]

The revocation to Rome was the beginning of the end for Wolsey. As the events surrounding Wolsey's fall have received particularly close attention in recent research, they will not be further investigated here.[5] Suffice it to say that Henry threw him to the wolves who always await the political corpse of a disgraced minister. This marked a new stage in Henry's dealings with Rome. The Parliament which met soon after passed a handful of strongly anticlerical bills whose ulterior motive was to put pressure on the pope. Indeed, the toppling of Wolsey itself, it has recently been argued, was part of that same policy – an indication that Henry was prepared to strike even at a prince of the Church in pursuit of his aims.[6] The point was driven home late in 1530 when three bishops who appealed to the pope against the legislation (Fisher of Rochester, Nicholas West of Ely, and John Clerk of Bath and Wells) were briefly imprisoned.[7] Henry's subsequent policy on the divorce, however, was two-pronged. Some time after the failure of the legatine tribunal, a suggestion by a Cambridge theologian, Thomas Cranmer, came to Henry's ears. This was that the universities of Christendom should be canvassed for opinions on the Levitical prohibition and on the pope's authority to dispense from it. The campaign was soon under way, with opinions solicited from Cambridge, Oxford, Paris, and Orleans, among others. Precisely what Henry hoped to gain from this, apart from propaganda victories and the exertion of moral pressure on the pope, is far from clear. There may have been an element of 'Gallicanism' in the appeal to the universities, an attempt to force the pope's hand by producing against him a consensus of the Church. But the division of academic opinion and the notorious use of bribery by both sides left matters where they started. Most universities judged according to the instructions of their political masters. The English universities came down in Henry's favour – although opposition was vocal. The French universities, with the exception of Angers, judged likewise – with François I's decisive intervention. Henry did not consult the Spanish universities, but Catherine's supporters found it rewarding to do so. In Italy and Germany, the outcome depended on financial inducements or the influence of local political authorities.[8]

In Rome itself, delay was still the policy. And it has been plausibly argued that Henry, fearful of an adverse decision, was beginning to share the pope's preference. From late 1530 new notes are struck in the royal campaign for the divorce – questions about the nature of papal jurisdiction over the king, denials that a king of England could be lawfully summoned outside his realm, and hints that an unsatisfactory papal decision would be referred to a future general council (a familiar recourse of kings in dispute with popes). The Duke of Suffolk's claim in September that Henry was emperor and pope in his own kingdom is perhaps the earliest hint of this from sources around the king. At much the same time, Henry was telling the papal nuncio that he could not be summoned to judgement outside his realm, and next month he consulted a committee of lawyers and clergy on whether Parliament could empower the English clergy to grant the divorce irrespective of the pope.[9] In the fascinating collection of texts relating to the divorce, 'Collectanea satis copiosa', are a number of passages called in evidence of such claims, and also of more general claims about the prerogatives of provincial or national churches. It was from material accumulated here that the doctrine of the royal supremacy over the church was to be derived.[10] The importance of all this activity is hard to assess. Its objective was probably still to have the case tried in England. 'Constitutional' claims were being advanced not out of commitment to principles but out of political exigency. It was becoming clear that the divorce case was a major jurisdictional conflict. But it must be emphasised that even at this point, in 1530, no absolute autonomy from the papacy was being formally claimed.

The emergence of the doctrine of the royal supremacy is inextricably bound up with the pursuit of the divorce. In analysing the doctrine, it is essential to distinguish it from a number of the ideas and images with which it was successfully foisted upon the English people. The doctrine that within his realms a king was not only the head of State (to use a slightly anachronistic term) but also the head of the church – that he was the source of not only temporal but spiritual jurisdiction – was unprecedented. Even Roman law, which gave the emperor wide powers in ecclesiastical matters, went nowhere near so far – and in fact recognised that the bishop of Rome was the 'head of all the holy churches'. The notion of 'imperial monarchy', then much in vogue among European monarchs, which extended to kings the prerogatives accorded the emperor under Roman law, was, as the examples of the Holy Roman Empire, Castile and France illustrate, compatible, despite recurrent tensions, with all the usual Catholic teachings on the papacy except for that of the pope's claim to depose errant rulers. The English common law, which also upheld the king's pure sovereignty, was similarly compatible, as generations of English kings had shown. Outside the Catholic Church, none of the Protestant leaders proposed any doctrine like the royal supremacy. Luther and Melanchthon concluded that Henry had simply usurped the powers of the pope, and Calvin, writing many years later, thought Henry's title blasphemous. Erastus, writing in the 1560s, perhaps came closest among Continental Protestants to the Henrician position, but there is a subtle difference between 'Erastianism' – the subordination of the church to the State as a sort of government department – and the royal supremacy, which left the church as an independent estate, but vested its headship in the person of the king.

The doctrine of the royal supremacy emerged gradually in the context of a campaign to persuade the English clergy to support Henry's call for a divorce and thus put further pressure on the pope. The degree of support for Catherine among the clergy, especially the higher clergy, was disturbing, and if the policy of resolving the problem within the kingdom was to be successful, the clergy had to be brought to heel. So in 1530 a writ of praemunire was issued against a group of English prelates, including Fisher and other prominent supporters of Catherine. Shortly afterwards, the entire clergy was charged under the praemunire statute for the simple crime of having exercised their spiritual jurisdiction. The underlying justification for these proceedings can be discerned in a work published in 1530 by a leading common lawyer enjoying close contacts with the king's council. Christopher St German's second *Dialogue between a Doctor and a Student* launched the novel argument that there was little or nothing in contemporary ecclesiastical legal practice that properly fell outside the jurisdiction of the king's courts. The concept he developed of the subordination of canon law to common law and thus to the king was an indispensable element in the emerging royal supremacy.[11] It was also essential in the manipulation of the ancient statute of praemunire against a target it had never been designed to hit. The bombshell was dropped in January 1531. Southern Convocation wilted under the assault and begged pardon from the king, sweetening their petition with a *douceur* of well over £100,000. In return, pardon was granted under a special statute for all past offences (another statute gave a free pardon to the laity). The act made no provision about future offences and left unresolved the problem raised by the continued existence of both the spiritual courts and the praemunire statute. Although no new claims were voiced during these proceedings, there was an implicit claim of jurisdiction over the entire machinery of the spiritual courts by the mere fact of making them the subject of statute and pardon. If nothing else, the possibility of similar proceedings in future remained. From this broken Convocation Henry then extracted the concession of the title 'supreme head' of the Church of England. In the event, this was granted only with the rider 'as far as the law of Christ allows' – with a significant minority registering dissent. Nevertheless, the first breach in the clergy's defences had been made.[12]

Printed propaganda played a major role both in preparing opinion for the divorce and in attacking the jurisdiction of the clergy. Late in 1530 the dearly bought opinions of the foreign universities were divulged in a proclamation which was Henry's first public statement on his matrimonial problem. They were reissued with a lengthy treatise on the king's marriage in April 1531, under the title *Gravissimae Censurae*. An English version was available later that year, and this was followed by several shorter works in favour of the divorce. A fourteenth-century anticlerical tract, the *Dialogue between a Knight and a Clerk*, was printed in Latin (and later English) by Thomas Berthelet, the king's printer, around 1531. St German's *Dialogue* was reprinted several times, supplemented by his *New Additions* (1531), and in 1533 he published a lengthy attack on clerical privilege, *A Treatise concerning the Division between the Spiritualty and the*

*Temporalty*, which ran to five editions by 1537. When Thomas More took up the cudgels against him, a voluminous controversy ensued: More published his *Apology* (1533); St German his *Salem and Bizance* (1533); More his *Debellation of Salem and Bizance* (1533); and St German concluded with *Additions of Salem and Bizance* (1534). It was in this context that royal policy unfolded.[13] The St German programme, as we might call it, was embodied in the 'Supplication against the Ordinaries', a document, probably drafted by Thomas Cromwell, presented to Henry by the Commons on 18 March 1532. This formed part of a royal campaign to secure the unconditional submission of the clergy to royal jurisdiction. It was presented to Convocation in April, and elicited a reasoned reply. In May, however, an irate king demanded that Convocation submit all past and future legislation to royal scrutiny and assent – in effect, that the Church of England abdicate its legislative autonomy in spiritual matters. What has been aptly described as a 'Rump Convocation' acceded to his demands on 15 May. Around the same time, a bill came before Parliament designed to cut off the payment of annates to the pope. The Act in Restraint of Annates was to take effect in a year's time at the king's discretion if the pope had not earned a reprieve – presumably by granting a divorce. But its most ominous provision was that, should the pope refuse to confirm an episcopal nomination because of the non-payment of annates, no retaliatory excommunication or interdict he might issue was to take effect in England. This was, potentially at least, an unprecedented attack on papal authority.

The diplomatic, legislative, and literary activities of the king and his supporters in the years 1529–34 could easily be seen as a 'high road' to the supremacy. They were no such thing. The path to the supremacy was a tortuous one, and while nobody disputes the importance of Thomas Cromwell in bringing it about, there remains room for debate about when, if ever, irrevocable decisions were taken. The ideological origins of the supremacy doctrine were equally complex.[14] It had roots in the conflict between common law and canon law; it drew on fourteenth-century conflicts between papacy and temporal princes; it owed something to Roman law concepts of imperial authority; it gained strength from the focussing of moral and spiritual aspirations on the monarchy; and this diverse material was integrated in an image of kingship modelled on that found in the Old Testament. It is hardly worth asking, and certainly impossible to answer, in precisely whose mind these various skeins first came together in what was to become the English royal supremacy, or at precisely what stage the 'turning-point' came.[15] Thomas More detected a crucial change in the submission of the clergy on 15 May 1532 and resigned the next day. Yet that submission did not receive statutory confirmation and thus become binding under English law until late 1534. Stephen Gardiner, a far from negligible figure in the royal counsels, was apparently unaware of the direction policy was taking as late as April 1532. By drafting Convocation's answer to the Supplication against the Ordinaries he brought down upon himself the king's wrath – hardly a characteristic mistake for such a tactful and subtle diplomatist.[16] As far as one can tell, the royal supremacy, like most major policies, was made 'on the run'.

Even after the submission, royal policy seems strangely unhurried. Negotiations with France followed whose apparent aim was to bring French pressure to bear on the pope, as if the plan was still to obtain a papal divorce. It was perhaps only with the death in August 1532 of the Archbishop of Canterbury, William Warham (whose initial support for the divorce had latterly become less than lukewarm), that a unilateral solution came within reach. In September, Cromwell was already drafting the bill against appeals to Rome that would enable the case to be resolved within England. Only after this it seems, perhaps with a firm promise and sure hope of marriage, did Anne Boleyn surrender to Henry's advances. When by the end of January 1533 she proved to be pregnant, proceedings at once become marked by haste. Henry married Anne in a secret ceremony. He decided that the serviceable Cranmer should be the next Archbishop of Canterbury, and the requisite bulls were sought from Rome. The hapless pope complied, anxious to placate Henry as far as possible. In the meantime, the Act against Appeals was passed in March. At the same time, Convocation was invited to declare that marriage to a deceased brother's wife was utterly unlawful in cases where the original marriage had been consummated, and that the pope had no power to dispense from this prohibition. Once this enabling legislation was in place, preparations for a trial began. Cranmer summoned both parties to a tribunal and, after due process, declared the king's old marriage null and void on 23 May. Within a week he had validated the new marriage, and on 1 June there followed the triumphal coronation of Anne Boleyn as the new queen.

The divorce and the second marriage were achieved not only in defiance of the papacy but in the face of significant opposition or at least dissent at home. Henry's pursuit of a divorce was almost universally unpopular, and Catherine was soon cast as the wronged wife. Women in particular sympathised with her – when two royal emissaries came to Oxford in 1530 to elicit an opinion on the marriage, they were pelted with rubbish by the women of the town – and she had many friends among the higher clergy. She was on good terms with some prominent noble families, such as the Poles and the Courtenays. Moreover, the divorce was an open invitation to papal retaliation, and Clement VII issued a bull excommunicating Henry which came into effect in September 1533. The crux was what response such a move would find among the English people, especially as Catherine's powerful nephew Charles V might be tempted to intervene. It was therefore essential to defuse domestic opposition. The spiritual leader of Catherine's supporters, John Fisher, was placed under house arrest the day after Convocation paved the way for a divorce, and was not released until it was a *fait accompli*. But a potentially far more serious focus of opposition existed in close proximity to London – Elizabeth Barton, the Holy Maid of Kent. This charismatic nun had taken a strong line against the divorce, the attack on the church, and the protection and patronage of clerics of dubious orthodoxy. One need look no further back than Joan of Arc to see what a popular peasant visionary might achieve with clerical support. Fisher had accepted the validity of her prophetic claims from an early date, as had Warham – whom she probably dissuaded from supporting the divorce. Such was her reputation that she even obtained audiences with Wolsey and the king. Based as she was in one of England's more politically volatile counties, Henry cannot have looked on her without disquiet. This must have turned to dismay when she began to warn that if he put away Catherine he would cease to be king in six months. She was arrested and interrogated. Her public recantation and humiliation in November 1533, when she admitted that her prophesies were fraudulent, was more than a personal act of revenge by Henry. It not only discredited her and her friends, but was also the first stage in a prolonged campaign to secure consent to the settlement of the succession and to the constitutional changes necessary to achieve and maintain it.[17]

The dynastic settlement was from the start legally and politically insecure. For centuries England had accepted the final jurisdiction of the papacy in matrimonial cases and much else besides. Although the submission of the clergy and the judgements of Convocation in May 1533 had been designed to circumvent papal jurisdiction, their legal basis was far from clear. The Act against Appeals was the only statutory backing for what had occurred, but while it theoretically curtailed any further legal proceedings over the divorce, it left many questions open. The crisis was resolved by the policy of 'reform by statute' associated with the name of Thomas Cromwell.[18] In a series of statutes running from the Act against Appeals in 1533 to the Act against the Authority of Rome in 1536, he and his king carried out a constitutional revolution. They swept away the legal basis for the exercise of papal authority in England, securely established the royal supremacy, and resolved the underlying dynastic problem. Nor did reform by statute stop there. The potential of statute as an instrument of the royal will was made manifest by the success of the legislation of this period, and throughout the rest of Cromwell's ascendancy and, to a lesser extent, the rest of Henry's reign, statute remained the favoured, though by no means the only, tool for change. It is important to remember that it was statute, not Parliament, whose strength was established in this period.

Although Cromwell has been seen as an exponent of parliamentary government, his essentially monarchical predilections are surely reflected not only in what he did for Henry but also, and more explicitly, in the way his client, William Marshall, transmuted Marsilius of Padua's advocacy of representative government into an exposition of absolute monarchy.[19] The reform statutes were drafted and pushed through by Cromwell and the king's council. There was discussion and debate in Parliament, even occasional opposition and amendment. But concessions by the regime were few. Parliament was a tool. It was there to make law of the royal will, and that was what it did. However, Cromwell's policy helped establish the supremacy and omnicompetence of statute law (against which Thomas More took a stand in 1535). This was a major constitutional change, and, like all constitutional changes, was a reflection of political conflict – in this case, a conflict which was far from over. On the other side, the pope continued to assert his supremacy (a claim which still had significant temporal content), and the liberties of the Church of England as guaranteed by Magna Carta still had their defenders (among them More). The twin dangers of imperial invasion and domestic rebellion under papal sanction offered a prospect which shaped home and foreign policy for most of the 1530s. Abroad, England sought allies among the Emperor's enemies – France and the Lutheran princes of the Schmalkaldic League. At home, an unprecedented programme of legislation and an administrative effort unparalleled since the Domesday survey consolidated allegiance to the new order. It is this domestic effort which most directly bears on religious questions.

The first step in securing the new order was the Act of Succession, passed early in 1534. This confirmed the former Queen's reduced rank, bastardised her daughter, and imposed on all adult male subjects an oath (whose text was not specified) to the new dynastic settlement and to 'the whole effects and contents of this act'. A commission to administer the oath was issued to the Archbishop of Canterbury, the Lord Chancellor, and the Dukes of Norfolk and Suffolk on the day of royal assent, 30 March 1534, and was soon being implemented. The same session of Parliament passed a number of other important acts. The Act for the Submission of the Clergy gave statutory effect to Convocation's submission of 1532, empowered the king to establish a commission to revise English canon law, and established the right of appeal from any ecclesiastical court to the king's court of Chancery. The Act of Attainder against the Holy Maid of Kent and her adherents was a particularly important part of the enforcement strategy. Humiliation of the Maid did not satisfy Henry. As so often, he exacted the ultimate penalty from his opponents. Since the normal course of a trial for treason was deemed unlikely to succeed (the Maid had after all revealed her allegedly treasonable prophecies to the king in person), it was decided to proceed by way of Parliamentary attainder (a declaration of treasonable guilt). Attainder offered several advantages to the regime. Cromwell extended to the bill his novel practice of tacking propagandistic preambles onto parliamentary legislation. In this case, he included the bulk of the sermon preached at the Maid's public exposure in November. In addition, attainder afforded the chance to strike at bigger political game – Thomas More and John Fisher, who were included on a charge of misprision (concealment) of treason in the bill that went before the Lords. More had always exercised the utmost circumspection in his dealings with the Maid, and was able to convince the Lords to delete his name from the bill – an event unique in the crowded annals of Henrician attainder. Fisher had not been so careful and was not so lucky. Although his defence, that he could hardly be guilty of concealing what was both public and royal knowledge, was morally sound, it was not legally so. The general object of the exercise was to soften up the opposition before the oath was administered. The particular aim with regard to Fisher and More was to induce them to acquiesce in the king's proceedings. In their case, it did not work. They refused the oath to the succession when it was proffered in April. But on the public stage, the execution of the Maid with six companions on Monday 20 April ensured ready compliance. The oath was presented to the citizens of London the very same day, with the dismembered corpses of the victims displayed on the city gates. The commissioners who took the oath around the country met equally little resistance. Gardiner, for example, informed Cromwell of how he and his fellow commissioners had assembled the gentry, heads of religious houses, and parochial clergy of Hampshire at Winchester early in May in order to administer the oath to them and to obtain from them lists of every male in the county over fourteen years of age (who were to be sworn subsequently by commissioners touring the county) – all of which was done 'very obediently'.[20] Over the country as a whole, a few senior clergy (including three canons of the royal chapel at Windsor) followed Fisher in refusing the oath, but More was the only layman to do so. Oddly enough, the Act of Succession laid down no penalties for refusal. All the council could do was gaol dissidents and hope they bowed under pressure.

When the Reformation Parliament reconvened on 3 November 1534, it returned at once to the legislative programme with the Act of Supremacy, which gave statutory recognition to Henry's new title as Supreme Head of the Church of England, and clarified the vast extent of his jurisdiction in this capacity. The act was not unopposed. According to a much later recollection of Stephen Gardiner's, Parliament 'was with most great cruelty constrained to abolish and put away the primacy from the bishop of Rome'.[21] This short act, which was carefully phrased to avoid seeming to confer either title or jurisdiction, attributed to the king powers if anything more extensive and less subject to restraint than those previously exercised by the pope. Strangely, it laid down no penalties for denying or opposing these powers. Two Acts of Attainder legitimated the imprisonment which had already been the fate of those who had refused the oath to the succession earlier in the year, and the Act of Treasons early in 1535 laid down legal penalties for 'maliciously' denying the royal supremacy. This act too met with 'much sticking' in the Commons, over either the insertion or the interpretation of 'maliciously' – a qualification which, though given great importance in the debate, subsequently turned out to be entirely vacuous.[22] Although some concept of treasonable words had previously been known under English law, there was nevertheless a widespread and justified feeling that this act represented a massive extension of the concept of treason in applying it to merely verbal offences.

The new Act of Treasons gave Cromwell the tool he needed for checking dissent by means of judicial terror. Its first victims were from the cream of English monasticism, the Carthusians. Three Carthusian priors presented themselves to Cromwell to protest that they were unable to accept the supremacy. They were rapidly put through the legal mill, to be followed in short order by three confrères. Their sorry fate was used in a final attempt to induce Fisher and More to capitulate. But More's silence baffled even the new law – only with the 1536 Act against the Authority of Rome did it become treason to refuse an oath to the royal supremacy. Fisher was not More's equal in caution or guile. He either slipped or was tricked into a forthright denial. Any denial of the supremacy, it transpired, was as such malicious, and his defence was therefore shattered. He was convicted in June 1535, and More a week or two later (on the perjured evidence of Richard Rich, who was later to provide the equally decisive and implausible testimony against Cromwell). They were executed with little delay, to the horror of the academic community of Europe, Catholic and Protestant alike. Such was the outcry that Cromwell and Henry found it necessary to justify the deed. Cromwell circulated a letter to all English representatives abroad, alleging unspecified treasons against the two martyrs and passing over the true content of their indictments. Gardiner was deputed to provide a more intellectually satisfying defence of Fisher's execution, though his effort did him little credit.[23] And the official line served only to elicit a withering reply from a German friend of the victims, John Cochlaeus.

Cromwell's regime appreciated the power of the press and the pulpit to a greater extent than any previous English government.[24] The power of the press was exploited to the full in an attempt to secure obedience to the royal supremacy, with a series of publications ranging from high academic theology through racy polemic (*A Little treatise against the muttering of some papists in corners*) and exhortatory homilies (Simon Matthew's

*Sermon*) to brief declaratory articles (the *Articles of the Council*). The fullest defence of the supremacy was Edward Foxe's *De Vera Differentia*, intended for the academic and European audience rather than for domestic consumption – and hence not translated into English for many years. Foxe's work was a direct product of the researches carried out by a whole team of scholars under his leadership during the divorce controversy. Much of its material had been gathered in the manuscript 'Collectanea satis copiosa'.[25] It was notable for its attempt to provide a historical basis for the supremacy, and took a high view of the royal office and dignity, founded on predominantly Old Testament texts together with the inevitable Romans 13, setting against this a conception of the papacy as a purely human rather than divine institution. The treatise owed much to medieval imperial and contemporary Protestant antipapal rhetoric. It thus stood at one extreme of contemporary English attitudes to the papacy, which varied quite widely. Some propagandists, like Foxe, availed themselves wholesale of Protestant antipapal rhetoric: Cranmer, for example, decried the pope as Antichrist early in 1536.[26] The conservatives, however, confined themselves to presenting the pope as tyrant and usurper. Their attack was moral and historical rather than theological, although some were happy to grapple with the Petrine texts on which papal claims were founded. The best-known conservative defence of the supremacy was the pamphlet with which Stephen Gardiner won back royal favour late in 1535. His treatise *On True Obedience* struck the key note of Henry's Reformation. Its case rested on divine law (as illustrated by the Old Testament) and on perfect obedience to it (as illustrated by the life and teaching of Christ in the New Testament). In presenting Henry's divorce as conscientious obedience to the Levitical law, Gardiner was not indulging in mere flattery. He was unlocking the secret of Henry's conscience: a firm belief in obedience to divine law is the principle which underlies many of the apparently unrelated initiatives of his Reformation. On the royal supremacy as such, the argument remained obstinately on a general level: true obedience entails obeying both divine law and divinely instituted authorities, supreme among which are princes, God's images and vicars on earth, whose headship carries over into the realm considered as church, and upon whose authority scripture places no limits other than divine law. Consideration of papal claims was restricted to breezy generalities. Instead of grappling with the papal arguments, Gardiner simply listed the major 'Petrine texts' and blithely announced that their true interpretation had recently come to light – without even saying what it was. And despite the bluntly antipapal rhetoric of the work, Gardiner perhaps kept his options open for a future reversal of policy by admitting that Peter's spiritual gifts made him in some sense 'first' and even 'supreme' among the apostles, and by expressing willingness in principle to respect a supremacy of some kind were the contemporary papacy only to live up to it.

Obedience was the central theme of the propaganda for the royal supremacy and indeed of the entire Henrician Reformation. To some extent this betrayed the insecurity of the regime. In the 'seditious time' which followed the break with Rome, there was a constant fear of rebellion and invasion, which the Pilgrimage of Grace did nothing to allay. The obsession with obedience evinced by so much of the official literature of this period was justified by the circumstances. But it was more than this. Many of the religious reforms introduced under Henry can be explained in terms of the need to establish and confirm the obedience of his subjects. In a sense, obedience was both cause and effect. The habit of obedience to the powers that be was already deeply ingrained in English hearts and minds, and this was what allowed Henry's changes to take effect. The introduction of the royal supremacy led to an increased emphasis on obedience in the theology and preaching of the Church of England, while subsequent religious changes not only drew strength from that reinforcement of obedience, but were themselves often designed to reinforce it further. The imposition of the English Bible was expressly intended to foster obedience by revealing to people the biblical foundations for what was now made the paramount Christian virtue. Henrician propaganda about preaching the 'word of God' might sound at first like evangelical enthusiasm for the

25

plain text of scripture. But it was code – code broken for us by a revealing comment of Richard Sampson's: 'the word of God is, obedience to the king rather than to the pope'.[27] In many ways, this theme represented the adoption into official rhetoric of the argument proposed by William Tyndale in his seminal work *The Obedience of a Christian Man* – which Henry had apparently read with approval. Tyndale of course had been responding to the charge that the new doctrines entailed sedition – a claim only too plausible in the aftermath of the German Peasants' War of 1525. He adapted Lutheran political theory for an English readership, maintaining that scripture inculcated obedience even to wicked rulers in all things that were not directly contrary to God's law, and that even in such cases resistance should be passive rather than active. For Tyndale, however, as for Luther, Christian liberty and faith alone remained at the heart of the Gospel. Henry's Reformation in contrast made obedience the centre not only of its political but also of its religious thought. Gardiner's *On True Obedience*, as a Lutheran critic noted, in effect substituted 'obedience alone' for 'faith alone' as the channel of salvation. Cromwell's propagandist Richard Morison made the point even more succinctly in the wake of the Pilgrimage of Grace, observing 'Obedience is the badge of a true Christian man', and claiming that of all the commandments, the most necessary was – 'Obey ye your king'.[28]

The campaign of propaganda which justified the supremacy was waged on several fronts. Among its most important elements was the rewriting of English history. The Act of Appeals itself appealed to 'sundry old authentic histories and chronicles' in support of its claim that England was an empire. But the medieval chronicles of England were clerical in origin, and tended to take a clerical and even papalist view of several crucial historical episodes. Their celebration of the mission of St Augustine at the behest of Pope Gregory I, which began the evangelisation of the English, was typical of their benevolent view of the papacy. By recording the mythical despatch of missionaries by Pope Eleutherius to King Lucius of Britain in the second century they were able to present the British church as a direct foundation of the Church of Rome. The murder of Thomas Becket in 1170 was presented as martyrdom for ecclesiastical liberties, and the papal interdict of the realm under King John as a due punishment for his tyranny and immorality. In the 1530s this papalist view of history came under heavy fire. As the need to establish royal supremacy and independence of Rome became pressing, the role of the papacy in English history was either written out or written off. The mission of St Augustine was played down or portrayed as the origin of papal corruptions. Greater emphasis was laid instead on the mythical accounts of the origins of British Christianity. The episode of Lucius and Eleutherius was reinterpreted to show the primacy of royal initiative: Lucius invited the Pope to send Roman law, but Eleutherius, calling him a 'vicar of God' and admitting his sovereign jurisdiction, assured him that, since he had the Bible, he had all that was needed to rule his kingdom justly. For the most radical Henrician revisionist, John Bale (who called for a full rewriting of English history in 1544),[29] even the limited role of Eleutherius was too much, and he went back to the mythical arrival of Joseph of Arimathea in Britain in order to separate the origin of Christianity in these islands from all papal taint. Still more drastic revision was applied to the stories of Becket and John. In 1538, Becket was publicly proclaimed a traitor. The papal interdict under King John was represented as unwarranted interference in English affairs. Pope Innocent became the tyrant, and John an unfortunate patriot, persecuted by the pope, harried by the clergy, and murdered by a monk. Fabyan's *New Chronicles* (1516) were reprinted in 1542 with substantial alterations to the accounts of Becket and John. All mentions of Henry II's 'tyranny' or Becket's saintliness and martyrdom were excised, while the Parliament of Northampton which sparked off their quarrel was now said to have been called 'for the reformation of many privileges that the clergy had'. A moralistic passage ascribing John's misfortunes to his 'disobedience' to the pope was omitted. The disappearance of the traditional history is symbolised in the fact that the most popular pre-Reformation chronicles, Higden's *Polychronicon* and Caxton's *Brut*, were not reprinted after 1530. The new view of history is best seen in Hall's *Chronicle*, written under Henry VIII though not published until the following reign. Although it did not go back beyond Henry IV, its commitment to the Tudor dynasty and its anticlerical tone embody the essence of Henrician historiography.[30] And perhaps the most effective rewriting of a single episode was Bale's morality play *King John* (written during his assocation with Cromwell in the later 1530s), which not only presented the new version of his reign in lively fashion, but ended with the figure of Imperial Majesty (Henry VIII) striding on stage to foretell the eventual vindication of John's stand against papal tyranny.

The image of English kingship which Bale put on stage had undergone profound changes in the 1530s. The theme had again been stated in the programmatic Act against Appeals: 'this realm of England is an empire'. The claim to imperial status was a claim to full sovereignty, the denial of any superior jurisdiction on earth.[31] It was not an entirely original claim on the part of the English monarchy. The 'crown imperial' had appeared on English coinage since the reign of Henry VII, and references to the 'imperial crown' pepper early Tudor English documents. But the Act against Appeals was, as Professor Elton argues, the first claim of imperial status for the realm as such rather than the crown, and imperial pretensions were undoubtedly advanced with a greater sense of purpose from this time.[32] This can be seen even in the king's favoured style of address. 'Highness', 'grace', or 'sovereign lord' had long sufficed as descriptions of the king in statutes, proclamations, and similar official documents. But in 1534 the more grandiose term 'majesty' (already current unofficially) appeared for the first time in both statutes and proclamations, and henceforth appeared so consistently as to betray official instigation. As a translation of the Latin 'maiestas', the property of the emperor under Roman law, it had obvious imperial connotations. The growing imperial pretensions of the king were part and parcel of the cult of monarchy which accompanied the extension of royal power under the early Tudors. This cult was expressed in a host of media, such as the coinage – Henry VII was the first English king to adopt the Renaissance fashion of issuing coins bearing his own image – and royal portraiture as such – Henry VIII is the first English king of whom we have full-length portraits. The royal supremacy was part of this cult, marking a return to earlier medieval traditions of sacral or theocratic kingship. Henry VII had begun the sacralisation of English kingship by resuming the custom of touching for the king's evil and by pursuing the cause of canonisation of Henry VI. Although Henry VIII apparently did not share his father's enthusiasm for their unfortunate predecessor, it is noteworthy that the title he won from the pope in 1521, 'Defender of the Faith', bore a strong resemblance to the liturgical title accorded Henry VI, 'Defender of the Church' (with which Henry VIII's title was often in practice confused). The adoption of the royal supremacy in the 1530s was both the culmination and a reorientation of this sacralisation. It is hardly surprising that the 1530s saw the reappearance of two early medieval epithets for the sacral king: 'vicar of God' and 'image of God'. When Thomas Paynell assured his king that God would not permit rebellion 'to prevail against a Christian prince, his very image in earth', he was expressing an altogether new level of respect and worship for the royal person. And Sir Thomas Elyot detected 'a divine influence or spark of divinity' in Henry's majestic performance at the trial of the heretic John Lambert late in 1538, while his dedication of his *Dictionary* to the king expatiated at some length on the divinity of kingship.[33] But the most important element of the new sacral kingship was the systematic and programmatic use of Old Testament models to justify and define the supremacy.[34] The jurisdiction of a David or a Solomon over the priests of the Temple was invoked to confirm Henry's power over his clergy, and in royal iconography Henry began to appear in the guise of these biblical figures – most famously as Josiah. Many of his later religious policies, as we shall see, can best be understood as attempts to fulfil the role in which he cast himself.

At the popular level, the sermon was undoubtedly the main medium of propaganda for the royal supremacy. The break with Rome unleashed a wave of preaching on a single topic perhaps unparalleled in English history. Following up the administration of the oath to the succession, instructions went out to clergymen throughout the land laying down the proper form of bidding prayers in church and imposing the obligation of preaching in favour of the king's proceedings. Every preacher was to 'preach once in the presence of his greatest audience against the usurped power of the bishop of Rome'. The campaign was soon under way. One of Cranmer's chaplains was explaining to the people of St Alban's in March 1535 how they had long been deceived by the bishop of Rome.[35] The recalcitrant inmates of the London Charterhouse were singled out for special attention, and a succession of talented Catholic preachers was sent early in 1535 to win them round: Archbishop Lee, Bishops Gardiner and Tunstall, and Dr Buckmaster (vice-chancellor of Cambridge). The campaign was intensified on 3 June 1535, when royal letters instructed all bishops to ensure that priests with cures of souls preached every Sunday and feast day on the royal supremacy and the renunciation of the bishop of Rome. These instructions seem to have been put into effect promptly. Rowland Lee, Bishop of Coventry and Lichfield, promised that, although he himself had never preached before, he and his chaplains would obey zealously. In fact he continued to fight shy of the pulpit, although he caused his chaplains to preach regularly on his judicial tour of the West Midlands. Cuthbert Tunstall, writing from Durham, was able to tell Cromwell smugly that he had begun to preach on the supremacy even before the instructions arrived. Archbishop Lee of York lamented to Cromwell that there were few preachers in his diocese up to the task. But for the less able he wrote and circulated a prepared statement. Gardiner too circulated a prepared text to the clergy of his diocese, while Longland had one printed. Nor were the bishops alone active. Archdeacon Thomas Magnus took an Austin Friar with him to preach the supremacy in his visitation of the East Riding. The irrepressible lay theologian Sir Francis Bigod took the evangelical Thomas Garrett around the North Riding for the same purpose.[36] Garrett was one of four men who received licences from Cranmer in summer 1535 to preach throughout the realm (the others were Thomas Swinnerton, John Thixtill, and John Chekyng). Similar licences were available from Cromwell. Richard Croke, a member of Henry VIII's divorce team, boasted early in 1537 of having preached 60 sermons in several counties under Cromwell's licence.[37] The centrepiece of the preaching campaign was England's most prestigious pulpit, Paul's Cross. The Bishop of London himself, John Stokesley, commenced the series on 11 July 1535. Cromwell thought this platform so important that he transferred control of it from the hands of Stokesley, whom he considered too conservative, to those of the pliant new Bishop of Rochester, John Hilsey. Hilsey was so zealous for the supremacy that he even made Catherine of Aragon's funeral at Peterborough Abbey the occasion for a sermon on it. Cromwell and Hilsey ensured that Paul's Cross was regularly filled by conservatives who had to demonstrate their loyalty to the new order and by evangelicals whose doctrinal tendentiousness could be tolerated for the sake of their enthusiastic denunciations of the papacy.[38]

The relative ease with which the constitutional revolution of the 1530s was accomplished has long been a matter for admiring or surprised comment among Tudor historians. There remains room for argument about how welcome the exchange of papal for royal supremacy was, but overt opposition was indeed remarkably limited. Even in the Pilgrimage of Grace, the greatest internal threat Henry ever faced, the issue of the supremacy was something of an afterthought. Historians have advanced various explanations for the lack of opposition. The least convincing merely ring the changes on the propaganda with which the Henrician regime justified the supremacy: that it changed very little, and was thus hardly noticed; that it was merely the culmination of a centuries-old political battle between the English crown and the papacy; and that the papacy was the object of widespread hostility or indifference. While it is true that the kings of England had for centuries exercised great influence on the English church, and that they, like other kings, had at times found themselves in dispute with the papacy, the English kings and people in the later middle ages were probably more attached to the papacy than any of their European counterparts. It was a king of France who had endeavoured to break Pope Julius II in 1511 by convoking a general council of the Church at Pisa. Henry VIII's proclamation of war with France in 1512 denounced this as schism and vaunted his own loyalty to his father the Pope and his mother the Church. And no anti-papal or anti-curial statements that may have emanated from England in the centuries before the Reformation smacked of anything like the bitterness of the grievances of the German nation aired in the Imperial Diets of the 1520s. In fact, the Lancastrians, the Yorkists, and the Tudors until 1530 were all loyal sons of the papacy. Even in the early fifteenth century, at the height of both the Great Schism in Europe and the Lollard crisis in England, the crown, Parliament, and Church of England remained firmly attached to the papacy. Wycliffe's rejection of the papacy was specifically included in his condemnation by the English church, which was upheld by Henry IV's statute for the burning of heretics and given universal significance by its inclusion in the acts of the Council of Constance (thanks to the efforts of the English delegation). Despite the problems that arose over Henry Beaufort's acquisition of a cardinal's hat with legatine powers from Rome, the Lancastrian regime held studiously aloof from the antipapal agitation of the Council of Basel; and its Yorkist successors were generous to both the English church and the papacy in their anxiety to secure political support. Henry VII, for all that he retrenched upon some of the concessions extended to the clergy by the Yorkists, took the precaution of securing papal confirmation of his title to the throne. Diplomatic relations with Rome were becoming ever closer in the fifteenth century. Edward IV was the first English king to appoint a 'cardinal protector' – a curial cardinal to take special care of English interests at Rome. The policy was continued under Henry VII, and was upgraded by his son, who sent Christopher Bainbridge to Rome in 1509 to fulfil that role as the first English curial cardinal for a century.[39] Although military and political obstacles prevented Henry from despatching English delegates to the Lateran Council in the 1510s, relations with Rome remained close. Henry not only obtained the cardinal's hat for his great minister Wolsey, but persuaded the pope to issue a conditional grant vindicating his claim to the French throne: even the papacy's temporal claims could be useful to an English king. Henry's love affair with the papacy culminated in his refutation of Luther, the *Assertion of the Seven Sacraments*, which contained a brief but firm affirmation of papal primacy and earned him the title 'Defender of the Faith'.

High diplomatic relations are one thing, popular attitudes quite another. The evidence here is scattered and difficult to interpret, but will hardly support claims of widespread hostility or indifference. Especially revealing is the undoubted commitment of the English clergy to the Roman primacy, which was made clear in their response first to Lollardy and later to Lutheranism. English theologians may not have subscribed to the extravagant account of papal power current in the Roman curia, but they were not conciliarists. John Fisher and Edward Powell, products respectively of the Cambridge and Oxford divinity schools, produced in the early 1520s lengthy justifications of papal primacy which, while tactfully silent on papal infallibility and temporal power, embodied the medieval consensus on papal headship of the Church. The position they defended against Luther was that defended by the Carmelite friar Thomas Netter against Wycliffe a hundred years before. Few clerics were highly trained theologians, but even sermon handbooks for humble parish priests presented a clear picture of the papal primacy. And the widespread reluctance among quite humble clergy to erase the pope's name from their service books in the later 1530s testifies to their true opinions. Among the laity, the papacy was something more than a distant Italian principality. There was a steady stream of English pilgrims to Rome, although such journeys were mostly the prerogative of the wealthy or of merchants. The pope, like the king, and ahead of him, was prayed for every Sunday in English in every church in the realm. Saintly popes were depicted in many churches. The evident popularity of papal indulgences, secured for local charitable purposes by English clergy and laity, and made widely available through the printing press, brought the papacy into everyday religious life. Direct contacts with Rome were frequent. Hundreds of English clerics needed dispensations of various kinds in order to pursue their ecclesiastical careers. Rather fewer lay people had such pressing needs, but many marriages depended on papal dispensations (enough to cause widespread concern among the gentry when papal bulls were declared null in the 1530s) and, among the gentry in particular, spiritual privileges such as the appointment of a personal confessor were much sought after. There can be no doubt that a full acceptance of papal primacy was part and parcel of pre-Reformation Catholicism in England. The traditional English hostility to 'popery' was an effect, and not a cause, of the break with Rome. The creation of that tradition was one of the most enduring achievements of Henry's Reformation.

The assumption of popular indifference or hostility to Rome is belied by the evidence of widespread discontent which came to Cromwell's attention in the 1530s. His surviving archives are littered with the relics of his close interest in the acceptance of the supremacy at every level of society. Whispers and rumours of the lightest words against it came to his ears, no doubt in great part because of the dangers under which the new Act of Treasons placed not only those who uttered treasonable words but also those who heard them. Professor Elton's brilliant analysis of this material in his *Policy and Police* has uncovered a world of disaffection previously unsuspected by historians, and has shown how discriminatingly Cromwell dealt with the myriad reports which reached him. Individuals guilty of nothing more than drunken bravado got off with a fright. The merely reluctant were induced to acquiesce: and the number of those who changed their minds after an interview with Cromwell is testimony to the force of his intellect and personality. Only the systematically recalcitrant, of whom there were few, experienced harassment, imprisonment, or the full rigours of the law. This is not to deny that Cromwell created a climate of fear. The dramatic increase in the use of attainder consequent upon the break with Rome is evidence enough for that. Between 1534 and 1547 the number of people attainted was 122, as against a mere 2 in the preceding 25 years of Henry's reign.[40] And irrespective of the justice of the convictions or the evident discretion of Cromwell in prosecuting those accused of treason, a total of over 300 executions for treason between 1534 and 1540 cannot have been without its effects on the English people. Even before the executions began, Cuthbert Tunstall, Bishop of Durham, was scared out of his resistance to the supremacy by a raid on his palace at Bishop's Auckland early in 1534. It is impossible to tell how many others conformed against their conscience out of fear. Only in a few cases can we be certain. George Crofts, chancellor of Chichester, who having sworn the oath was subsequently and fatally implicated in the Exeter conspiracy of 1538, confessed under interrogation that there was 'none act or thing that ever he did more grieved his conscience than the oath which he took to renounce the bishop of Rome's authority'.[41] The truly astonishing feature of the Henrician revolution is that a manifestly unpopular and unwanted policy was imposed so successfully and with so little public disturbance.

In seeking to understand the success with which the supremacy was imposed, it is necessary to view it against the background of the 'Church and State' conflicts of the middle ages. It was in fact entirely novel for a king to declare himself independent of the pope. In previous schisms, it had been popes who acted first, excommunicating kings or putting entire kingdoms under interdict. Nevertheless, it was possible to see the schism between Henry VIII and the papacy in the traditional light as a jurisdictional quarrel which would be patched up once its causes were resolved (for example, by the death of Catherine of Aragon or Anne Boleyn or both). Did Henry's démarche really seem in England or Rome any worse than the attempt by Louis XII to depose Julius II? There certainly were Englishmen, such as Robert Hobbes, the Abbot of Woburn executed for treason in 1538, who saw the schism in this perspective. While he accepted the royal supremacy and went through the motions of erasing the pope's name from service books, he was distinctly unenthusiastic, failing to inculcate the supremacy in his sermons. When ordered to surrender all his house's papal bulls, he did so promptly – but not before having copies made against the day of reconciliation. It is likely that even Gardiner entertained such secret hopes. Despite his acceptance of the new *status quo*, his true sympathies are betrayed by his appearance in a papal dispensation of 1533 allowing a few English clergy to celebrate religious services even under interdict, by his occasional and risky contacts with papal diplomats in the 1530s and 1540s, and by his much later claim (probably wishful thinking) that after the death of Catherine of Aragon and the execution of Anne Boleyn Henry had been considering a rapprochement with Rome.[42] Other instances of clergymen predicting or expecting a return to the Roman obedience turn up in Cromwell's papers: for example Robert Austin, a London Carmelite, early in 1535.[43] It is likely that similar expectations underlay the many cases in which priests failed to erase the pope's name from their service books. It is certain that such hopes lay beneath the many reports from all over the land of priests urging their flocks against the royal supremacy under the sacramental seal of confession. Confession was the rite which gave Catholic priests their most direct access to the minds and hearts of their flocks. Its secrecy offered a rare window for free speech, one exploited to the full by conservative clergy under the Cromwellian regime. Some priests of Syon Priory were banned from hearing confessions in 1534 because of reports that they used its secrecy to undermine the royal supremacy. A similar ban was placed on the London Crossed Friars in 1536. Treason in confession was alleged against the friar John Forest, executed in May 1538 for heresy. And the parish priest of Bilsington, John Bromfield, was telling his parishioners in confession early in 1539 that he expected an imminent reconcilation with the pope.[44] It is hardly surprising therefore that Cromwell encouraged preachers who attacked auricular confession. What is surprising is that Henry's own commitment to the sacrament was not undermined by its use to foster dissent from his supremacy.

The royal supremacy, then, was far from popular. But the control which the king and his council had over the ruling elite in the localities ensured for the most part that discontent would not turn into rebellion. The examples made of such notable dissidents as the Holy Maid of Kent, John Fisher, Thomas More, and the Carthusians, kept that elite – particularly the all-important clergy – from openly expressing its discontent. Afraid to oppose, people confined their resistance to grumbling and grudging acquiescence. Fundamental suspicion of the royal supremacy was nourished, largely through confession, on the hope of a speedy resolution to the schism. These hopes were frustrated by Henry's growing attachment to his new self-image as the head of the Church. Even the deaths of Catherine of Aragon and Anne Boleyn, which cleared the way for reconciliation, left him unmoved in his commitment to his new-found dignity. For, although the Catholics may have hidden it from themselves as best they could, the break with Rome was of a different kind from the medieval 'Church and State' conflicts: it was the king who had thrown off the pope, not the pope who had excommunicated the king. The result had been a massive extension of royal power and authority. The first fruits of this were quite literally tangible in the diversion of ecclesiastical revenues from papal to royal coffers. The king's traditionally wide range of ecclesiastical patronage was further extended and given firm intellectual and legal foundation. The royal visitatory power offered the chance of new influence at every level of the hierarchy and beyond into the ranks of the humblest laity. Finally, there was the enticing prospect of exploiting the massive and hitherto untouchable endowments of the church. For the remainder of his reign, Henry was to flex the muscles of the royal supremacy, vindicating in practice the quasi-papal powers to which he had successfully laid claim and living up to the model of Old Testament kingship to which he was increasingly inclined to assimilate himself. The remainder of this book will investigate how the supremacy functioned in the various dimensions of religious and ecclesiastical activity. The first and most obvious area to examine will be the exercise of that supremacy with regard to the administration, endowments, and hierarchy of the church.

# 2

## CHURCH AND CROWN

The royal supremacy represented the extension of full royal authority over the church. Its most immediate application was in relation to the administration, finances, and personnel of the ecclesiastical hierarchy. The influence of the king over the church in this restricted sense (which will remain its sense throughout this chapter) had already been considerable even before the break with Rome. The king had wide powers of patronage within the church, and was accustomed to rely on it as a source of revenue. Through the common law, the kings of England had in addition established some control over the temporalities of the church, and had set limits on papal intervention in matters of patronage. But they could not touch the endowments of the church, which were sacrosanct, and the internal government of the church continued to enjoy the autonomy guaranteed under Magna Carta. With the establishment of the royal supremacy, all this changed. The personnel of the church found themselves under the royal thumb. The government of the church found itself subject to crown, Parliament, and common law. The endowments of the church were suddenly within reach. These temptations proved irresistible. In a host of ways, some more important than others, Henry VIII and his councillors consolidated their grip on the machinery of the church and manipulated it for their own ends.

The church which Henry formally took over in 1534 was

a wealthy institution with a sophisticated though not always effective administration. It consisted of twenty-one dioceses, grouped into two provinces. The province of Canterbury comprised the archdiocese of Canterbury itself; the English dioceses of Bath and Wells, Chichester, Coventry and Lichfield, Ely, Exeter, Hereford, Lincoln, London, Norwich, Rochester, Salisbury, Winchester, and Worcester; and the Welsh dioceses of St Asaph's, St David's, Bangor, and Llandaff. The province of York comprised the archdiocese of York and the dioceses of Carlisle and Durham. The dioceses were all rich landholding institutions, although their wealth varied widely. According to the *Valor Ecclesiasticus*, the valuation of ecclesiastical property carried out in 1535, the richest was Winchester, with a net annual income of nearly £4000, the median London with about £1100, and the poorest Bangor, with less than £150.[1] The dioceses varied as much in size and population as in wealth. The vast dioceses of Lincoln and York covered areas which could have swallowed up many southern dioceses, while that of London contained a disproportionate fraction of the English people. Each diocese was composed of one or more archdeaconries (numbering sixty before the Reformation), which themselves varied enormously in size. Lincoln was divided into eight archdeaconries, while Rochester contained only one. The vast northern archdeaconries of Chester (Coventry and Lichfield) and Richmond (York), functioned almost as dioceses in their own right. Every archdeaconry was further divided into deaneries, the units of episcopal visitation. And deaneries themselves were composed of parishes, the basic administrative units of the church. But other ecclesiastical entities lay outside the parochial system altogether: firstly the monasteries and religious houses, often exempt by papal grant from episcopal jurisdiction (St Alban's abbey, for example, exercised jurisdiction over what amounted to an autonomous archdeaconry of Hertfordshire); and secondly, the cathedral chapters and other collegiate churches, answerable to the bishop, but free from the archdeacons. In addition, the international but centralised religious orders (such as the Cistercians or the Dominicans) organised themselves into provinces which bore no relation to existing ecclesiastical, or even in some cases national, boundaries. The ecclesiastical map of England was therefore a patchwork of exempt, peculiar, and overlapping jurisdictions.

The machinery of ecclesiastical government operated through this system of territorial division. While the Church of England, as part of the international Catholic Church, followed Roman canon law and was bound by the decrees of popes and general councils, it had its own legislative and executive apparatus. The normal legislative body in each province was the *Convocation*, a sort of clerical parliament, where the bishops, abbots, archdeacons, and cathedral or collegiate deans sat by right, together with elected representatives of cathedral chapters and diocesan clergy. Convocations were usually summoned to coincide with Parliaments, from which they had hived off in about 1300. Although Convocations originally existed simply to vote revenues to the king, separation from Parliament had led them to take on the aspect of provincial church councils, which thereafter became rare in England. Occasionally, a national council of the whole English church was convoked by a papal legate (for example by Wolsey in 1519), and below the provincial level diocesan *synods*, with representatives from each deanery, were in theory held every three years (it depended on the zeal of the bishop). But these synods tended to be more exhortatory than legislative. The ordinances of Convocations and synods were implemented by means of the *visitation*, the fundamental executive process of the medieval and Tudor church. Duly authorised officials (the bishop or his archdeacons, or their appointed representatives, the 'commissaries' or 'vicars-general') would visit the relevant unit (deanery, college, chapter, abbey, or priory), publish a set of *injunctions* embodying provincial or diocesan legislation, and question those present with a set of visitation *articles*. Any breach of regulations or proprieties would be suitably reprimanded or punished either on the spot or in the church courts. For the most part, bishops or their vicars-general visited cathedrals and religious houses, while archdeacons or their deputies visited deaneries and colleges. Exempt religious orders and houses were either not visited at all, or else were visited by provincial officials of their order or by papal legates. In practice, the visitation was not always the finely tuned administrative instrument it could become in the hands of a vigorous bishop. Its procedures too often degenerated into mere routine, and its fees and fines into peculation and corruption.

The early Tudor Church of England stood in clear need of rationalisation. Demographic shifts and growth were powerful arguments for increasing the number of dioceses, while such sprawling dioceses as Coventry and Lichfield, York, and Lincoln were administratively unwieldy (the smaller dioceses seem on the whole to have been better managed).[2] A redistribution of wealth among the dioceses might also have been advisable – the disparity between Winchester and Bangor was explicable but hardly justifiable. At the local level, the kaleidoscopic patterns of jurisdiction made the task of the reforming bishop unnecessarily complicated. Yet it remains one of the most startling features of the English Reformation that the opportunity for thorough reorganisation was not seized. The need had been perceived even before the break with Rome. Early in 1529 Cardinal Wolsey had obtained authorisation from Rome to establish new dioceses. His plan was apparently to convert monasteries into cathedrals, using their endowments rather than entrenching on those of the established bishops. Unfortunately, no precise proposals survive, and it is hard to say how close his scheme might have been to those subsequently discussed around 1540 and introduced piece-meal over the next few years.

It has often been suggested that the clergy were even more in need of reform than the system in which they served. A long historiographical tradition has lambasted the late medieval clergy for their lack of education, training, moral fibre, and spiritual commitment, making their greed, ambition, arrogance, and negligence into the fuel of a widespread anticlericalism which motivated the entire English Reformation. In recent years this tradition has been questioned. It is therefore worth sketching the outline and character of the ecclesiastical hierarchy before we go on to consider the question of anticlericalism as such. At the peak of the hierarchy stood the bishops, whose major role in English political life derived from a long-standing co-operation with the crown. The bishops had for centuries been crown appointees, and under the early Tudors the commonest route to high office in the church was through service to the king – the superior educational attainments of the clergy made them valuable in administration and indispensable in diplomacy. Only later in the sixteenth century, as laymen displaced clergymen from the highest administrative and diplomatic positions, did clerical promotion became more purely a matter of ecclesiastical service. The English bench of bishops under Henry VIII was one of the most impressive groups of men ever to have held such office. They had all received a university education, and many were men of genuine intellectual distinction. John Fisher, Bishop of Rochester, was the country's most famous preacher and a theologian with a European reputation. Cuthbert Tunstall (Bishop of London 1522–30, and of Durham 1530–51 and 1554–59) and John Stokesley (Bishop of London 1530–39) were renowned thanks to the praises of Erasmus, among whose friends and patrons were many of the English bishops. Even those whose careers offer us little evidence of academic distinction were often generous patrons of education. Founding colleges and schools had long been a tradition of the English episcopate, and it was continued in Henry's reign by Wolsey, Fisher, Fox, Longland, Holgate, Veysey, Oldham, and many others.[3] Their administrative talents are revealed not only in their service to the king but also in their care for their dioceses. Although the highest royal servants were often obliged to be absent from their sees, even they seem mostly to have kept their dioceses in good order, albeit through deputies. And a recent survey has revealed rates of episcopal residence which belie the impression of negligence and absenteeism derived from Reformation polemics. Studies of Fisher, West, Sherbourne, and Longland among others have uncovered a previously unsuspected degree of pastoral care and zeal.[4] On the moral level, the bishops of England were far superior to their German and French counterparts. Few bishops in Henry's reign – most notably Cardinal Wolsey – are known to have fathered illegitimate children, and, even in Protestant polemics, charges of sexual laxity against the English bishops were rare and never rang true.[5] Other charges, such as greed, ambition, arrogance, and cruelty, were similarly routine, although sometimes with rather more basis in fact. Allegations of cruelty were based on the dutiful performance of traditional responsibilities for suppressing heresy. Ambition and arrogance were occupational failings, especially visible in men such as Gardiner or Bonner. And the naked greed of a Ruthal or a Wolsey, though offset by a liberality and munificence which probably made as many friends as enemies, is undeniable. Nevertheless, the Henrician bishops were mostly a conscientious and talented group, and many of them earned high praise from such observers as Erasmus.

Just below the bishops stood a social and academic elite which staffed the diocesan administrations, filled the cathedral chapters, occupied the wardenships and plumper canonries of the secular colleges and hospitals, held the fellowships in the educational colleges, and had the pick of the richer parishes, especially the fashionable parishes of London. These men were recruited primarily from the universities, and came mostly from the families of the gentry, yeomanry, or burgesses. From Oxford or Cambridge they would seek minor offices and benefices in an episcopal or noble entourage, and from there they would climb a ladder which could culminate in the royal administration with a bishopric or even a cardinal's hat. It was among this section of the clergy that pluralism was prevalent – not to say rampant. A successful cleric could build up a substantial position without ever assuming the burdens or honours of the episcopate. Thomas Magnus, a Tudor royal servant who amassed one of the century's most impressive collections of benefices, could boast a clear income of more than £800 a year from his four collegiate masterships, three rectories, two prebends, vicarage, and archdeaconry. This made him wealthier than many bishops. Even Magnus was outshone by the untalented and undeserving bastard son of Wolsey, Thomas Winter, whose income was estimated in 1529 at £2,700 a year. But individual cases can be deceptive as well as instructive. A collective analysis is more informative, and one can be atempted for 1535, when the *Valor Ecclesiasticus* presents us with an unparalleled snapshot of the English church (although gaps in the surviving original returns mean that these figures must be underestimates). In that year, the 60 archdeaconries of England were held by 55 men, who between them held at least 300 benefices worth in total more than £10,000 a year. The mean clear income of the archdeaconries was about £70 a year, but the mean clear income of the archdeacons was nearly £200 a year. If money be the root of all evils, there was certainly some point in the mocking question of medieval theologians, 'can an archdeacon be saved?'.

Overlapping to some extent with this elite was the vast body of parochial clergy. The parish priests of late medieval England, be they incumbents (rectors or vicars) or curates, seem for the most part to have been decent, respectable, and tolerably educated men. There was a trend for increasing numbers of incumbents to be graduates. This holds true over the century preceding 1535 for such different places as Chester, London, and Lincoln.[6] Bishops were especially keen to use their patronage to promote graduates in the early sixteenth century. However, the increasing proportion of graduates did not necessarily cause any improvement in pastoral care, for they were often diocesan administrators or pluralists, absentees who drew the revenues but left the work to salaried underlings. Despite the myth of an illiterate clergy still prevalent in some quarters, literacy was virtually indispensable to the job of the parish priest, and seems to have been widespread even at the lowest levels of the secular clergy. It was not simply a matter of reading church services from liturgical books – which could probably be managed by rote. A more specialised but increasingly common call upon a parish priest's talents was the drafting of wills for his dying parishioners. The abundance of wills surviving from the early sixteenth century testifies to the ability, not to say zeal, of the parish priests – often mere curates – in this regard. To judge from the number of books printed for priests by the presses of London, their literary interests were deemed to extend beyond the minimum necessary for the performance of the liturgy. The relatively frequent mentions of books in clerical wills, and their almost total absence from lay wills, confirms that literacy was more common among the clergy than the laity. The profusion of school foundations in late medieval and early Tudor England gives us good cause to believe that literacy in general was increasing.[7] And the occasional cases recorded in episcopal registers where candidates for ordination were turned away on the grounds of illiteracy suggest that the requirements of canon law in this regard were not systematically flouted.

It was the moral rather than the academic qualifications of the parish clergy, however, which were of the greatest concern to their parishioners. This concern focused on clerical sexuality, an area where attitudes are just as significant as facts and just as hard to assess. Much depended on the conventions and expectations governing lay and clerical behaviour, and these varied from region to region. In England, for example, the medieval campaign against clerical marriage had been remarkably successful. Elsewhere in Europe, for example in Germany, Poland, Scandinavia, and many mountainous or isolated districts, it was common for priests to live in a long-term monogamous relationship. If the ecclesiastical authorities paid any attention to this, it was merely to exact regular fines which became more like fees. This state of affairs did not exist in early Tudor England. Early Tudor Wales, however, was a different country, and there clerical concubinage was still common. For England, in contrast, allegations of sexual immorality by the clergy concentrated on casual fornication, prostitution, and adultery. Even within England, variations can be observed. It is unlikely that clerical sexuality was of paramount importance to the laity of the north-west. There the gentry commonly kept mistresses in conditions tantamount to bigamy, and ecclesiastical records abound with the sexual offences of the laity. The clergy of that region probably seemed paragons of chastity in comparison with their lay neighbours.[8] And throughout England it is remarkable how few charges of sexual immorality were laid against the parochial clergy – despite the difficulty of keeping relationships secret in small communities. Archival and anecdotal evidence thus combine to suggest that parish priests, those with whom the people of late medieval England came into closest and most frequent contact, earned the respect of their flocks. It is surely no accident that the only cleric in the *Canterbury Tales* who appears in an entirely favourable light is the simple parish priest.

It is at the parochial level that we might expect the traditional clerical failings of pluralism and absenteeism to have made the most impact. After all, if services were not provided, complaints would be made. However, recent research has shown that these problems were not so widespread as was once assumed. Pluralism was certainly the main cause of absenteeism, but it was predominantly a vice of the elite. Dispensations for non-residence from benefices with 'cure of souls' stipulated that clerics should provide for the celebration of the requisite religious services during their absence. And work on diocesan records for several counties and dioceses has shown that it was rare in the early sixteenth century for benefices to go without religious services for anything other than casual and temporary vacancies. Access to the spiritual ministrations of the late medieval church was not restricted by absenteeism before the Reformation. Indeed, one of the few areas in which there was a shortfall of priests in the early Tudor period was Lancashire, which poverty made a net exporter of priests.[9] It is clear that in the north of England the educational attainments of priests were lower than elsewhere and the parochial system itself was underdeveloped and overstretched. Yet the north, with the worst clerical provision was, far from anticlerical, the most religiously conservative region of England.

It was the lowest group among the secular clergy that gave priests a bad name. Despite attempts to ensure that men could only be ordained if a secure place in the church existed for them, the attractions of a clerical career begot numerous expedients to circumvent these limitations. The expanding demand among the laity (and especially the dying) for the services of priests (and especially the mass) ensured that there was a constant stream of occasional labour for the unbeneficed: temporary chantries or obits, chaplaincies with confraternities and guilds, household chaplaincies, and even illicit services. These provided the livelihood of those described in contemporary literature as 'massing priests' and 'hedge priests'. Above this lowest level were the minor benefices: chapels, chantries and 'choral vicarages' (posts fulfilling duties in collegiate churches or cathedrals on behalf of absentee canons). Not all chantries, it should be said, were meant for this 'clerical proletariat'. Some were well endowed, often better than parishes, as they were often founded in towns during the later middle ages to supplement pastoral care in crowded parishes. These posts attracted the middling sort of clergy. But most minor benefices paid little and attracted candidates only of the lowest calibre. For this reason surviving visitation records for collegiate churches generally provide more lively reading than those for parishes or monasteries. The visitations of Southwell Minster (Nottinghamshire) for the years around 1500 tell a sorry but consistent tale of negligence, drunkenness, violence, and womanising by the resident vicars choral and chantry priests. The vicars choral of the collegiate church of St John, Chester, seem to have been equally undisciplined, as were those of St Mary, Leicester. And the high frequency of disciplinary action taken against vicars choral in the cathedrals has been contrasted with the rarity of such action against their superiors.[10] Drastic reform was certainly necessary at this level of the clergy, whose idleness and immorality provoked much of the satirical and sermonising literature against clerical misconduct cited by those who give anticlericalism a major role in the success of the Reformation.

Besides the *secular* clergy, as those described so far were known, stood another numerous clerical body, the *religious* – members of the religious orders. When Henry VIII became Supreme Head of the Church of England in 1534, there were about 750 monasteries, priories, convents and dependent cells in England and Wales. Relatively few were models of piety or learning. The need for reform was manifest. Of all the orders, only the Carthusians and the Observant Franciscans could be described as flourishing. Some of the greater Benedictine houses were also in excellent condition – for example, Glastonbury, Bury St Edmund's, and Winchcombe – but most houses of whatever order seem to have made little effort to rise above mediocrity. In discussing the state of the religious orders, however, we must bear in mind two crucial divisions: firstly, between the male and female orders; and secondly between the monastic and the mendicant orders. In theory, the monastic orders pursued a communal life of prayer in retreat from the world, while the orders of mendicant friars, though likewise committed to communal life and prayer, lived much more in the world, and took an active part in it through preaching, hearing confessions, studying and teaching, and ministering in various other ways to the spiritual needs of the community outside. The different orientations of these two modes of religious life are best illustrated by this contrast: monasteries were mostly self-sufficient units, often physically isolated in rural areas, and supported by landed endowments; friaries were integrated with the local community, were almost always located in towns, and were supported by charitable donations. The English male religious houses numbered about 610, more than half of them belonging to the three main monastic orders: 82 Benedictine houses; about 160 of Augustinian Canons; and 74 Cistercian; with a further 34 cells dependent on some of the major houses of these orders. In addition there were 29 Premonstratensian and 16 Cluniac houses, 9 Carthusian priories, and a handful of houses from other orders. The remaining 200 male houses were all of friars, mostly from the four major orders: 58 Dominican, 62 Franciscan (the latter including 6 Observant houses), 39 Carmelite and 35 Augustinian houses. The division between monastic and mendicant orders was not so important for women. Although some of the mendicant orders had established female branches, the weight of conventional opinion had soon restricted them to a way of life little different from that of the female monastics. England had 124 convents of nuns in 1534, the vast majority of them enjoying incomes of less than £200 a year. Finally, there were 21 houses of the native English order, the Gilbertines, which consisted of parallel establishments of canons and nuns.[11]

It is impossible to summarise adequately the social role of the monasteries in late medieval England, because it varied so much from region to region and even from house to house. Their obvious role as landlords is easily described. Although once viewed as probably more generous than their lay counterparts, recent research has shown that on the eve of the Reformation this was not so. Most of their tenants would have had little to do with the monks anyway, as the lands were often at some distance from the monasteries and were generally administered by lay stewards, as were the lands of the king, bishops, and major secular landowners. Those who as abbots, priors, subpriors and so forth tended to run the monasteries were for the most part of noble, gentle or at least yeoman stock, and they tended to manage their households and estates in much the same way as their lay counterparts. Indeed, the tendency of the monks to be assimilated in all but their notional celibacy to the landed gentry was one of the weakest features of late medieval monasticism across Europe. Having said that, it was at least to the credit of English monasticism that the abuse prevalent in Scotland and France, by which bishops, clerics, or even laymen held abbacies '*in commendam*' without participating in the communal life, was almost unknown (there were some cases, notoriously Cardinal Wolsey's acquisition of St. Alban's). However, the world found many other ways into the cloister. Visitation records frequently lament the aping of contemporary fashions in dress and personal adornment by the supposedly unworldly monks. Heads of houses and other senior officials were increasingly withdrawing from community life into privileged apartments within, or manors beyond, the monastic walls – rather as, outside, the peerage and gentry were withdrawing into private chambers separated from the rest of their household. The estates were viewed more and more as the property of the monks at the time (rather than of the community across time), and even as the personal property of abbots and priors. In many ways the dissolution, when it came, was simply the culmination of an inherently secularising trend within the orders themselves. Those heads of houses who lived out their lives under the later Tudors as substantial country gentlemen probably felt little serious change in the pattern of their lives as a result of the dissolution.

Popular attitudes to the monasteries are an equally insecure subject for sweeping generalisations. Such attitudes tended to concern monasteries rather than monasticism (which was a fact of life), and it is the neighbours rather than the tenants of monasteries (although the two categories often overlapped) whom we must look at. Robert Aske's famous defence of the monasteries is doubtless somewhat idealised, but the fact remains that through providing education, hospitality, help for the poor and care for the sick, and a range of religious services, many monasteries commanded considerable local loyalty.[12] The connection of the Pilgrimage of Grace with the dissolution is undeniable and argues a strong loyalty to local institutions. If some allowance has to be made for the fact that the risings took place in the relatively less disciplined north, we should remember that when the Premonstratensian house of Bayham (Sussex) was dissolved and appropriated to Cardinal's College in 1525, the canons briefly reoccupied their house with the assistance of the local inhabitants and the connivance of Lord Bergavenny. But local loyalties could be matched or even outweighed by local rivalries or enmities. The Benedictine cell of Lytham (Lancashire) was embroiled in disputes over land with the local gentry and commons in 1530. Several hundred of the townsfolk rioted and perpetrated the 'iconoclastic' act of pulling down the monastery's boundary markers – which, as was usual for monastic lands, were crosses embellished with the image of the patronal saint (in this case St Cuthbert).[13] And the relationship between great monasteries such as Bury St Edmund's and Reading over the townships within their jurisdiction was fraught with tension. Although such tension was primarily jurisdictional rather than religious, it was enough to create enduring ill-feeling between such monasteries and their neighbours.

If anticlericalism, the allegedly long-standing and bitter resentment of the layman against the character and pretensions of the clergy, was really widespread in late medieval England, then explaining the Reformation becomes simple. Once the Lutheran doctrine of the priesthood of all believers or the Henrician doctrine of the royal supremacy had provided a theological justification for abolishing or restricting clerical privileges, the put-upon laity would inevitably respond with enthusiasm. Yet the evidence customarily cited for the strength of English anticlericalism does not establish the case. It consists mostly of jurisdictional conflicts of the middle ages between popes and kings, sermons and satires depicting clerical vices in lurid colours, and court records of tithe disputes, slander, and even violence between laity and clergy. Spiced with Lollard expostulations against the efficacy and legitimacy of a sacrificing priesthood, the mixture is heady, but historians have had difficulty reconciling the picture of a discontented laity straining against the clerical leash with the mass of archival and anecdotal evidence for the popularity of 'popular' religion. One explanation has been that the ritual and liturgical provision of the Church was so important to people that they were prepared to pay the price of an arrogant and avaricious clergy: anticlericalism was a persistent itch rather than a terminal illness. In recent years even this moderate view has been called into question. Professor Scarisbrick starkly contrasts the popularity of late medieval religion as evinced by wills, churches themselves, and churchwardens' accounts with the traditional picture of persistent anticlericalism, and concludes that the massive lay investment in parochial life in the fifteenth and early sixteenth centuries simply belies the presumption of endemic conflict between the parish priest and his congregation over tithes and morals. And Dr Haigh rejects the very concept of anticlericalism as inappropriate to late medieval England. The traditional evidence, he maintains, is a rag-bag of disparate items testifying to separate attitudes or problems, all of them blown up out of proportion.[14]

Much of the evidence cited is literary, and such inherently ambivalent evidence has often been crudely interpreted. Sermons such as that of John Colet, castigating the moral shortcomings of the clergy, were in general delivered to clerical audiences, and employ an obviously exaggerated rhetoric in order to achieve the desired end of moral reform. Colet himself was anything but anticlerical. He was an avid disciple of the late classical 'Pseudo-Dionysius' whose writings on the heavenly and ecclesiastical hierarchies coined the concept of 'hierarchy' (rule by priests) and put it into circulation. Colet regarded ordination as the paramount sacrament of the Church and was unhesitating in his elevation of spiritual authority and dignity over temporal. If he castigated the clergy, he did not spare the laity, assuring them that they got the clergy they deserved.[15] Satire, although directed to a more general audience, had similarly moralistic aims, and is notoriously unreliable as a basis for generalisation. Moreover, its targets were not exclusively clerical. We are often reminded that Chaucer's vision of the clergy in the *Canterbury Tales* is unflattering. Among several clerical figures only the parish priest conforms to any religious ideals (although the clerk is presented sympathetically). Yet the lay pilgrims fare no better. The pompous and irascible knight, the gluttonous franklin, the lecherous wife of Bath, and the rowdy miller are for the most part rogues, albeit likeable rogues. And it is commonly overlooked that most of the literature labelled as anticlerical was produced by orthodox authors for a largely orthodox readership. Chaucer's own piety and orthodoxy can hardly be called into doubt except by those to whom any good medieval writer must be a forerunner of the Reformation, while clerical satirists like Gower and Lydgate leave even such critics no room for manoeuvre. Given that the *Canterbury Tales* included among its readers such a notoriously devout person as Lady Margaret Beaufort, it seems that the potential of this kind of literature for inspiring, focusing, or reflecting religious discontent has been greatly exaggerated.[16] Even when widespread popular feelings can be assumed to underlie literary anticlericalism, as in the attacks on Wolsey's character in the 1520s by such authors as John Skelton and William Tyndale, the significance of these feelings can easily be overestimated. Although Wolsey's failings were notorious, it is doubtful that he was any more unpopular in the 1520s than Cromwell or Cranmer in the 1530s. In any case, literary evidence can cut both ways. Isolated texts can be selected to present the reverse of the usual case. For instance, William Barlow puts into the mouth of the clergy in one of his dialogues the claim 'none presumed till now a late / Against the clergy to bear any hate', presenting anticlericalism as a result rather than a cause of the Reformation.[17] General surveys of religious literature just before the Reformation suggest that the vast bulk of it evinced nothing other than complete though implicit satisfaction with the religious provision of the late medieval Church.[18]

None of this is to deny that there was frequent tension, mostly of a financial or jurisdictional character, between clergy and laity. The clergy of Tudor England were as litigious as their lay contemporaries, and were often over eager to vindicate their rights through the ecclesiastical courts, which deployed the penalty of excommunication with a readiness that can only have undermined its solemn significance. The most notorious example of this is the case of Richard Hunne, the London citizen who in 1511 picked a quarrel with his curate over the burial fee for his infant son, was ordered to pay by the archbishop's court in 1512, and challenged that court with a writ of praemunire in 1513. Late in 1514 he was detained on a charge of heresy in the episcopal gaol, where he was subsequently found hanged. Apart from fulfilling what was (according to Thomas More) Hunne's ambition to go down in English history as the protagonist of 'Hunne's case', the case, although extreme in its outcome, was typical in its origins as a financial dispute between a stiff-necked parson and a stiff-necked parishioner. Burial fees ('mortuaries') and tithes were certainly the commonest causes of conflict between clergy and laity. But the significance of such conflict has been exaggerated in the historiography of anticlericalism.[19] Recent studies have shown that the vast majority of parochial clergy were never involved in litigation over such matters. Out of thousands of parishes, and tens of thousands of priests, tithe disputes in the first fifty years of the Tudors can be numbered in the hundreds at most. Some areas, of course, produced more than others. Out of 106 parishes in the city of London about a third saw tithe cases go before the church courts in the period 1520–46. This must have been the worst record of any part of England, and reflects a fundamental jurisdictional conflict between church and city resolved only by the transfer of tithe cases to civic jurisdiction in 1546. Yet even in London, it has been observed, evidence of other kinds 'calls into question the real prevalence of anticlericalism'. In fact, tithe disputes often derived from the difficulty of applying in an urban and commercial context a system of taxation designed for an agrarian world, or from basic disagreements over valuations in an economy racked with inflation. Inflation was probably the chief reason why tithe disputes proliferated throughout England in the 1530s and 1540s, from Lancashire to London. Many of the Lancashire disputes were caused by priests trying to reject customary cash payments and return to the older practice of taking tithes in kind.[20] They were not over the principles involved, but over the application of the principles. And after the break with Rome, doubts about the future of canon law (on which tithe depended) further encouraged the laity to withhold tithes: in 1536 a temporary statute was passed giving legal force to tithe, because withholding had broken out 'in more temerous and large manner than before that time had been seen'.

Until recently, anticlericalism so dominated approaches to the subject that no attempt had been made to investigate the wider question of popular attitudes to the clergy. But in some recent research the phenomena of anticlericalism have been set in a new and more satisfactory perspective. The high place accorded to the priesthood in late medieval theology (for example by Colet) was indeed reflected in popular attitudes, and it was above all the priestly power to consecrate the body of Christ in the mass that set priests apart. Their sacred power and status made them focuses at once of reverence and anxiety. Expectations of their behaviour were high, and their failings were consequently taken more seriously than those of the laity. To do. violence against a priest was seen as especially heinous. The taboo was so strong that, in some cases, priests could unwisely presume on its ability to protect them from the consequences of misbehaviour. For priests themselves to resort to violence was equally shocking. Expectations of the moral, and in particular the sexual, purity of priests were high. The fear of a sinful priest polluting the sacrament he consecrated heightened both suspicions and vigilance about priestly morality. It was what underlay the frequent provision in early Tudor wills that masses should be said for the testator's soul by an 'honest priest' (honesty and chastity were often synonyms). But parish priests seem for the most part to have lived up to the high expectations held of them. The social and material penalties of failure – popular contempt and ecclesiastical censure – were a powerful deterrent. It has therefore been suggested that it was the sacred role and status of the priesthood as such that prevented the inevitable shortcomings of individuals from precipitating genuine anticlericalism. But when Henry's Reformation undermined the social status of the priesthood, and the Edwardian Reformation then stripped away its sacramental power, human weakness was no longer cloaked by the office, and anticlericalism began to emerge in increasing legal, verbal and physical attacks on priests, in declining financial support, and in falling recruitment.[21]

All the revision in the world can neither disprove nor disguise the fact that the late medieval secular clergy fell short in many respects of Christian pastoral ideals. Nor can it be doubted that the average Anglican clergyman of the early seventeenth century was far better educated than his early Tudor predecessor. Nevertheless, improvement in clerical standards can hardly be attributed to the Reformation under Henry VIII, or even under Edward VI. On the contrary, standards of education and provision actually declined from the 1530s to revive only under Elizabeth (and in the latter part of her reign at that). There was some legislation under Henry which ostensibly aimed at the reformation of clerical abuses – most notably the laws of 1529 limiting pluralism and absenteeism. But these laws were more a political lever against the hierarchy and the pope than a disinterested drive for reform. Pluralism was hardly a significant problem at the parish level. It flourished rather at the higher levels of the clergy, and was driven by the need of kings and bishops to recruit and reward talented servants and officials. There was certainly no noticeable diminution in pluralism in the latter years of Henry's reign. Some rough figures give a general idea of how little things changed. The papal registers for the years 1504–7 record an annual average of about 75 dispensations for pluralism of various kinds for English clergy. In comparison, the Archbishop of Canterbury's Faculty Office registers for 1535–47 record an average of about 70 a year. Admittedly it cannot be assumed that these figures are either exhaustive or precisely comparable. Even before the Reformation it was possible to obtain dispensations for pluralism without direct recourse to Rome: papal nuncios often had limited powers to dispense for pluralism, and Wolsey obtained extensive powers of this kind. And after the break with Rome, dispensations could be obtained direct from the king. Nevertheless, the figures suggest that the scale of the practice did not change dramatically.[22]

The first effect of the Henrician Reformation was to put a new pinnacle on the ecclesiastical pyramid – the king instead of the pope. A resident royal pope could be expected to exercise his supremacy more forcefully than a distant bishop nervous of offending a king, and this is exactly what happened. Although the traditional division of the Church of England into two provinces was retained, the royal supremacy gave that church a degree of administrative unity it had never previously enjoyed. The Convocation of the northern province showed no signs of independent life after its shortlived opposition to Henry in 1532–33, and henceforth meekly followed the lead of its southern counterpart. Parliament in any case took over many aspects of ecclesiastical legislation, and Henry made his almost priestly view of his supremacy impinge on every aspect of ecclesiastical life. His episcopal view of his office can be seen in the title of 'vicar-general' which he bestowed on Cromwell to run the church in his name. As vicar-general or 'vicegerent' of the supreme head, Cromwell successfully claimed presidency and precedence in the southern Convocation of 1536.[23] He pushed through a set of injunctions which he then enforced by means of a royal visitation carried out by his own agents across the whole country. Indeed, one of his greatest achievements was to raise the ecclesiastical visitation to new heights of effectiveness and to implement it on a national scale and uniform basis. The papal power of granting dispensations from canon law was transferred to a new office, the Faculty Office of the Archbishop of Canterbury, under a further statute of

1534, though dispensations could also be obtained directly from the king or Cromwell, whose own vicegerential court also exercised functions previously carried out at Rome.[24] Cromwell's appetite for business led him to intervene directly in diocesan and monastic administration all over the realm, appointing, dismissing, judging, and advising in such a way as to make the royal supremacy a reality at every level of the church.

Cromwell's ambitious plans for Henry's church included a thorough revision of canon law. As the storehouse of papal ideology, canon law was plainly incompatible with the royal supremacy. Its revision was therefore provided for under the Act for the Submission of the Clergy in 1534, although such law as was not contrary to the royal prerogative or statute was allowed to stand pending revision. A new code was drafted in 1535 along traditional lines, but was never promulgated, and was soon rendered obsolete by further religious changes. The repudiation of the old law was confirmed by the prohibition of its study in the universities that same year, and the consequent legal vacuum put a question-mark over the basis of tithe which inspired a proliferation of tithe disputes. Further statutes of 1536 and 1544 vainly renewed the call for a revision, but delay prevailed, and Henry was still discussing the matter with Cranmer as late as 1546.[25] A more drastic revision was indeed prepared under Edward VI, but this too proved abortive. Its passage into law was preempted by Mary's accession, and the project was not resumed under Elizabeth. The church courts, like the canon law which they existed to enforce, found themselves in a state of crisis after the break with Rome. Their future was at first as uncertain as that of the canon law itself, and even though they remained in operation, they seem to have suffered a consequent crisis of morale and authority. This can be seen not only in the general decline in the levels of business (apart from tithe cases) coming before them, but also in the increasing contempt with which their main penalty, excommunication, was treated from the 1540s. But given the prominent place of grievances against the activities and procedures of church courts in the anticlerical agitation of the early 1530s, it is surprising how little was done to reform them. As with canon law, and indeed so much else of the ecclesiastical administration, the story of the courts in the Henrician church is one of lost opportunities.[26]

Even before the assumption of the royal supremacy, the English crown had looked upon the Church of England as a regular and reliable source of revenue.[27] Yet royal financial needs were constantly increasing, and the royal supremacy heralded a new era in the financial exploitation of the church. The first stage of this was the transfer of certain ecclesiastical taxes (which were at the same time increased and extended) from the papal to the royal treasury. Under an act of 1534 (26 H. VIII c. 3), 'first fruits' (the first year's net revenues) of all benefices (rather than simply of bishoprics and abbacies) were henceforth to be paid by each new incumbent not to the pope but to the king; in addition, an annual levy of a tenth of the net revenues was imposed on all benefices. This change led to one of the greatest administrative achievements of the age, the compilation of the *Valor Ecclesiasticus* – a systematic valuation of ecclesiastical assets throughout the entire country, carried out by commissioners in every diocese. Commissions went out dated 30 January 1535. The job was done in nine months, and the collated information was ready for use by early 1536. Comparisons of the *Valor*'s valuations with the evidence (where it survives) of leases and accounts suggests that it probably undervalues monastic wealth slightly (mostly in respect of occasional revenues, such as receipts from the felling of timber or offerings made by pilgrims). Nevertheless, the *Valor* was under the circumstances remarkably accurate.[28] The wealth it revealed was prodigious, and doubtless whetted the appetite of the king and his advisers.

The most dramatic development of Henry VIII's Reformation was undoubtedly the dissolution of the monasteries, an enterprise in which the rhetoric of reformation soon became little more than a cloak for naked expropriation.[29] No policy of his reign had so direct an impact on so many people or on so much of the English landscape and skyline. And no aspect of Henry's Reformation has undergone such a dramatic revision in understanding within the last hundred years. The propaganda with which Cromwell justified the suppression retained its hold on English minds until Cardinal Gasquet stood it on its head 350 years later. Since Gasquet's time a host of local and general studies has produced a balanced account of the dissolution which commands widespread assent. It is unlikely that future work will significantly alter the outlines of the story, although there still remain gaps to be filled by detailed studies of the fates of lands and communities. There is also room for further thought on the significance of the dissolution in religious terms.

The early Tudor monasteries stood in clear need of reform and pruning, and efforts in this direction were under way before the dissolution. A few smaller houses and cells had been amalgamated. And more than thirty had been dissolved since 1500 so that their endowments could be reappropriated to educational or charitable purposes. Houses of monks, canons, and nuns were used to endow Cardinal Wolsey's colleges in Oxford and Ipswich, and St John's College in Cambridge, while Jesus College (Cambridge) occupied the site of a former nunnery as well as taking over its endowments. Henry VII appropriated the property of a house of canons to support an almshouse attached to his chapel in Westminster Abbey. Wolsey himself, as we have seen, was planning to convert some monasteries into cathedrals, and had in addition obtained powers to amalgamate undermanned religious houses. Similar reappropriations were being carried out elsewhere in Europe, and were recommended on a grand scale by the Catholic reformers at Rome who drafted the *Consilium de Emendenda Ecclesia* in 1537. There is little reason to doubt that the increasing preoccupation with education in Tudor England would have taken this policy further. Indeed, much of the initial support for the dissolution, from evangelicals and Catholics alike, was based on the assumption that the proceeds would be used this way. These hopes, voiced by such diverse figures as Thomas Starkey, Hugh Latimer, and Robert Crowley, were to be cruelly disappointed.

The policy of large-scale dissolution was, however, radically different, and it is not entirely clear how it originated, although there seems little reason to doubt that it emerged from the inventive brain of Thomas Cromwell. Cardinal Pole reckoned that the elimination of the monasteries was on his political agenda from the start of his association with Henry VIII, and while this accusation has won little credit, it is by no means inconceivable. The policy was not unthinkable. John Fisher warned in 1529 that the anticlerical legislation of that year might be the thin end of a wedge of wholesale expropriation.[30] And the polemic against clerical wealth current in the fourteenth century had received a timely restatement in Simon Fish's *Supplication of the Beggars* (1528). The *Dialogue between a Knight and a Clerk* published probably with official approval in 1531 brought the same notions into a more respectable arena. Cromwell himself, already sympathetic to a Lutheran brand of Reformation, must have been aware of how German princes and cities were availing themselves freely of former monastic wealth. And he personally reprimanded monks as early as summer 1535 for an excessive trust in the value of their religious vows.[31] Nevertheless, neither of the two steps which with hindsight appear as indispensable preliminaries to the dissolution need necessarily have been taken with that object in view. The first, the *Valor* of 1535, was merely a tax assessment. And the second, the nationwide visitation of religious houses set in motion by Cromwell later that same year, was primarily intended as an assertion and practical demonstration of the royal supremacy. True, these measures gave rise to rumours of an impending assault on monastic endowments.[32] Yet even towards the end of 1535, when the *Valor* was largely complete and the visitation was under way, Cromwell and other crown servants gave no hint of planning a dissolution in the legislation they were preparing for the Irish Parliament of 1536.[33]

The policy of dissolution seems to have emerged in the course of the visitation. The visitors – chiefly Dr Richard Layton, Dr Thomas Legh, John ap Rice (notary public), and Dr John Tregonwell – set out with a series of articles and injunctions which differed little from their medieval counterparts except in the prominence given to the royal supremacy and some gratuitous attacks on monastic ceremonies and the cult of relics. These perhaps show some influence of evangelical ideas, but were far from amounting to an attack on either monasticism or relics in principle. The visitations themselves, however, were carried out without the general attention to fairness that had characterised medieval proceedings.[34] And the increasing haste of the English visitors towards the end of 1535, together with the systematic exaggeration of monastic abuses, suggests that something beyond mere internal reform was soon being contemplated. Dr Layton and the others rarely spent more than a day in any house, and sometimes dealt with two houses a day. Their reports to Cromwell show how limited was the real scope of their investigations. The gathering or manufacture of rumour and evidence about sexual misdemeanours, and the reporting of dubious relics and popular superstitions connected with them, form the staple of their letters. Their reports display a consistently high estimate of the sexual appetites of monks and nuns which is not borne out by the evidence of surviving pre-Reformation visitations. Dr Layton in particular was of a salacious mind, and his indiscriminate readiness to believe any malicious gossip fed his imagination. Some of his letters contain statements which even after four hundred years can be nailed as lies. But it is noteworthy that at some houses – Glastonbury, Leicester, and Waverley – even he found nothing to report. The other visitors were less prejudiced than Layton, and give us cause to regard several houses with some respect: for example, St Alban's, Bury St Edmund's, Durham, and Ramsey.

At any rate, Cromwell was drafting a bill for the suppression of poorer houses early in 1536. The evidence gathered by the visitors was collated for presentation to Parliament and, according to Latimer, was decisive in rallying support for the bill, which became law in March. In theory all houses with an annual income of less than £200 (a very substantial sum of money) were to be dissolved. This would have shut over 300 of them, including most of the English nunneries. But in fact many were reprieved, perhaps 70 or 80, generally by petitioning for exemption.[35] This first dissolution was emphatically not an attack on monasticism in principle, nor was it envisaged as the first stage of a wholesale dissolution. Had this been the case, the act would hardly have given a hostage to fortune by praising the quality of the religious life in the larger houses. Nor would the inhabitants of the dissolved houses have been given the option of transferring to another establishment. Although nearly 1000 people opted to abandon the habit in 1536 and 1537, without even the incentive of a pension, many others chose to move. It was this choice that necessitated the reprieve of numerous houses in some areas. In Yorkshire, for example, there were 23 nunneries, none of them worth more than £100 a year, housing perhaps 250 nuns. Yet only nine were closed in 1536. Few nuns voluntarily chose to leave the religious life – with neither independent income nor matrimonial prospects, that option must have looked bleak indeed. Yet Yorkshire monks seem to have been nearly as reluctant as their sisters to abandon their profession. Elsewhere, life inside was more repellent, or life outside more appealing. The dissolution in Sussex was far swifter. Eight of the eleven monasteries and nunneries were closed in 1536. Out of 52 monks thus released, only four moved to other houses.[36] Precisely how one is to account for these regional variations in response to the first dissolution is far from clear. Areas where monks chose more frequently to persist in their vocations were often involved in the Pilgrimage of Grace. It may well be that the monasteries in such areas were better integrated into local society. But what may in turn have underlain regional variations in attitudes to the monasteries is again a knotty problem.

In the aftermath of the Pilgrimage of Grace, further steps were taken on the road to suppression. Those monasteries which the rebels had restored to their former occupants were soon emptied again by the Duke of Norfolk early in 1537. A further handful of religious houses followed them into liquidation on account of their support for the rebellion. The abbots of Whalley, Sawley, Barlings, Jervaulx, and Kirksted and the prior of Bridlington were all attainted of treason and executed, and their houses and estates, by a novel interpretation of the law of attainder, were taken into the king's hands. These were far wealthier than the monasteries hitherto suppressed, many of them yielding over £500 a year in addition to the considerable value of their movable property. The new interpretation of attainder was also to be used in 1538 to dispose of two houses with indiscreet abbots – Lenton and Woburn. A more significant development, however, had taken place in 1537 in the cases of Furness and Holm Cultram. The abbot of Furness had been implicated in the rising, but not deeply enough for an example to be made of him. Instead, he and his monks were persuaded to surrender. The abbot of Holm Cultram, who had been suspected of some unrecorded treason even before the Pilgrimage, was executed in 1537 for complicity in the rising, and his house too was induced to surrender itself into the king's hands early in 1538. It was this method of 'voluntary' surrender that was to finish off English monasticism.

The evolution of the suppression policy in the later 1530s exhibits a tragic rather than an historical inevitability. The initial attack of 1536 seems to have shaken public confidence in the security of religious donations and endowments. The first victims of this were the friars, who depended for the most part on casual donations. We have little direct evidence about the pattern of charitable giving to the friars, but testamentary bequests, for example, declined sharply around 1535, and this decline was probably reflected in other forms of giving. In addition, Cromwell's attack on shrines and images hit the friars hard. Many friaries housed images or relics which were held in high esteem and generated considerable income. Malchus's ear and an unspecified image were reckoned to be worth twenty marks a year to the Dominican priory at Bangor. Cromwell's ban on preaching about the miracles performed through images, and his discouragement of donations to them, presumably cut off this source of income. Finally, the manpower of the friaries was haemorrhaging at two points. The spread of evangelical ideas, encouraged by both Cromwell and Cranmer, was causing many of the best friars to become disillusioned with their religion. Between 1535 and the middle of 1538, when the suppression of the friaries began, about 120 English friars obtained dispensations to become secular priests (although some may have been responding to financial crisis rather than answering the call of the new gospel). This certainly underestimates total leakage. John Bale, the former Carmelite prior, does not appear in the Faculty Office Registers. Neither does Richard Ingworth, the former Dominican prior and leading agent in the final dissolution of the friaries, who told Cromwell in 1538 that he had lost his friar's heart two years before shedding his friar's coat.[37] Nor do the figures include those who simply walked out. At the other end of the doctrinal spectrum, those with a conscientious commitment to their vows were inclined to flee the country. Many Observant Franciscans had fled as early as 1534 rather than accept the royal supremacy.[38] Some Dominicans also fled, notably Robert Buckenham, prior of Cambridge, and Richard Marshall, prior of Newcastle. The latter left an explanatory letter to his *confrères*, pointing out among other things that their rule rendered their order 'immediately subject to the Roman pontiff'.[39] The departures were particularly marked among the educated elite of the friars, which amplified their impact both within the orders and in the eyes of their traditional clientele, which was generally interested in their services as preachers and confessors. The sharp decline in clerical recruitment which set in at about this time was especially marked in the religious orders. With all these problems, the friaries quickly went into crisis. They were forced to liquidate their few assets in order to service mounting debts, and by the time the visitors called in 1538–39, it was in most cases an act of mercy to close the house.

The friars were not the only ones to feel the pinch. Although the monasteries, with their ample endowments, were better equipped to weather the storm, the steady trickle of suppressions in the aftermath of the Pilgrimage seems to have given them an intimation of impending doom. Their reaction embodied exactly that perception of the ecclesiastical endowment as personal property which ran so counter to the spirit of the monastic life and which was identified by the Roman *Consilium de Emendenda Ecclesia* ('plan for reforming the Church') as the pervasive vice of the late medieval Church. In short, the monasteries realised assets in the short term by granting long leases on low rents to favoured friends, relations, and clients. By an irony of history, the actions of the monks precipitated the very cataclysm they sought to pre-empt. As late as December 1537 the king apparently had no intention of eliminating monasticism. For when the abbey of Chertsey surrendered, Henry himself refounded it, with promised endowments worth some £700 a year, on the site of the previously dissolved monastery at Bisham. While this might be interpreted as a Machiavellian stratagem, it seems more reasonable to take it at face value, especially as the dedication of the new monastery, to the Holy Trinity, was what Henry later chose for most of his other religious foundations and refoundations. However, as early as November 1537 the great Cluniac priory at Lewes made its final mark in history by becoming the first religious house to be closed by voluntary surrender to the Crown. By January 1538 Cromwell was aware that rumours and panic selling were sweeping through the monasteries. The decision to set about a wholesale dissolution was probably taken in response to this information, just before Cromwell's encyclical letter to heads of houses in spring 1538 telling them that no such decision had been taken, and instructing them to cease pre-emptive leasing. It is in this context that we should view the curious praemunire charge levelled against Bishop John Stokesley of London in May 1538, namely that in admitting two brothers and a nun to Syon Priory he had illegally acted by the authority of papal bulls. Since he was no sooner convicted than pardoned, the real objective may well have been to curtail further monastic recruitment. And the surrender of Henry's new foundation at Bisham on 17 June 1538 confirms the regime's drastic change of course.[40]

When the commissions to receive the surrenders of the monasteries were issued in 1538, the writing was on the wall. The commissioners were empowered in the case of houses refusing surrender to dissolve them in any case, paying no pensions to the obstinate and imprisoning them at pleasure. Harsh though the alternatives were, the absence of vigorous resistance is an indictment of the calibre of the English religious life far more damning than anything turned up in the reports of Cromwell's minions. In many cases the task of the commissioners was made easier by the fact that the royal supremacy had for several years been used to ensure that 'conformable' superiors were installed wherever vacancies occurred. Only in a small minority of houses was there resistance. The austere Carthusians of Mountgrace, having been encouraged by Tunstall's fleeing chaplain Dr Richard Hillyard, were led in stiff opposition by their prior John Wilson, whose cousin Dr Nicholas Wilson was a prominent conservative who had spent three years in the Tower before accepting the royal supremacy. It took a trumped-up charge of murder to bring the abbot of Vale Royal into line. The Benedictine nunnery of Romsey in Winchester diocese appears to have refused to surrender. No deed of surrender survives for the house and no pensions for its nuns are listed in the records of the Court of Augmentations. In the majority of cases, however, things ran more smoothly. Between 1538 and 1540 the commissioners suppressed some 200 monasteries, 200 friaries, and 40 nunneries, evicting some 8000 religious. All monks and nuns except the obstinate few received pensions until they died or (in the case of priests) secured some benefice. These pensions, mostly five pounds a year or more, were arguably adequate, but their real value declined in the mid-Tudor inflation. It is difficult to generalise about the fate of the former religious, which varied according to their pension, their talent, their circumstances, and their response to the changes around them. The heads of houses received ample compensation, often including a former manor of the abbey, sufficient to set them up as substantial gentry. For most priests, long-term security depended on obtaining a benefice, which in turn depended on education and connections. Many senior or better educated monks soon found stalls in collegiate or cathedral churches as well as good parsonages or vicarages. Monks from houses which had held a lot of parochial benefices also had better chances, as the authorities often appointed them to those benefices in order to save their pensions. And even when benefices were not forthcoming, many monks doubtless found work as chantry priests or curates. Nuns for the most part were less generously treated and had fewer opportunities to better their lot. But by returning to live with their families, or else by clubbing together in unofficial communal life, they could get by. The friars probably did worst of all: no endowments, no pensions. All they received with their marching orders was a small cash sum. The better educated found little difficulty in securing benefices. The prior of the York Franciscans, for example, was soon ensconced in a city rectory. The less able had a leaner time.

The final phase of the dissolution was well advanced before it was given a firm legal foundation. In the Parliament of 1539, the second Act of Dissolution validated the king's title to all monastic properties surrendered hitherto or thereafter. It was accompanied by a statute enabling Henry to found new dioceses, cathedrals, and collegiate churches by letters patent. Since, as Professor Scarisbrick has pointed out, there was nothing to stop him doing this anyway, this act was probably intended merely to sweeten the pill of dissolution. Its expansive preamble held out the prospect of large-scale charitable and educational foundations. What transpired in reality was less glorious, but makes a fitting commentary on the true nature of the dissolution. Eight monastic cathedrals were refounded as secular cathedral corporations of dean and chapter, six more monasteries were refounded as new cathedrals, and two others (Burton-on-Trent and Thornton) became secular colleges. Of the old monastic cathedrals, Norwich was secularised as early as May 1538. The other seven – Canterbury, Carlisle, Durham, Ely, Rochester, Winchester, and Worcester – were refounded between March 1541 and January 1542.[41] In most cases, the last prior of the monastery became the first dean of the secular cathedral, and a few of the most able monks were retained among the new canons. The monasteries selected for conversion into cathedrals for new dioceses – Bristol, Chester, Gloucester, Oseney-Oxford, Peterborough, and Westminster – were Henry's only positive contribution to serious administrative reform of the church. Some grandiose schemes for new dioceses were considered around 1539–40, but these were probably opposed by Cromwell on grounds of cost or principle: he had no love of bishops, and the projected endowments were substantial. In practice, diocesan reform was worked out by two conservative bishops, Gardiner and Sampson, and no action was taken until after Cromwell's fall.[42] Neither the refounded nor the newly founded cathedrals retained the entire wealth of the former monastic institutions. Henry held back a considerable portion of their lands, and the new foundations in particular were chronically underfunded. Even the established dioceses suffered financially at the king's hands. By a series of mostly unfavourable exchanges of land and property, many of the bishops lost valuable country manors and stately London residences to the king and his cronies. Although the trickle only turned into a flood in the reigns of Edward and Elizabeth, it has been estimated that even by the end of Henry's reign the English bishops had lost about 10 percent of their manors. The total loss was not as great as this figure might imply. The bishops were mostly compensated with the 'spiritual' incomes of rectories and tithes. The total income of the English episcopate was on paper about the same in 1547 as in 1535. But this concealed both a major shift from 'temporal' to 'spiritual' income and a lowering of the average by the foundation of the new dioceses.[43] The vast bulk of the ecclesiastical booty was lost to the church forever. Much was retained by the crown, under the management of Cromwell's superb administrative creation, the Court of Augmentations. But more was rapidly liquidated in order to finance the wars of the 1540s and to consolidate political support for the Reformation among the nobility and gentry. Not the commonwealth, but the king, peers, and landowners were the true beneficiaries of the dissolution.

Amidst the widespread plunder of Henry's reign, it is remarkable that the secular cathedrals themselves survived largely unscathed. An attack on them was by no means unthinkable. Simon Heynes, the reforming Dean of Exeter, put to Cromwell proposals for a radical reorganisation of the chapter there. And William Barlow, Bishop of St David's, proposed an ambitious plan to translate his see to Carmarthen and reorganise the diocese around it. Nothing came of these plans, and no cathedral suffered anything worse than unfavourable land exchanges. But a number of secular colleges were induced to surrender voluntarily to the king. The imposing Southwell Minster surrendered in 1540, apparently on the understanding that it would be converted into a cathedral. In the event, Henry changed his mind, and Southwell – uniquely – was reconstituted as a college in 1543. From 1541, a succession of colleges surrendered permanently, including Mettingham in 1542, Warwick in 1544, and Tattershall in 1545. That year, the proceedings were put on a firm legal basis. Henry secured, after some struggle in the Commons, an act empowering him to dissolve colleges and chantries at will. Despite the advance of popular Protestantism in the 1540s and its approach even to the heart of the court, this act eschewed even the pretext of reform. Its motive was explicitly financial, and the avowed basis was no longer the word of God, but simply the will of the supreme head. With the king facing heavy financial demands in the wars of the 1540s, no ecclesiastical corporation could now feel safe. Even the colleges of Oxford and Cambridge felt threatened, though in the event they lobbied so effectively that they each obtained a new royal foundation, or refoundation, in the colleges of Christ Church and Trinity. Nevertheless, the trickle of suppressions continued, and by the end of the reign a quarter of England's 140 colleges had been put down.[44]

Henry's Reformation also led to certain limited changes in the pattern of clerical recruitment and in the patronage of ecclesiastical offices and benefices. The dissolution of the monasteries transferred the patronage of hundreds of benefices into lay hands, with the king emerging as far the greatest gainer. Parochial patronage now became for the first time predominantly lay rather than ecclesiastical, marking a fundamental shift in the relationship between the clergy and the laity. More radically, benefices formerly appropriated to monasteries were reappropriated to laymen, with the result that spiritual revenues – tithes – were henceforth paid to lay people, who then employed vicars to perform the spiritual functions on their behalf. And when Thomas Cromwell secured his own election as Dean of Wells in 1537, he inaugurated a brief period during which laymen without any clerical pretensions could occupy ecclesiastical benefices (admittedly only those without cure of souls). A statute of 1545 took this further by permitting married laymen qualified in Roman law to exercise jurisdiction in church courts (37 Henry VIII c. 17). The increase of royal power and patronage was manifested in many ways. At the universities, for example, the royal visitation and injunctions of 1535 saw the government intervene not merely in the administration but in the curriculum itself.[45] And the elections of masters in Oxford and Cambridge colleges became subject to direct royal intervention. So too, by virtue of a special act of Parliament (26 H. VIII c. 14), did the appointment of suffragan bishops, whose role was to assist diocesan bishops by performing sacramental functions without exercising episcopal jurisdiction.

The administration of the Church of England under Henry VIII was not the disinterested pursuit of reform that it purported to be. No aspect of his reign better fits Raphael Hythloday's condemnation of various political arrangements as a 'conspiracy of rich men procuring their own commodities under the name and title of the commonwealth'.[46] Little was done to set the administration of the secular church on a more rational basis. The failure to clarify the nature of ecclesiastical jurisdiction or to implement the reform of canon law betrays the lack of true reforming purpose. The abolition of papal authority and thus of exemptions dependent on it, and the dissolutions of the monasteries in the 1530s and of the collegiate churches in the 1540s, eliminated many of the jurisdictional anomalies confronting bishops and archdeacons. But there remained a number of episcopal exemptions and, apart from the erection of the new dioceses, nothing was done to amend the diocesan map. The new dioceses were a step in the right direction, but were insufficient and underfunded. Their efficiency was hampered by debt for years. The dissolutions were motivated from the start by financial exigencies. For all the idealistic schemes of reformers of all persuasions, the commonweal undoubtedly suffered on all counts, whether of charity, education, or hospitality. Some sops were thrown to local communities, in the shape of former monastic buildings for use as parish churches, grammar schools, or town halls, but little was saved from the wreck. The only winners were the king and the ruling elites at the centre and in the counties, who made or increased their fortunes out of the booty. And while the reform of the church was undoubtedly a financial expedient for the crown, it was at the same time an expression and an extension of royal power. Only under the royal supremacy was action against church endowments conceivable, for under papal canon law it was impossible for churchmen to alienate their institutional patrimony, and sacrilege for laymen to take it. Although Parliament gave legal sanction to the dissolutions, they remained an expression of royal rather than parliamentary authority. Even during the first phase, it was the royal will which decided which of the poorer houses should stand and which fall. In the second phase, seizure under attainder and surrender by communities were essentially prerogative actions, even if they were retrospectively legitimated by statute. The chantries act further increased royal power, leaving it up to Henry to dissolve such institutions at pleasure. The expropriations thus made the nature and extent of the supremacy clear. There was nothing it could not touch short of divine and natural law. It was in every respect as extensive as the papal jurisdiction it replaced, and it was more immediate, more arbitrary, and more far-reaching in its effects.

# 3

## POPULAR RELIGION

For the majority of his people, Henry's Reformation was notable chiefly for its effect upon their parish religious life. They were far from unmoved by the break with Rome, as Cromwell's papers show, although perhaps neither this nor the subordination of the clergy to the crown made much practical difference. The dissolution of the monasteries, though resented, probably made less of a mark upon mental than upon physical horizons. But Henry's elimination of much of the traditional fabric of popular devotion brought change home to every man, woman, and child in unmistakeable fashion. Shrines, relics, images, indulgences, and pilgrimages, together with a host of liturgical and 'para-liturgical' practices, fell victim to the reforming zeal of the supreme head and his ministers. Most of this activity was concentrated in the later 1530s, the period of Cromwell's vicegerency, with its leanings towards Protestant evangelicalism. Yet even in the 1540s, after the 'conservative reaction' had set in, there was no official retreat from the positions adopted during that more radical phase. In place of traditional popular piety, Henry's church offered a religion of 'God's word', an affair of the printed page rather than the painted picture. There was in effect a shift from a ritually and visually rich religious culture to something more spartan and cerebral. The exploration of this new culture of the word which Henry tried to impose will be reserved for the next chapter. This chapter will confine itself to the attack on traditional popular religion, first sketching the religion of Tudor England in the first third of the sixteenth century, then looking at the development and justification of the attack on popular religion by the Henrician regime.

Before examining the religious life of early Tudor England, it is worth summarising the religious view of the world in which late medieval Catholics were in theory instructed, as this alone explains the nature of the religious activities in which they engaged. This world-view, which made sense of and gave value to what, in the absence of religious beliefs, must otherwise become the intrinsically meaningless phenomena of human existence, was dominated by three concerns: first, the attainment of salvation; second, the constitution and preservation of human society and community; and third, the securing of worldly and material benefits – chiefly health, welfare, and children. That Catholicism was taken to be – and to a large extent really was – constitutive of human society, or at least of that society in which the English found themselves, hardly needs saying. From the cradle to the grave and beyond, it surrounded and protected them, its moral rules guiding society, its rituals marking rites of passage, its oaths guaranteeing human relationships, and its ceremonies defining and holding together local communities. It is hardly surprising that in such a context the heretic should be regarded with fear and loathing, as one whose deviance inevitably threatened disorder, sedition, and moral turpitude. And in an age of limited technological and governmental resources, it is hardly surprising that the Church, the best organised institution in Western Europe, offered and controlled most of what limited education and health care was available, supplementing material welfare provision with prayers to appease the wrath and implore the favour of God. But what Catholicism offered above all was salvation, a life of eternal blessedness with God after death. The means of salvation were believed to have been revealed by God in the scriptures and to be made available through the Church founded by his incarnate Son Jesus Christ and guaranteed by the Holy Spirit. Salvation was necessary because of 'original sin', by which the ancestors of the human race, Adam and Eve, had sinned against God in such a way as to deprive themselves and their descendants of his friendship, to prevent them obeying his will, and to expose them to temporal death. The race could only be reconciled with God by some adequate act of recompense, so God became a man in the person of Jesus Christ in order to effect the reconciliation himself. Jesus's passion, death on a cross, and resurrection atoned for sin, and made salvation available by grace (i.e. the divine favour) to those who repented of their sins, believed in him, and lived according to his will. Access to the saving grace offered by Christ was gained through membership of his Church, the mediator or dispenser of grace. Membership of the Church was established by baptism (a ritual of purification in which initiates were mystically made part of Christ's body) and manifested by attendance at the eucharist (the ritual memorial meal and sacrifice in which Christ's body was mystically eaten by the faithful). Membership of the Church could be lost or denied by unbelief, excommunication, or apostasy. The Christian life within the Church involved obedience to the Ten Commandments; and a communal existence based on the sharing of certain ritual acts, chiefly the seven sacraments (baptism, confirmation, the eucharist, penance, marriage, holy orders, and extreme unction), and on the good works of prayer, fasting, and almsgiving.

It was not thought possible for Christians to live in this world without repeatedly losing God's favour through sin, so repentance was an indispensable element of the Christian life. Reconciliation was available through the sacrament of penance or confession, in which sinners revealed their sins to a priest, expressed their sorrow, and in return received absolution together with instructions to perform specific good works – 'penances' – as satisfaction. These penances varied according to the gravity and frequency of the offence, and had originally been extremely severe. Defined in terms of time spent in penitential activity (anything from forty days to the rest of one's natural life, or more), this regime had been relaxed in the course of the middle ages for the average Christian, as it was scarcely possible except for monks or hermits. Relief came from the doctrine that the Church was a spiritual community – the communion of saints. Just as worldly goods were (in theory) shared among its members, so too were spiritual goods. Anybody could pray for anybody else, and those who were on better terms with God – the saints, and in principle anyone who was not cut off from grace by sin – could intercede with God for both spiritual and material benefits. Access to the 'intercession of saints' could be facilitated by access to their remains or relics – their bones, graves, clothes, belongings, or even images. This gave rise to the keeping of shrines, the veneration of images, and the making of pilgrimages. Fresh comfort to the average Christian was derived from the doctrine of 'purgatory', a further opportunity to complete unfinished satisfaction for sin after death.[1] As souls in purgatory remained members of the Church, they could benefit as much as the living from intercessory prayer. The eucharist (or mass) was seen as the most efficacious prayer because it was believed to be a special representation of Christ's saving sacrifice for sin upon the cross. The performance of masses for the dead therefore became one of the commonest religious practices of the later middle ages. Connected with the doctrine of purgatory was that of indulgences. Purgatorial suffering was taken to be the equivalent of performing the full penance due for sin in this world. An indulgence was a release from that suffering, granted by popes or bishops (by virtue of the power Christ had vested in them to forgive sins) in return for specific good works – such as going on crusade or pilgrimage, reciting specified prayers, or contributing to charitable causes. Indulgences varied from a basic forty days' remission to the 'plenary' indulgence, which satisfied the punishment due for all sins a person had committed, repented, and duly confessed as of the date of issue. The emphasis laid on the three last named doctrines – the cult of the saints, the sacrifice of the mass, and purgatory (with indulgences) – is what most readily distinguishes medieval Catholicism from other periods and varieties of Catholicism and Christianity. These doctrines underpinned the bulk of voluntary religious activity in the middle ages, and it was against them that the theological attacks of the Protestant Reformers were most directly aimed.

The basic religious instruction deemed suitable and necessary for the English people had been laid down during the middle ages in provincial legislation which was frequently re-enacted – for the last time by Wolsey for the northern province in 1518.[2] Parish clergy were to instruct their flocks four times a year in the Creed, the Ten Commandments, and the seven sacraments, virtues, deadly sins, and works of mercy (these groups of seven were structured around the seven petitions of the Pater Noster or 'Our Father'). The creed summarised the essence of Christian doctrine, and the commandments the essence of moral obligation. The remaining material presented a model for the Christian life. A considerable body of instructional literature was produced in the later middle ages to assist parish priests in their catechetical work: the sermons in Mirk's *Festival*, for example, or the *Lay Folk's Catechism*, or the verse teachings of the *Prick of Conscience* and the *Speculum Vitae* (*Mirror of Life*). Nor were books the only instructional aids. The parish churches of early Tudor England were richly decorated with paintings, carvings, and statues, many of which combined a catechetical purpose with their more obviously devotional or decorative character. Carvings around pulpits or fonts illustrated the seven sacraments, and wall-paintings illustrated scenes of sacred history from the Bible or the lives of the saints. It was a commonplace of the time that such visual material, suitably expounded, could render the details of Christian doctrine or practice more readily accessible to the congregation: images were 'laymen's books'. Outside the church, moreover, stood a further dimension of religious instruction, the sacred drama of miracle and morality plays from which the English dramatic tradition in part descended. The great cycles that still survive from such towns as York, Wakefield, Coventry, and Chester illustrate the range of religious teaching that this medium could handle. And such plays were not limited to the major towns. Travelling players took them round the countryside, and their performances must have been not only a highlight of popular entertainment but also an important vehicle by which the community expressed and passed on its religious values. The instructional medium *par excellence*, however, remained the sermon, often almost as much a form of entertainment as the play. Sermons at

Paul's Cross, the kingdom's premier pulpit, could attract thousands. As contentious and divisive preaching emerged in the 1530s, one certainty amid the doubts was that almost any preacher could quickly gather an audience – even a bricklayer preaching from his bedroom window.[3] And the appearance of permanent stone and wooden pulpits in hundreds of churches throughout the land in the century before the Reformation (a fact verifiable from churchwarden's accounts and in some cases from visiting the churches today) testifies to the growing role of the sermon in parochial life. Although pulpits served other functions than preaching – such as the reading of the litany and bidding prayers – they were usually erected at the expense of the parishioners themselves, and probably indicate popular demand for sermons.

In the light of Protestant polemic about Catholic 'dumb dogs' in the late medieval church, it is important to draw attention to the widespread and growing provision of sermons in early Tudor England. The early Reformers, in denying that the 'word of God' was being preached, rarely meant that no preaching was going on – rather that preaching inculcated not God's word but 'human traditions', in which they included not only the lives of the saints but also much of what they saw as the 'works religion' of Catholicism. Distasteful though its content undoubtedly was to the Reformers, there was a great deal of preaching in England on the eve of the Reformation: parish priests, cathedral preachers, monastic preachers, preaching friars, episcopally licensed preachers, preachers sent out from the universities, and preachers in collegiate churches and chantries. The endowment of sermons by the pious laity was catching on. Among the best known of such foundations was that by which Lady Margaret Beaufort provided early in the sixteenth century for a Cambridge graduate to preach six sermons a year at a number of specified places around the country. Around the same time, Cambridge University itself obtained a papal licence to appoint a dozen preachers a year to preach anywhere in the kingdom. Within twenty years, some 150 graduates had been involved in this scheme, and many were subsequently famous preachers – among them the Reformers Bilney, Latimer, and

Cranmer, and the conservatives Robert Ridley, Henry Gold, and Nicholas Wilson. Further preaching was provided by the orders of friars. It was a commonplace of contemporary literature that friars regularly went on preaching tours, and over thirty priors of mendicant houses can be identified as preachers in the early sixteenth century – enough to suggest that many houses tried to live up to their ideals by evangelising the urban communities in which they were situated. Sermons were also provided in the cathedral churches. Many of the early sixteenth-century deans and canons of secular cathedrals were sufficiently talented to be invited to perform at the court or on State occasions – among them John Colet and Richard Pace (successive Deans of St Paul's), Edward Frowcester (Dean of Hereford), and Edward Powell (canon of Salisbury). Even among the bishops more and more preachers were to be found – Fisher at Rochester, Alcock and West at Ely, Longland at Lincoln, and Tunstall at London and Durham – while almost all bishops kept talented preachers among their chaplains. At the parochial level, we have little direct evidence about the provision of preaching by incumbent or visiting clergy. But there was plenty of scope for literate and conscientious priests, even if they lacked creative genius themselves, to derive sermons from published handbooks and compilations. No precise quantification of preaching in early Tudor England can be attempted. But impressionistic evidence indicates that provision was plentiful and growing.

It is impossible to judge in modern terms the success of the late medieval catechetical effort. In an age of religious conformity and limited literacy, there was neither the means nor the motive to conduct detailed investigations of popular religious knowledge. The very idea of such an investigation is anachronistic. Nevertheless, the sheer scale of popular religious activity in the later middle ages shows that, by whatever channel, much of the message got through. The overwhelming concern of late medieval Catholics was the attainment of salvation. So urgent was this preoccupation that late medieval Catholicism has been described as in practice 'a cult of the living in the service of the dead'.[4] Although there is some truth in this judgement, it is largely an illusion created by an excessive concentration on wills as evidence for religious belief and practice. Much popular religious activity was indeed directed to reducing the time to be spent in purgatory by oneself and one's friends and relatives. Wills often heaped up dizzying piles of intercession: masses were ordered by ones and twos, by thirties ('trentals'), by annual memorials ('obits'), by hundreds or thousands (as by Henry VII), or in perpetuity ('chantries'). The prayers of the poor were reckoned of especial influence with God, and many wills leave quantities of money to be distributed to the poor at funerals. A glance at any published collection of early Tudor wills indicates the extent and extravagance of such practices. For the less well-off, membership of pious guilds or fraternities, arranged before or after death, could secure a share in a permanent medium of intercession. Fraternities held regular masses and prayers for their deceased members and benefactors, whose names and generosity were recorded on the 'bead-roll'. Within this life, the obtaining of indulgences was perhaps the most powerful insurance against purgatory. The number of printed indulgences which survive in stray fragments can but hint at the popularity which these documents enjoyed in early Tudor England. Numbers printed and issued are literally impossible to estimate, but they clearly formed a major slice of Pynson's production, and for comparison it is worth recalling that a contract survives recording the production by a Barcelona printer of 18,000 copies of an indulgence available for offerings made to the leading Spanish shrine of Our Lady of Montserrat.[5] Late medieval English prayer books and commonplace books frequently contain detailed instructions about how to gain vast indulgences by reciting specified prayers. And indulgences regularly added to the appeal of sermons, almsgiving, and even the burnings or recantations of heretics.

But Catholicism in early Tudor England was for the living as well as for the dead, and seems by all available evidence to have been thriving. The incessant requests in wills and on funeral monuments for passers-by to recite the Pater Noster, Ave Maria, Creed, or De Profundis, show that knowledge of basic Latin prayers was presumed to be universal (and incidentally that a good many passers-by were thought able to read the requests).

The visitations of the Reforming bishops under Edward VI testify back-handedly to this. Bishop Hooper found in Gloucester that while everyone knew their Pater Noster, few had as yet succeeded in mastering the Our Father. Latimer himself observed how the English version was scornfully rejected by people for whom the old-fashioned Pater was quite enough. All the seven sacraments (except perhaps extreme unction, popularly regarded as a death sentence) were in great demand. Baptism was universal. Popular concerns about its validity which emerged under Edward VI, when Cranmer's new rite radically pruned the traditional rituals, show the seriousness with which it was taken. Evidence about confirmation is slender, but it seems that it was usually administered in childhood, or even infancy. Marriage is not susceptible of close analysis before the parish registers begin in the 1530s, but was presumably the norm for those who did not opt for ordination or the religious life. And ordination rates remain impressively high in episcopal registers right up to the 1530s, when the Reformation started to dent clerical recruitment. The mutually connected obligations of annual confession during Lent and of annual communion at Easter were widely known, and, as far as we can tell, widely observed. The laity were anxious to receive their 'rights' (as Easter communion was known) and priests could and did refuse communion to those they thought had not gone to confession. And the popularity of indulgences, which in theory depended on recent confession, suggests that many people confessed more than once a year. The obligation of attendance at mass on Sundays and feast days was equally well known, and evidence of non-attendance is rare – even among Lollards. The Reformation polemic against the 'private mass' should not mislead us (a private mass was a mass sung for a 'private' or specific intention – public attendance was in no way excluded). We should not imagine that England was full of solitary priests mumbling mass in deserted chapels. The mass was enormously popular. Daily attendance was such a common practice that those who, like Lady Margaret Beaufort, wished to exhibit special devotion would hear mass as many as four or five times a day.[6] And the laments of preachers from the end of the fourteenth century until the abolition of the mass testify to the magnetic appeal of the consecration. Rapt sermon audiences would be enticed by a ringing bell away from the pulpit to whichever altar was about to display the elevation of the host and chalice. Both this behaviour and its subsequent condemnation by Protestant Reformers as superstition and idolatry merely testify to the hold which the mass exercised over people's imaginations.

The popular religion of late medieval England remained a strongly visual and ritual activity. This is most apparent in the continued popularity of shrines and pilgrimages. There were many national and regional pilgrimage centres in early Tudor England: shrines and images of Our Lady at Walsingham, Ipswich, Doncaster, Caversham, and Penrhys; crucifixes (or 'roods') at Boxley and Boston; the Holy Blood at Hailes; shrines to saintly bishops in almost every cathedral (for example, Becket at Canterbury, St Richard at Chichester, and St Hugh at Lincoln); and shrines to particular saints such as St Anne at Buxton, St Modwen at Burton-on-Trent, and St Derfel Gadarn at Llanderfel in Wales. Anecdotal evidence confirms the popularity of these shrines even in the 1530s. Latimer tells us that the Blood of Hailes was daily attracting crowds along the Fosse Way. Royal commissioners in Wales reported that between five and six hundred pilgrims visited the statue of Derfel Gadarn on a single day (5 April 1538). Robert Testwood was irritated by the crowds of westcountrymen who flocked daily to the shrine of Henry VI at Windsor.[7] William Barlow, Bishop of St David's, told Cromwell with obvious distaste early in 1538 of an allegedly miraculous candle which burned before an image of Our Lady in Cardigan priory and was 'now used for great pilgrimage' despite Cromwell's injunctions and Barlow's opposition.[8] Other shrines remained prominent in local religious life: St Blaise at Bromley in Kent, the Rood of St Paul's, Our Lady of Grace at the Cambridge Blackfriars, Our Lady of Worcester, St Edmund at Bury St Edmund's – the list could fill pages. While anecdotal evidence confirms the general strength of the cult of the saints, records of the offerings made by the faithful at particular shrines, though rare and not always reliable, hint at the rise and fall of various cults. Takings at the shrine of St Thomas at Canterbury were apparently falling in the early sixteenth century, but those at the shrine of Henry VI at Windsor and at Our Lady of Ipswich (associated with Cardinal Wolsey's new college there), were rising.[9] The best proof of the strength of pilgrimage in general is perhaps the economic dependence of some settlements on their shrines. Canterbury felt the economic ill-effects of Henry's abolition of pilgrimage by the end of the 1530s. And the case of St Kenelm at Halesowen perfectly illustrates both local loyalty to a cult and economic dependence on it. In 1538 the parish church of Halesowen purchased a picture of the local martyr St Kenelm auctioned at the dissolution of the nearby abbey. But Kenelmstowe, the hamlet within that parish which housed the popular shrine and holy well of the saint, went into rapid decline after the prohibition of pilgrimage. The offerings at its chapel were valued at £10 a year in the *Valor*, yet in the 1540s a note on Kenelmstowe in the Office of First Fruits and Tenths observed the decay of the place since 1538. Its decay proved irremediable: Kenelmstowe simply disappeared.[10]

Shrines, relics, and images were used as means of seeking or giving thanks for special favours, such as fertility and safe childbirth. In an age of massive perinatal mortality, prayer offered the only hope of improving chances of successful pregnancy, easy delivery, and healthy offspring. From the king and queen downwards, couples would go to Walsingham to implore the gift of children. When Alice Cowper of London had a serious fall in pregnancy, her neighbours urged her to go on pilgrimage to St Lawrence for the safety of the unborn child.[11] After the onset of labour, images or relics could be brought to the mothers. The image of St Modwen was equipped with a staff which used to be taken to women in labour for them to lean upon. Similar practices explain the frequency with which the girdles of female saints are found in the lists of relics held at churches and monasteries. In visiting the monasteries of south-west England in 1535, Dr Layton found such relics at Bruton and Farley priories, and reported that they were sent out to help and comfort women in labour.

'Our Lady's smock' at Maiden Bradley priory was doubtless used for the same purposes, and the abbey of St Werburge in Chester possessed a girdle of their patroness which was 'in great request by lying-in women'.[12] This last example may offer us an explanation of the origin of these curious relics. In the verse life of St Werburge by the early sixteenth-century Chester monk Harry Bradshaw there is a story of how a woman in labour received a vision in which the saint commanded her to take a linen cloth to the church, wind it around the altar, remove it, and then wind it around her womb. The woman obeyed, the labour was successful, and she made an offering of the cloth in a silver case to the church.[13] It is highly likely that this was the 'relic' subsequently taken out to women in labour, and it may be that other such relics originated in the same way. In other words, they were not so much relics as votive offerings, albeit credited with a sacred power akin to that of relics themselves.

But pilgrimage cannot be reduced to a fertility cult. Physical health was another concern of those who had recourse to images and shrines. There were several holy wells scattered throughout England to which the faithful might go for relief from rheumatic, arthritic, or muscular complaints. The well of St Winifred at Holywell in Flintshire remained a popular pilgrimage site throughout the sixteenth and seventeenth centuries, despite the Reformation, and St Anne's spring at Buxton reopened as a spa within a generation of its closure as a shrine.[14] Cures of headaches were sought from the many skull relics, such as the head of St Ursula (of which Dr London collected at least two examples in December 1538), or the cap of Henry VI which pilgrims used to place on their heads at Windsor. An image of the Virgin at Higley in Herefordshire was said to restore sight to the blind.[15] More worldly benefits could also be sought. Henry VII made a pilgrimage to Walsingham when he heard of the outbreak of Lambert Simnel's revolt, and after his victory at Stoke in 1487, he sent his banner to the shrine as a votive offering. His gratitude was enduring. In his will he bequeathed to Walsingham a gilded statue of himself. We should not conclude from the *Canterbury Tales* and Erasmus's account of his trip with John Colet that pilgrimage was nothing more than an excuse for a holiday – although the joys of leisure and travel were not least among the attractions of pilgrimage. Nor should we conclude that the motives were purely material. All shrines which offered special indulgences on certain feasts were obliged to provide facilities for confession in order to help pilgrims gain them. And the benefit sought from the Rood of Grace at Boxley or the Holy Blood of Hailes was nothing less than certainty of being in a state of grace.[16]

The continuing vitality of popular Catholicism in late medieval and early Tudor England is demonstrated not only by the flourishing of established cults and shrines, but also by the continued emergence of new cults. The penultimate abbot of Glastonbury, Richard Bere, built a shrine there modelled on the Holy House of Loretto (a rapidly growing international shrine in northern Italy). The cult of St Bridget of Sweden (canonised in 1391) was particularly buoyant. It was promoted by the fashionable Abbey of Syon near London, the only English house of the religious order she had founded, and it was manifested not only in images, but also in the immense popularity of the 'Fifteen Oes' (a prayer to Jesus attributed to her authorship) and in the wide readership of her mystical revelations. Bridget herself was of royal birth, and her cult (along with Syon abbey) enjoyed royal patronage in England.[17] An even more impressive royal cult was that of Henry VI, which originated in popular devotion under the Yorkists but was taken up enthusiastically for reasons of dynastic legitimation by Henry VII. Only his avarice and his son's indolence prevented an official canonisation. There is some evidence that Henry VI's son, Prince Edward, was venerated at Tewkesbury; and Bishop Fisher of Rochester may have been trying to foster another Tudor royal cult. His funeral sermon for Lady Margaret Beaufort reads like the life of a saint, and he wrote a full account of her life (now lost) which is more likely to have been a hagiography than a biography. A notable growth area in new cults was the field of pastoral clergy. The most prominent was that of Master John Shorn, the fifteenth-century parson of Marston in Oxfordshire. His image there (resorted to for cures from ague) was a popular pilgrimage centre, as was his tomb at St George's chapel in Windsor. His cult became one of the *bêtes noires* of the Reformers. Similar cults were also arising around Richard of Caistor in Norwich and Thomas Woghope at Smarden in Kent. At Ely there was an incipient cult of John Alcock (bishop, 1486–1500), venerated by his flock for his devotion to their care. And in Exeter cathedral the tomb of Bishop Edmund Lacey had been the site of pilgrimage and miracle cures since his death in 1455.[18]

Popular veneration for living holy men and women was another feature of medieval Christianity which retained its vigour in early sixteenth-century England. This is illustrated in general by the esteem in which hermits were widely held. More particular evidence can be found in the careers of three holy maidens who achieved fame in this period. The fraud of the Holy Maid of Leominster in Henry VII's time has been recorded for posterity by Thomas More. A young girl claiming to be nourished on nothing more than daily communion set out her stall in the roodloft of Leominster parish church. Her fame attracted sizeable crowds from the surrounding area, but an investigation conducted under the auspices of Lady Margaret Beaufort soon discovered that she was receiving several square meals a day from her accomplice, the curate (with whom her relationship was suspiciously familiar). This story of exposure not only reveals the ready credulity of the people but also suggests that official investigations of such phenomena were more than mere formalities. This is worth recalling when the other two cases are considered. The first was that of the Holy Maid of Ipswich (a daughter of the local knight Sir Roger Wentworth), who enjoyed a brief spell of fame in 1516 when she was miraculously cured of epilepsy at the shrine of Our Lady of Ipswich, after which she retired to the house of Franciscan nuns in London. But the most notorious of these girls was Elizabeth Barton, the Holy Maid of Kent, who came to prominence in the later 1520s. Afflicted with epilepsy in 1526, she successfully prophesied her own cure on Annunciation day at the Marian chapel of Court-at-Street in Kent. Soon after, she joined the nunnery of St Sepulchre's in Canterbury, and her regular mystical trances thereafter were accompanied by miracles, special revelations, and prophecies. These were publicised by a circle of clergymen led by her spiritual director Dr Edward Bocking (cellarer of Christ Church Abbey, Canterbury). The Maid's career follows the pattern of medieval visionary nuns like Elizabeth of Schöngau, Bridget of Sweden, and Catherine of Siena. Marked parallels between her career and that of Catherine may owe something to the fact that Dr Bocking used to read to her from that saint's life. But what is most noteworthy is that Elizabeth Barton exercised what was virtually a female ministry. Regularly at her convent, and occasionally in visits to the chapel at Court-at-Street, she would play a part in preaching and calling pilgrims to penance. Dr Bocking would deliver an introductory sermon, and then the Maid would appear in a trance and utter inspired words – encouraging hearers towards orthodox religious practices, especially confession and the mass, and exhorting them against the errors of the Lutherans. The high point was the Maid's ability to remind individuals in detail of their particular sins and thus inspire them to repentance.[19] Counter-Reformation Europe was to produce many similar examples of visionary nuns, and these women were often great forces for reform within religious orders. But none of them had the public role and impact of the Holy Maid of Kent.

Excessive emphasis on the multifarious and often bizarre manifestations of the medieval cult of saints can, however, be as misleading as excessive concentration on the 'cult of the dead'. It can seem to substantiate the common charge, first levelled by the early Reformers, that late medieval Catholicism allowed the person of Christ to become obscured by the cult of the saints with its profusion of rites and ceremonies. Only in the case of one saint could such an argument conceivably be sustained – that of Our Lady, the Blessed Virgin Mary, Mother of God – who alone shared with her son the distinction of being depicted (usually more than once) in every church or chapel in the land. If any saint's cult in reality rivalled or jeopardised the worship of God, it was hers. And it was traditionally very strong in England, which had boasted at least since Richard II's time of being 'Our Lady's Dowry'. The cult of Mary easily eclipsed those of other saints. The Ave Maria was perhaps the most frequently uttered single prayer, and cycles of prayers such as the rosary, recited with the aid of strings of beads, were widely used. There were more feasts of Mary than of any other saint in the ecclesiastical calendar, and new Marian devotions from the Continent such as the Angelus were rapidly assimilated in England. Judgements on the relationship of the cult of Mary to the worship of God will inevitably depend on the historian's theological preconceptions (if any). Certainly it was incompatible with Protestant theologies of Christ and salvation. But within the Catholic tradition, Marian devotion in practice helped focus attention on Christ and his incarnation, and was well integrated into patristic and scholastic theologies. The close positive correlation between Marian and eucharistic devotion is obvious in the history of the Catholic Church, and, Protestant polemic notwithstanding, there is little evidence to suggest that either the cult of Mary or those of other saints in fact undermined devotion to Christ.[20]

Devotion to the person of Christ was on the contrary intense and passionate in the later middle ages. Great veneration was paid to the crucifix and to the consecrated host, and to other signs, relics, and images of Christ, including the true cross, the crown of thorns, the holy lance, the five wounds, the seven sheddings of blood, and the name of Jesus. All these things inspired hugely popular cults in early Tudor England, and indeed throughout Catholic Europe. Expenditure on rood lofts, where images of the saints were set in proper symbolic relationship to the crucified Christ, was one of the most frequent features of churchwardens' accounts. And the candle burning before the rood was, together with that burning before the reserved eucharistic host, one of the most important devotional focuses within the parish church. The cross was so universally represented that even a hundred years of official English iconoclasm did not suffice to eliminate it from the realm: the Puritan zealots of the Civil War still found plenty to put beneath the hammer. As late as 1533 Henry himself demonstrated his acceptance of the Catholic devotional system by donating a fragment from Christ's crown of thorns to the royal chapel at Windsor.[21] The materialistic superstitions often attached to such images, relics, and devotions testify to the central place of Christ's person, and especially of Christ's passion, in late medieval religion. The very act of making the sign of the cross was a habitual response to evil of all kinds. But it was the consecrated host which dominated devotion. The mere sight of it at mass – 'seeing one's maker' – was popularly supposed to protect against sudden death and blindness that day, and we have already noted the magnetic attraction which the consecration and elevation of the sacrament had for early Tudor congregations. Indeed, the eucharistic host, the body of Christ, has been not inappropriately termed 'the ultimate relic'. Its power can be seen in a dispute at Lytham in Lancashire, where the local townspeople rioted against the monastery and tore down its boundary markers – crosses embellished with images of St Cuthbert. Although the people were undeterred from their violence by these sacred objects, they were overwhelmed when the monks faced them down with a consecrated host which compelled immediate veneration.[22] Considered as a relic, the host was undoubtedly the most popular in late medieval Europe.[23] And Christocentric devotions were the most widespread. In them we can see at its clearest the complex interaction of 'popular' and 'elite' religion. Sermons and books expounding and expatiating upon the sufferings and wounds of Christ, the instruments of the Passion, conformity to Christ in his Passion, and dedication to his person and Holy Name, fed a popular piety that lived in images and prayers. For all the elements of superstition that clustered around it, the core of this devotion was impeccably and centrally Christian, as can be seen from the verses inscribed beneath a crucifix venerated in St Alban's Abbey:

> Fly the falsehood of the fiend, for he will found thee.
> Dread not my dreadful dooms, for I died for thee.
> Call on me thy Saviour Christ, I can cheer thee.
> My mercy is more than thy miss, I may amend thee.
> See how my side was pierced for thee, and I shall
>     help thee.[24]

Throughout the middle ages there was a constant suspicion on the part of educated senior clergy of the religious practices and social customs of their lay inferiors. The fear that rural paganism survived under a thin veneer of Christian shrines and saints was often voiced. The employment of the sacred objects of Christian worship for superstitious purposes was regularly decried, and ecclesiastical legislation constantly endeavoured to control access to and disposal of not only the blessed sacrament, but holy water, blessed bread, candles, and relics. The line between superstition and religion was never easy to draw, and certain customs amounted to what Dr Scribner has called 'para-liturgical' practices. Originally classified as super-stitions, they could eventually find their way into local liturgical handbooks with the approval of the relevant authorities, and could ultimately ascend to the sphere of the elite in the form of new and officially sanctioned liturgical devotions – such as the Feast of the Name of Jesus or the Mass of the Five Wounds.[25] In addition, many perfectly orthodox and acceptable religious practices – such as the procuring of masses, or the saying of regular prayers like the Pater Noster and of special prayers like the 'Bone Iesu' – were encouraged in popular eyes by their connection with legendary stories like St Gregory's Trental or St Bernard's 'Scala Coeli' or else with the promise of stupendous and often spurious indulgences.

In the wake of the royal supremacy there developed within the Church of England a sustained campaign against many aspects of popular religion. An early victim was the indulgence. The depth of attachment to indulgences in pre-Reformation England must not be underestimated. Indulgences were avail-able for the recitation of prayers, charitable giving of all kinds, attendance at recantations and executions for heresy, and much else besides. Alongside the authentic indulgences issued by popes or bishops there was a fantasy world of spurious indulgences – mostly for improbably enormous yet minutely specified periods – attached in popular belief to various ritual acts and incantations. It is these, more than anything, that illustrate the hold of the indulgence on people's imaginations. But once the authority of the papacy had fallen, it would have been inconsistent in the extreme to retain a religious custom which was entirely dependent historically and theologically on that authority. The documents recording papal indulgences were implicitly covered by the anti-papal legislation, and the printing of indulgences seems to have petered out in the mid-1530s. The process was probably well under way when a specific proclamation against them was issued on 1 January 1536.[26] Its rhetoric is particularly revealing about the motive for the attack, arguing that indulgences encouraged people both to waste their money and to be negligent in keeping the commandments. From about this time, the vernacular Primers which were printed with a degree of official support omitted the detailed instructions on gaining indulgences which were commonly found in pre-Reformation Primers. Nevertheless, some backwoods clergy were still preaching the papal indulgences for Corpus Christi day in 1536.[27] As late as 1538, Cromwell's injunctions prohibited the ringing of church bells for the Angelus, 'lest people do hereafter trust to have pardon for the saying of their Aves, between the said knelling, as they have in time past'. So it is unlikely that popular attachment to indulgences was eliminated overnight. But they soon disappeared from public religious life, and the ease with which they were destroyed is one of the most remarkable features of Henry's Reformation. Their demise was bound up with the attack on the doctrine of purgatory that developed in the 1530s, unofficially at first but soon gaining official tolerance and even sympathy. The indulgence had to stand or fall with purgatory – in the 1530s, they fell together.

The exhibiting of relics was a matter of notorious abuse in the late medieval church. While there were undoubtedly many genuine relics in the possession of monasteries and churches, popular demand stimulated the manufacture of spurious relics where reality failed to come up to expectations. Even in the middle ages bishops and theologians were aware of the problems caused by excessive credulity, and attempts were made to authenticate relics held up for public veneration. When, for example, a 'bleeding host' (a consecrated wafer alleged to be miraculously exuding blood) created a popular sensation at the

London Carmelites in 1515, Wolsey ordered a prompt investigation which exposed it as an imposture.[28] But despite all efforts at supervision, abuses proliferated, and attracted the satirical pens of the Christian Humanists of the early sixteenth century. Erasmian satires ridiculed the quantities of Our Lady's milk and clothing and of the True Cross on display across Europe. Erasmus himself has made famous the disgust which he and John Colet felt on being presented with Becket's handkerchief on a visit to Canterbury around 1511. Committed as they were to the value of the written word, the humanists demanded documentary authentication before accepting relics. Thus, Erasmus's devotion (shared with many humanists) to the Holy House of Loretto can probably be ascribed to that shrine's claim to possess a number of documentary records of the miraculous appearance there of the Holy Family's Nazareth home in 1294 and of an investigation pursued there and in the Holy Land shortly afterwards which concluded that the house had indeed miraculously crossed the Mediterranean. Essentially humanist presuppositions about authentication seem to have underlain the monastic visitation of 1535. It is plain from the reports of Dr Layton and the other visitors that there was a systematic attempt to sort out the genuine from the spurious. When Dr Layton examined the relic of St Peter's chain at Bath priory in August 1535, his worst suspicions were confirmed by the fact that the monks were unable to say how they had come by it and had no written evidence about it. And John ap Rhys wrote from Bury St Edmund's in November: 'Among the relics we found much vanity and superstition, as the coals that St Laurence was toasted with, the paring of St Edmund's nails, St Thomas of Canterbury's pen-knife and his boots'.[29] Nevertheless, neither Erasmus nor the visitors of 1535 seem to have rejected the cult of relics in principle. It was the abuse, not the use, of relics that offended them.

A distinct change in official policy appeared in 1536, when Cromwell's radical injunctions for the Church of England opened a phase of sustained official hostility towards much of the apparatus of traditional popular religion. The injunctions were issued in the wake of the 1536 Convocation which had approved the Ten Articles drafted by the king and his advisers in an attempt to resolve certain disputed questions of doctrine and practice. Both the articles and the injunctions touched on popular piety, and it is instructive to note the variations in emphasis between the two documents. The articles were produced by a king and passed by a Convocation which were both predominantly conservative in religious sympathies. They deal with images and the veneration and intercession of saints, taking a moderate but essentially conservative line. The scriptural basis for the use of images was acknowledged, albeit balanced by the scriptural evidence for the dangers of idolatry. Images, especially of Christ and Our Lady, were declared to be of value as examples of and inducements to a holy life. Preachers were to make it clear that devotions paid before images were addressed not to the images or saints themselves but to God. The saints were to be honoured for what God had worked in and through them, and were to be prayed to not as if they had power in their own right, but purely in order that they might intercede with God. The only identifiable departure from the Catholic tradition in the three articles on saints and images is to be found in the terse rejection of the concept of the patron saint as a 'vain superstition'. Cromwell issued his injunctions in part to disseminate the articles, but in doing so he modified their message in a more radical direction. He effectively forbade sermons about images, relics, and miracles; attacked prayer to saints without conceding their role as intercessors; and strongly discouraged pilgrimages and offerings to images and relics. He mentioned neither the educational nor the moral value of images. His avowed concern was that 'all superstition and hypocrisy . . . may vanish away'. It is in these words that the significance of the injunctions and articles lies. The articles had alluded to the risks of abuses, superstition and even idolatry in the cult of the saints; Cromwell's injunctions made the same point more definitely. Henceforth an increasing body of popular devotional practice was to be dismissed in the new rhetoric of 'superstition' and 'idolatry'. The changes of 1536 probably had little practical effect on popular piety in themselves. But they undermined the basis of popular religion, indicated the likely direction of future change, and put into official circulation a new rhetoric which was to be taken up with enthusiasm by Reformers in positions of authority. Thus in 1537 Latimer went beyond both the articles and Cromwell's injunctions, asserting flatly in his own injunctions that idolatry, superstition, and other enormities were rampant in his diocese.[30]

Official suspicions about relics had been manifested as early as the visitation of the monasteries in 1535, although, as we have seen, Henry himself had donated a relic of the crown of thorns to Windsor as late as 1533. From early 1536, suspicion became downright hostility. At first, Cromwell seems to have envisaged acting through Parliament, for a draft statute survives which proposes suppressing pilgrimages and the worship of relics by means of injunctions.[31] In the event, he decided that injunctions would suffice without further statutory backing, and his injunctions of 1536, together with the Ten Articles, strongly discouraged pilgrimage and the cult of relics. From 1538 relics were sought out and destroyed. Perhaps the most famous relic in England was the Holy Blood of Hailes (Worcester diocese), believed to be a quantity of Christ's actual blood miraculously preserved in a crystal phial. For the Lollards this relic was the quintessential fake: they had for years dismissed it as duck's blood. In February 1538, John Hilsey took up this charge in a sermon at Paul's Cross. Later that year, the abbot of Hailes, himself a client of Cromwell's sympathetic to reform, asked the vicar-general to authorise an investigation into the relic. His request may not have been unsolicited – around the same time Cranmer made a similar request with respect to the relic of Becket's blood in his cathedral. On 4 October Cromwell issued a commission to look into the matter. His choice of personnel determined the result in advance: Latimer, Henry Holbeach (prior of Worcester cathedral), the abbot of Hailes himself, and Richard Tracy – all by this time committed reformers. They concluded that it was some kind of coloured gum, and locked it away. On 24 November 1538, Hilsey preached again at Paul's Cross, displaying the relic for public contempt and publishing the findings of Cromwell's commission.[32] Although in this case there was a conscientious attempt to investigate the nature of the relic, in most other cases the year 1538 simply witnessed the redefinition of relics as 'feigned'. Cromwell's injunctions themselves did not explicitly order the destruction of relics. But he ordered preachers to discourage people from putting trust in them, to prohibit them from paying devotions to them, and to recant publicly if they had ever previously extolled them to their parishioners. Reforming bishops avidly took up this theme. Echoing and amplifying the message of Cromwell's injunctions, Shaxton fulminated against the 'intolerable superstition and abominable idolatry' which surrounded relics in his diocese. He forbade the dispatch of girdles and similar items to women in labour, and ordered that all relics should be brought to him for inspection. He promised to return those that were found authentic, but it is unlikely that any passed his exacting standards. Further signals about the regime's hostility to relics were given in 1541, when Henry abrogated the two feasts of the Invention and the Exaltation of the Cross, which celebrated the cult of the crucifix. Public devotion to relics was presumably brought to an end by Cromwell's injunctions. Pilgrimages seem to have ceased almost at once. At Iddesleigh in Devon, pilgrimage offerings disappeared from the churchwardens' accounts after 1537.[33] But popular attitudes were harder to reform. In 1545 a London priest thought it worth attempting to fake a 'bleeding host' miracle. And relics of those executed for refusing the oath to the supremacy were prized among Catholic malcontents. Thomas Mudde, a monk of Jervaulx, excaped to Scotland with the head of his martyred *confrère* George Lazenby, while some former London Carthusians retrieved and hid away the arm of the Carthusian martyr John Houghton until they managed to smuggle it abroad in 1547.[34]

The feast day or holy day was an important element in the social experience of traditional Catholicism. As well as a religious celebration, the feast day was an opportunity for rest and recreation. It is no coincidence that it has given 'holiday' to the language. But the tendency of popular recreations to degenerate into vice had long been lamented by moralists, and there was a growing sense in the later middle ages that there were just too many feasts in the ecclesiastical calendar. A particular problem in the larger cities was caused by the parochial celebrations of patron saints. Since most parish churches were distinguished by different dedications, a single city could host a series of dedication feasts throughout the year. And the parish boundary was not so impermeable that fun-lovers from other parishes could not come along to join in. The opportunities that such feasts thus gave for idleness among servants and labourers was a growing concern of the more sober and established citizens. The first steps in reforming this problem were in fact taken before the break with Rome, by the humanist Bishop of London, Cuthbert Tunstall, at the instigation of the mayor and aldermen of the city. In 1523 he transferred all dedication feasts of churches within the city to 3 October, thus drastically reducing the temptations offered by frequent feast days. After the break with Rome, the regime turned Tunstall's reform into a national policy and took it much further. The Convocation of 1536 translated all dedication feasts to the first Sunday in October, prohibited patronal feasts, and ordered that, with certain exceptions, no feasts falling in harvest time (1 July to 29 September) or the law terms should be observed as holy days.[35] Henry VIII promulgated this in an encyclical letter to the bishops, and the message was reiterated in Cromwell's injunctions later that year. The abolition of 'superfluous holy days' was justified, much as it had been by Tunstall, in terms of the common good. There were some problems with the reform. It was found that the feasts of the evangelists Mark and Luke had been unwittingly abolished, along with that of Mary Magdalene. These were restored by proclamation in 1541. The same proclamation resolved a problem which had arisen with the abolition of the feast of St Laurence, namely that many people continued to observe the traditional fast on the vigil: it was now made clear that where feasts had been abrogated, associated fasts were implicitly abrogated likewise. The attack on the carnival aspects of religious observance in the interests of hard work and sobriety was continued in other ways. The 'superstitious and childish observances' associated with such feasts as those of St Nicholas and of the Holy Innocents (on which boys dressed up as priests and bishops and performed mock rituals) were banned in 1541 as more pagan than Christian. And in 1544 the performance of plays and interludes on Sundays and holy days was severely restricted.[36] Together with the attack on pilgrimage in the injunctions of 1536 and 1538, these changes represented a significant reduction in the lighter side of religious life, and were clearly moving in the directions later taken by the Puritans. This impression is confirmed by the report from Nottinghamshire in 1539 that whereas respectable people dutifully worked on the old feast days, the poorer sort continued to take those days off.[37] The whole campaign was directed towards the production of a disciplined and orderly society. The attack on pilgrimage was buttressed with claims that God was better pleased with a zealous performance of employment and family duties, and with the donation of surplus wealth to the poor, than with jaunts around the country. The injunctions of 1536 instructed parsons and parents to teach the elements of the faith to children and to ensure that the young were brought up 'either to learning or to some other honest exercise, occupation, or husbandry'. The concern with a 'work ethic' can be seen in Latimer's rosy report to Cromwell in 1538 about the moral improvement in Worcester since the overthrow of the cathedral's Marian shrine: 'by reason of their lady they have been given to much idleness; but now that she is gone, they be turned to laboriousness, and so from ladyness to godliness'.[38] His equation of idleness with idolatry, and of 'ladyness' with laziness, was central in the appeal of the Reforming message to the 'better sort' of people in England's towns.

The injunctions of 1536 fired the first shot in what was to be a prolonged campaign within the Church of England against the use of images in church and eventually against their mere presence. This campaign was intensified under Edward VI, reversed under Mary, reinstated under Elizabeth, and not finally completed until the Civil War of the seventeenth century. The iconoclasm of Henry VIII's reign differed from that elsewhere in Europe in one major respect: it was inspired from above rather than from below. There were several quite serious iconoclastic incidents earlier in Henry's reign, including a spate of attacks in East Anglia during 1531–32 in the wake of Bilney's execution.[39] But these cases involved few participants, and were wholly different from the riots which eliminated images from the cities of Germany and Switzerland. Nor were the English incidents always religiously motivated. One case in Sussex in the 1530s, when a few men emerged from an alehouse and went off to uproot a wayside cross, turned out to have rested on no more profound a belief than that a pot of gold lay buried underneath – a motive perhaps not far beneath the surface of the official iconoclasm of the later 1530s.[40] Despite the barely restrained hostility of Cromwell's 1536 injunctions, there was little effect on the cult of the saints until 1538, perhaps because the Pilgrimage of Grace deterred the authorities from sudden change. Some images fell with the smaller monasteries. For example, the Holy Cross of Bromholme (Norfolk) was sent to Cromwell by the dissolution commissioner Richard Southwell early in 1537. And evangelical bishops like Cranmer and Latimer did their best to enforce change (Latimer stripped Our Lady of Worcester of her vestments and ornaments in 1537), but even they found it an uphill task.[41] In 1538, though, Cromwell turned his attention once more to images and the saints. His second injunctions intensified the message of 1536, and on his instructions a campaign of iconoclasm was launched. Major shrines throughout the country were closed down, and their images, relics, and movable property sent to his London residence. The Rood of Grace from Boxley was burned at Paul's Cross on 24 February. The image of St Saviour was removed from Bermondsey Abbey shortly afterwards, and Derfel Gadarn was burned at Paul's Cross on 22 May. That event provoked one of the few cases of genuine mob iconoclasm during Henry's reign, the smashing of the rood at St Margaret Pattens (London) by a group of English and Flemish lads. However, this disorder inspired no widespread imitation, perhaps because of the destruction of much of that parish by fire a few days later, which was interpreted by conservatives as divine judgement. The official iconoclasm continued unabated and unopposed.

In the summer, statues of Our Lady were brought to London from Basingstoke, Caversham, Ipswich, Penrhys, Walsingham, and Worcester. St Anne at Buxton and St Modwen at Burton-on-Trent were taken down and sent to London in August, while St Paul's lost its rood and its Virgin. The Rood of Boston was burned in its home town on 7 September. The shrine of St Edmund at Bury was razed. St Thomas of Canterbury was proclaimed a traitor, his shrine stripped, his bones burned, and his feasts struck from the calendar.[42] The shrine of St Richard at Chichester was looted in December. Nor was it only the greater shrines that fell – they simply made the most noise. Smaller fry were also swallowed up: Dr London complacently told how he took down two Marian shrines and a rood at Coventry in October.[43] Across the country, as surviving churchwardens' accounts show, the lights burning before images went out, and the little confraternities that maintained them ceased to exist. Only the lights before the rood, the reserved sacrament, and the sepulchre were allowed to remain. The fact that they did so everywhere shows how little attitudes had changed. For some reason (probably the conservatism of Bishop Longland), the shrine of St Hugh at Lincoln survived the first wave of destruction. Like most major shrines, it was bedecked with fabulous wealth in gold, silver, and jewels. But it was brought to Henry's attention in June 1540, and he promptly gave orders for its suppression and the conveyance of its wealth to London.[44] The main campaign, however, was over by the end of 1538, presumably because its objectives had been achieved. And dramatic though it was, the extent of the iconoclasm must not be exaggerated. Wealthy shrines and miraculous images were stripped and smashed, and all veneration of images was forbidden, but most churches retained statues, paintings, and stained glass windows until the more radical iconoclasm of the following reign.

The conservative reaction of the 1540s took remarkably few steps backward from the positions of the late 1530s, and nowhere was this more true than in official attitudes to popular religion. Henry's personal commitment to the attack on the cult of the saints was revealed in 1542, two years after

Cromwell's fall, when, on a progress which took him as far north as Yorkshire, Henry discovered the extent to which the injunctions of 1538 had been at best fulfilled only according to the letter, and at worst flagrantly disregarded. Finding that many shrines remained intact, he ordered Cranmer to ensure that they were so completely dismantled that no vestige survived.[45] Official teaching remained equally hostile to saints, relics, images, and pilgrimages. The King's Book of 1543, which reflected Henry's conservative theological predilections, not only reiterated but even reinforced the relevant teaching of the more radical Bishops' Book of 1537. No concessions were made to pilgrimage, a practice irredeemably compromised by the rebels of 1536. The preaching of miracles, relics, and legends of the saints remained forbidden – which effectively cut off at the root both new cults and the revival of the old. The offering of money, the lighting of candles, and the addressing of prayers to statues and images was still condemned as idolatry. On the other hand, the lines drawn in the 1530s around the rump of the cult of saints were held firm. Prayer for intercession could still be addressed to saints, and images and pictures were permitted in churches for educational and commemorative purposes, provided that no idolatrous practices grew up around them. In other domains the attack on the cult of the saints was taken further. In 1544 Cranmer published the first vernacular Litany, replacing the old Latin Litany of the Saints. Where the traditional form individually sought the intercession of dozens of apostles, evangelists, martyrs, confessors, and virgins, the role of the saints in Cranmer's Litany was reduced to the barest minimum. There were two general petitions, one for the intercession of the angels and the other for the intercession of the saints. And when Henry finally issued his authorised Primer in 1545, the casual reader might have found it hard to believe that this was a descendant of the pre-Reformation Primer, the 'Hours of the Blessed Virgin'. The saints were almost completely expunged from it, and Our Lady herself was scarcely mentioned from one end to the other.

Notwithstanding the relentlessness with which the regime extirpated the cult of the saints, its attitude to traditional popular religion still fell considerably short of that of Continental Protestantism. On the Continent, the liturgical ceremonies of the medieval Church were swept aside, like the cult of the saints, as idolatry. Yet in England, the blessing of holy water, the offering of candles at Candlemas, the use of ashes on Ash Wednesday and of palms on Palm Sunday, and the paying of veneration and reverence to the crucifix and the consecrated eucharistic host kept their place in the annual liturgical round. Their place was apparently guaranteed by the Ten Articles of 1536, which emphasised in Erasmian fashion that their purpose was 'to put us in remembrance of those spiritual things that they do signify'. But it was by no means apparent at the height of Cromwellian reform that such ceremonies would remain inviolate. Cromwell himself protected and favoured preachers who inveighed against them, and his injunctions of 1536, although requiring that ceremonies should be observed, went out of their way to emphasise that they were not necessary to salvation, but rested on royal authority. By November 1538, enough people were disregarding ceremonies to merit censure in a royal proclamation. And while Henry commanded his subjects to observe 'laudable ceremonies', his casual aside 'which as yet be not abolished nor taken away by the King's highness' was to say the least ominous. In February 1539, a further proclamation followed this up by ordering parish priests to instruct their flocks in the significance of the ceremonies whenever they were used. Thus the use of holy water was to be expounded as a reminder of baptism, and creeping to the cross on Good Friday as a sign of humility before Christ and a memorial of Christ's passion. The point of all this was characteristically summed up: 'to the whole body it shall be greatly profitable . . . to see the whole congregation under the king's majesty's governance, so to profess and outwardly to declare a loving and charitable obedience'.[46] Moreover, Henry ostentatiously availed himself of holy water and other ceremonies around this time in an obvious attempt to restore their credit. This policy was taken further in 1540, when Cromwell informed the House of Lords that the king had appointed a committee of bishops to produce a definitive exposition of the ceremonies used in his church.[47] Their highly traditional exposition, entitled 'Ceremonies to be used in the Church of England', seems to have been presented to Henry and Cranmer, but was never officially promulgated, perhaps because Cranmer managed to dissuade or distract Henry from issuing it.[48] Cranmer's role can only be conjectural, but he did manage to hold the line against a number of other conservative initatives in the 1540s, and his hostility to traditional ceremonies was no secret. He countenanced the omission and rejection of ceremonies within his own diocese in the 1540s. And in January 1546, he tried to persuade the ageing king to ban them. But Henry backed off, claiming to have been persuaded by the arguments of Gardiner that the foreign policy repercussions would be dangerous.[49]

Our best opportunity to assess the impact of the Henrician attack on popular religion is afforded by the many series of parochial churchwardens' accounts which survive for this period. One conclusion commands universal assent. In so far as general support for the established religion can be deduced from the financial support accorded it, there is no reason to suppose that the late medieval church in England was anything other than hugely popular. The picture which these records paint is of a vigorous popular piety directed to the worship of God through the efforts of the whole community embodied in what was often the only communal building, the parish church.[50] It is arguable that the ideal of a Christian community united in belief and worship before God, an ideal pursued with such zeal by Protestant and Catholic Reformers alike, has never been so closely approximated as in the late medieval parish. This is not to say that there were no defects in their grasp of Christian doctrine, nor that they were notably successfully in upholding Christian moral standards; simply that, considered as communities, they effectively performed the worship they felt due to God and his saints. Nothing could be further removed from the truth than the common criticism of the Reformers that the proliferation of saint cults, and thus of guilds and altars, in the late medieval Church constituted a divisive influence in communities, 'setting altar against altar'.

But the other main conclusion which has emerged from a series of thorough local studies and can be verified by almost random sampling among the many series of published accounts, is that the parishes of England acquiesced in the Henrician assault with startling promptness and obedience. Generally speaking, orders to remove were fulfilled more promptly than orders to obtain: when told to take down relics and venerated images, churchwardens did so without demur; when told to purchase Bibles, they did so, but often after some delay. Obedience was prompt partly because the changes were piecemeal and partly because Henry's regime had a tight grip on the kingdom. But it is manifest that the changes in minds and hearts mostly succeeded rather than preceded the outward reforms. No churchwardens' accounts suggest any diminution in commitment to the cult of the saints even on the very eve of the 1538 injunctions. Donations to maintain lights before images or altars remained constant, or even increased, until the moment the practice was outlawed.[51]

Henry's attack on the popular religion of his subjects remains one of the hardest aspects of his Reformation to explain. Professor Dickens, making his own the rhetoric of the Reformers, sees it as the triumph of the pure word of God over the unscriptural accretions of late medieval Catholicism.[52] In fact it was royal power, not Gospel truth, that won the day. Another suggestion is that the policy emerged from an Erasmian concern to purify popular Catholicism. Yet the policy was originated by reformers whose evangelical leanings were more Protestant than Erasmian. It went beyond the Erasmian agenda and was repudiated by three leading English Erasmians – Tunstall, Longland, and Stokesley – who set their hands to a measured affirmation of the veneration of relics, the practice of pilgrimage, and the possibility of miracles at shrines.[53] The dissolution of shrines and abrogation of holy days probably owed as much to greed and a concern for social discipline as to the disinterested worship of God in spirit and truth. Yet it was no mere coincidence that the veneration of relics and images was abolished in the same injunctions that ordered every parish church to buy an English Bible. The 'word of God' rhetoric so frequently invoked to justify the changes of the 1530s resounded through Cromwell's injunctions. But once more we must have recourse to the image of Old Testament kingship if we are to make sense of Henry's policy. The iconoclasm of 1538 was perceived and presented by his supporters in terms of the achievements of a Josiah smashing the idols. An important preparation for this was the adoption by Henry's Church in 1537 of the 'Reformed' enumeration of the Ten Commandments, in which the prohibition of graven images is given special prominence by separation from the injunction to worship God alone (with which it is usually conflated in the Rabbinic, Catholic, and Lutheran traditions).[54] Having begun to see himself as a king according to the model of the Old Testament, Henry, like Josiah, was brought to a clearer understanding of God's word, and immediately set about enforcing it lest the wrath of God should strike his kingdom. His iconoclasm, like his supremacy, was justified by an appeal to the word of God. And the natural concomitant of this appeal was the official publication of an English Bible, to reveal to people the scriptural authority claimed for his policies. This portentous event stood at the end of one cultural development and at the beginning of another. It was the culmination of the emergence of a literate English culture during the later middle ages, and it was the start of an English culture based on the Bible which replaced the predominantly oral and visual culture of late medieval Catholicism.

# 4

## VERNACULAR RELIGIOUS CULTURE

The most lasting positive contribution of Henry VIII's Reformation to the popular religion of England was the official sanctioning of the English Bible. 'The BIBLE, I say, The BIBLE only is the Religion of Protestants!', William Chillingworth was to proclaim emphatically in 1638, a hundred years after royal injunctions first ordered that a copy of the English Bible should be purchased by every parish church in the realm.[1] And the particular version of the Bible which shaped the religion of English Protestants, the Authorised Version, was little more than a rehash of that which Henry had sanctioned – in turn essentially that of the Lutherans Tyndale and Coverdale. Henry not only introduced England to its Bible but also encouraged in many other ways the development of a popular religious culture that was literate and vernacular. This was something of a contrast with the visual and ritual past, although the novelty has been exaggerated by some historians. To some extent the Henrician changes merely amplified and redirected currents which had already been flowing in the late medieval Church. The increasing sophistication and uniformity of the English language in the later middle ages, together with the marked rise in lay literacy and the introduction of printing, had already stimulated demand for vernacular religious literature and perhaps even for vernacular scripture – to which the opposition of the early Tudor clergy was by no means unyielding. Henry's regime not only fostered but also sought to control these developments, primarily in the interests of promoting obedience. By publishing the Bible and disseminating the word of God in a language people could understand, he hoped to spread knowledge of the moral law, especially the law of obedience to princes, and of the divine sanction for the moral and political order. This policy certainly appealed to his new self-image as the Old Testament king: Moses, David, and Solomon had composed large portions of the scriptures; Josiah had restored them; and even the pagan monarchs Artaxerxes and Ptolemy had pleased God by having the scriptures respectively restored and translated. Henry was perhaps led to believe that the effects of a vernacular Bible would not be subversive, as had previously been feared. But when it seemed as though vernacular religious literature was indeed fomenting disorder and subversion, attempts were made to control the printing trade – a further extension of the scope of royal government, though far from wholly effective. Even so, print was potentially as much an instrument for conformity and uniformity as for dissent and diversity. Henrician policy aimed to encourage the former role and curtail the latter. From the break with Rome onwards there was a consistent pursuit of uniformity in religious literature, whether in Bibles, prayer books, or handbooks of religious instruction. The Edwardian liturgical projects of Thomas Cranmer, although constructed on radically different theological foundations, were expressions of a similar policy, and were enforced suitably enough by the two Acts of Uniformity.

It is well known that in the fourteenth century English was emerging as the culturally dominant language of the kingdom. A turning-point in this process was marked by the substitution in 1362 of English for French as the language of pleading in the king's courts (though Latin remained the language of record; see 36 Edw III c. 15). English was also displacing French as the language of the royal court itself: court poets such as Chaucer, Gower, and Lydgate turned to English rather than French. These developments reflected the strident nationalism that characterised the prolonged conflict between England and France. The language of the common people thus achieved a status it had not hitherto enjoyed, and a standard English, distinct from most local dialects, matured as a literary idiom. The vernacular culture also invaded English religious life. The aftermath of the Norman Conquest had seen the virtual suppression of a flourishing Old English religious literature and culture. For several centuries, vernacular religious writing in England was mainly done in Norman French: the earliest translations of parts of the Bible (Psalms and Kings) into French were carried out in England during this period.[2] Even at the end of the fourteenth century, an English nobleman owning the Bible would probably have it in French rather than English. But Archbishop Pecham's Lambeth Constitutions of 1281 had laid down the importance of vernacular religious instruction for all levels of society, specifying, as we have seen already, that such teaching should cover the Our Father, Hail Mary, Creed, Ten Commandments, seven sacraments, seven works of mercy, seven virtues, and seven deadly sins. In response, writers on religious subjects turned increasingly to English in the fourteenth century. William of Shoreham, for example, was composing religious instruction in verse for his Kentish parishioners around 1330. In 1357 John Thoresby, Archbishop of York, issued a more systematic book of basic religious instruction in both English and Latin. And the most successful effort in this genre, the *Prick of Conscience*, a verse exposition of the faith, survives in more manuscripts than any other vernacular work except the Lollard Bible. Nor was catechetical literature alone produced. Before 1350 Richard Rolle had carried out a verse rendering of the Psalms – the first scriptural translation into English – as well as a number of spiritual treatises. And by the end of the century, Walter Hilton had composed his *Scale of Perfection*, a manual of the spiritual life which was one of the earliest English works to be accorded the accolade of translation into Latin.

In the midst of these developments, in the 1380s, came the first attempt to render the entire Bible into English. The project was apparently undertaken by scholars of Oxford under the influence of the controversial theologian John Wycliffe.[3] The translation was certainly done by and for Lollards, but the common assumption that its readers must all have been Lollards is questionable. The English Bible was very popular, surviving in about 250 copies, mostly produced in the early fifteenth century. It far outscores any other medieval English work, its nearest rivals being the *Prick of Conscience* (over 110 copies) and Chaucer's *Canterbury Tales* (around 80). Although a decree passed by Convocation under Archbishop Arundel in 1408 condemned Lollard translations of the Bible, prohibited the carrying out of further translations except under episcopal supervision, and made possession of the English Bible dependent on episcopal licence, its effects may not have been as drastic as is usually thought. Possession of the vernacular scriptures did not on its own constitute heresy or decisive evidence of heresy, although it was powerful circumstantial evidence against those who incurred suspicion on other grounds: hence the interest of ecclesiastical investigators in the books owned by suspects. Nor was there anything intrinsically heretical in the bare text of the Lollard Bible, which was a largely accurate rendering of the Vulgate. Heretical doctrine was confined to Lollard interpretations of scripture, found in marginal annotations and in the so-called 'general prologue'. But this unquestionably heretical prologue survives in only eleven of the 250 extant manuscripts.[4] It was this prologue which was covered with hostile annotations by the rigidly orthodox Bishop of Coventry and Lichfield, Geoffrey Blythe, who unearthed a group of Lollard suspects at Coventry around 1511. And it was the presence of this prologue, together with heretical annotations in the owner's hand, in Richard Hunne's Bible which constituted Thomas More's main evidence that he was indeed a Lollard.[5] The sheer number of surviving manuscripts of the English Bible suggests that it was not in practice made absolutely illegal, although their early date suggests that the decree effectively curtailed further copying of the text. Although no formal episcopal licence for ownership of the English Bible is recorded, there is evidence that such licences were indeed granted. The anonymous translator of *The Mirror of Our Lady* around the mid-fifteenth-century obtained his bishop's permission to translate passages of scripture therein, and observed to the nuns for whom he was writing that they could read the psalms in English Bibles 'if ye have licence thereto'. The power to approve the possession of the English Bible was probably in practice devolved to qualified theologians. Bishop Pecock certainly thought they had such authority. One manuscript contains a note to the effect that it had been inspected and passed by Doctors Thomas Eborall and William Ive (successive masters of Whittington College, London in the years 1444–86). And Dr James Preston, the vicar of St Michael's Coventry (1488–1506), inspected and approved the English New Testament owned by Alice Rowley, the mayor's widow (although she was later found to be a Lollard, there is no reason to conclude that he was one).[6] Moreover, where surviving Bibles can be traced to particular pre-Reformation owners, those owners were mostly of impeccable orthodoxy: Henry VI, Henry VII, Duke Humphrey of Gloucester, the Carthusian priory of Sheen, Dame Anne Danvers, the priory of Syon, Fotheringay College, Sir William Weston (d. 1540, last English Prior of the Knights of St John), and the Dominican priory at Cambridge. It is more than likely that such owners had permission to keep and read their Bibles.

There was, however, an ambivalence within the Church of England over the use of the vernacular in religious contexts. This is manifest in the tribulations of the one pre-Reformation English Catholic theologian who made extensive use of the English Bible in his writings – Reginald Pecock, Bishop of Chichester. He chose to meet the Lollards on their own ground, answering their arguments in English rather than Latin, accepting the utility of vernacular scripture, and even citing scripture in the Lollard version. His enemies distilled error and heresy from his voluminous writings, forced him to recant and resign, and thus reduced him to silence. His real crime was to transgress the limits of an ambient theological conservatism.[7] Yet despite his discouraging fate, the development of a vernacular religious culture in England continued along different channels. The obstacles placed in the way of bible-reading and translating may account for the success enjoyed by 'para-scriptural' literature, mostly relating to the life of Christ, of which the best example is the *Mirror of the*

*Blessed Life of Christ*, a translation by the Carthusian Nicholas Love of a Latin life of Christ woven out of the four Gospels and commonly ascribed to Bonaventure. This version was submitted to Archbishop Arundel himself for approval, and survives in about 50 manuscripts. Another case is the early fifteenth-century translation of the medieval harmony of the Gospels, *Unum ex Quattuor*, of which over a dozen manuscripts survive.[8] It was not only literature which felt the impact of the vernacular. The early fifteenth century also saw English starting to figure in wills and in funeral inscriptions, both of them documents of religious significance. The traditional language of wills was Latin. The earliest known English will dates from 1351, and English wills were still very rare in the early fifteenth century. McFarlane noted the penchant for using English in the wills of his 'Lollard knights', and it may be that association of the vernacular with Lollardy set back the trend for English wills. At any rate, the fifty earliest English wills found in the registers of the Prerogative Court of Canterbury range from 1387 to 1439, standing out amid thousands in Latin. But the trend towards English grew apace in the later fifteenth century, and by the first decade of the sixteenth it is clear that English was the predominant language of lay wills. In Hull, for example, the earliest surviving vernacular will dates from 1453, with a handful more following until the 1480s, when a dramatic rise in the proportion of vernacular wills began. A quarter of Hull wills were written in English in the 1480s, two fifths in the 1490s, two thirds in 1500–10, and over nine tenths thereafter. The vast majority of Norwich wills in the first decade of the sixteenth century were already being written in English, with the few exceptions predominantly found among clergy and widows. Only among the clergy did Latin retain anything like its former popularity, though by no means all clerics used it. Even in the mostly clerical registers of the Vice-Chancellor's Court of Cambridge University, the majority of the wills are drafted in English from the beginning of the records early in the sixteenth century.[9]

The development with regard to funeral inscriptions parallels that of wills, although far fewer inscriptions survive. In the fourteenth century, inscriptions were in either Latin or French, Latin predominantly for the clergy, French for the nobility and gentry. French becomes extremely rare after 1400, and the first English inscriptions appear around then. But English remains rare until about 1450, and does not become common until about 1480. By 1500 it is vying with Latin, and by 1520 its dominance is plain. Latin remained fashionable among clergymen, and among such laity as wished to put on a show of learning. But by the late sixteenth century the Latin used was highly classical. The significance of the increasing use of English on funeral monuments is clear. The main purpose of such monuments was to request the prayers of passers-by for the souls of the dead. At a time when literacy was largely confined to the clergy, it made little sense for a monument to appeal for prayers in any other language than Latin. But as vernacular literacy spread among the laity, a new public of potential intercessors could be reached and was duly sought by the funeral monument. The connection of this trend with the rise of lay literacy is illustrated by a particularly interesting set of funeral monuments in Derbyshire: the brass plates in memory of Sir John Statham (d. 1453), his son Sir Thomas (d. 1470), and their wives. The monuments to Sir John appeal in both in Latin and English for intercessory prayer, indicating the different audiences envisaged. And an engraving on the plate to Sir Thomas's first wife Elizabeth portrays the Blessed Virgin Mary as a child being taught to read by her mother, St Anne. This topic was increasingly used as an illustration in manuscript books of hours being produced for the lay market in the later fifteenth century. The association which this iconography thus established between literacy and the two most popular female saints in fifteenth-century England is in itself a commentary on the new social value being attached – perhaps as much among women as among men – to lay literacy.[10]

The rise of the printing press in the later fifteenth century offers still clearer evidence of the increasing demand for the vernacular in literary and religious contexts. The press exploited even more fully the new medium of paper which had facilitated the vast expansion of manuscript production earlier in the century. In England, even more than on the Continent, printers showed a distinct preference for the vernacular. The production of liturgical texts (missals, breviaries, psalters, antiphoners, and hymn-books), which were necessarily in Latin and inevitably in constant demand, was carried out for the most part by French and Flemish printers for the English market rather than in England itself. This was partly because Continental publishers had dominated this market for some time, and partly because they were better equipped to print texts of high quality. Printing certainly gave new impetus to the development of the vernacular. The first occasion on which the enactments of an English Parliament were printed (in the reign of Richard III) was also the first occasion on which they were published in English. And the opportunities afforded by the press in an age of spreading literacy stimulated an unprecedented effort of translation. Demand for vernacular literature exceeded the available supply of original English works, and translation was the easiest way to generate more. So Caxton published translations of the Aeneid, of Boccaccio, and of much else besides, usually performing the translation himself. England also resembled the Continent in the strength of the market for religious books. In the first half century of English printing, religious books represented an enormous proportion of total publications, constituting one of three main market-sectors (the others were educational texts – grammar and logic manuals, mostly in Latin; and legal publications – statutes, proclamations, yearbooks, court books, and text-books, mostly in Law French or English). Of 812 editions by Wynkyn de Worde between 1492 and 1535, 214 were religious works, and a further 40 were liturgical texts – just over 30 per cent. This was exceeded only by his output of educational texts, a staggering 330 editions (all but two in Latin), or rather more than 40 per cent. Excluding educational texts printed for a manifestly specialised and restricted market, the proportion of religious books was therefore around 50 per cent, a level at which it remains if analysis is confined to vernacular books.[11] Romances, fables and poems provided the next most popular genre, accounting for nearly 30 per cent, with the rest mostly accounted for by works of law, history, and practical advice. Production patterns varied between different printers, doubtless reflecting different market decisions. The press of Robert Redman, active between 1525 and 1540, produced 210 surviving works. Nearly two thirds of them were legal texts, and most of the rest were religious. Of about 600 items produced by Pynson's press between 1490 and 1529, about two fifths were religious, although nearly half of these were ephemeral sheets such as indulgences (a market he clearly dominated). Legal texts represented a quarter of his output, and educational texts a sixth, with works of romance and history accounting for much of the remaining sixth.

The advent of printing did not fundamentally alter popular taste in religious literature. Works which had already circulated widely in manuscript were soon made available in print. The 'para-scriptural' *Mirror of the Life of Christ* had several editions before 1530, as did the increasingly popular *Imitation of Christ*. Lives of the saints had long been popular, for example in the translations by Lydgate and by the Augustinian canon Osbern Bokenham. One of Caxton's most successful efforts was his translation of the *Golden Legend*, the best-known medieval compilation of saints' lives. Collections of sermons were also made more accessible by printing. The *Festival* of John Mirk, already widely copied in manuscript, went into several editions by 1530. And the best-selling original English religious composition of the first quarter of the sixteenth century was John Fisher's *Sermons on the Seven Penitential Psalms*, of which at least seven editions were published between 1508 and 1530 (among vernacular sermons published in Tudor England, only Latimer's and the official Anglican *Homilies* enjoyed greater success). Books of religious instruction, mostly expositions of the basic prayers, similarly retained their popularity. The fashionable religious literature of the period, whether before or after the advent of printing, was characterised by a concentration on the person of Christ and a concern with a private and almost individualistic devotional life. Personal penance and the passion of Christ were at the heart of the literate devotional life. But while devotional and catechetical literature flourished in the vernacular, other areas of religious literature were notably absent. New translations of scripture had effectively been outlawed by Arundel's Constitution. The Catholic liturgy remained entirely in Latin throughout this period: although some books were published giving vernacular commentaries on the liturgical action, no translations as such were printed in English. And professional theology remained the preserve of the academic clergy, conducted entirely in Latin.

Despite the prevailing conservatism of vernacular religious literature in the first fifty years of English printing, there are signs that pressure to extend the range of such literature was gradually pushing at traditional limitations. This can be seen in the production of one of the most common religious texts for the lay readership, the Book of Hours of the Blessed Virgin Mary, otherwise known as the Primer or the 'layfolk's prayer-book'. Some vernacular versions of the Primer had been produced in the late fourteenth and early fifteenth centuries, but the Lollard crisis curtailed this development. It was probably not so much that such translations were intrinsically suspect as that their production suffered in the spirit of suspicion created by the repression of Lollardy. So when Primers began to be printed in large numbers for the English market towards 1500, they were all in Latin. However, the demand for vernacular instruction led to the inclusion of increasing quantities of vernacular rubrics to tell readers what they were reading and when and how they should read it. Gradually, paraphrases and translations of certain important prayers and passages of scripture began to appear in these volumes. Conventional limits on the use of the vernacular in such books were being quietly pushed back. Popular para-liturgical prayers such as the Fifteen Oes, a series of invocations of Christ attributed to St Bridget, were among the first to be translated. Basic prayers such as the Pater Noster – which everybody knew in Latin – started to appear in English as well. Even passages of scripture began to be rendered, although here there was a tendency to evade the letter of Arundel's Constitution by recourse to paraphrase rather than translation. Rhymed versions of psalms began to circulate, reflecting a growing lay demand. It is even likely that one of the reasons for the popularity of Fisher's *Sermons on the Penitential Psalms* was that they provided, albeit spread through the text, a complete though free rendering of all seven psalms, including the two most popular psalms of the time, the Miserere and the De Profundis (psalms 50 and 129). The question of why the Bible was not freely available in English when it was so in French was far from unthinkable. The printer Richard Pynson addressed it in a preface written in 1506, giving the traditional though scarcely adequate reply that, compared with French, English was not sufficiently sophisticated a language.[12]

The advent of the Reformation in England was closely connected with the increasing lay demand for vernacular religious literature. This is not to suggest that the fashion for the vernacular was intrinsically subversive, but that the ultimate success of the Reformation in England owed much to the success of the early Reformers in aligning themselves with the aspirations of an increasingly literate laity. For there can be no doubt that the Reformation brought about an immediate and considerable expansion in the scope of vernacular religious culture. This is most obvious in relation to scripture, which in the 1530s became for the first time widely available to the English public in a language they could understand. Yet the influence of the vernacular also manifested itself in two other areas during Henry's reign. The first was that of theology, which became the stuff of popular vernacular as well as of academic Latin debate. Thus, in England, the duel between Tyndale and More marked an important shift in attitudes.[13] Whereas Pecock had incurred the hostility of the clergy through his efforts to meet the heretics in their own language, More was positively encouraged by the clergy to do exactly the same thing. One can scarcely even imagine a layman of Pecock's time attempting what More was to attempt – although one can readily guess the fate of anyone who might have had the temerity so to do. Finally, Henry's reign saw the first steps towards the translation of the Church's liturgy into English, a process which was to be triumphantly completed by Cranmer with a reduced range of truncated texts in the following reign. These first steps were tentative, extending only to the private liturgy of the Primer, and to the public Litany of the Saints. But they were nonetheless significant for that.

The processes by which the vernacular Bible and Primer developed from unofficial, indeed forbidden, endeavours into authorised versions exhibit marked parallels, exemplifying the way in which so much of the policy of the Henrician Reformation was formulated. It is well known that when Tyndale, having failed to interest Cuthbert Tunstall in his project, decided to publish a new version of the New Testament in English, he found it necessary to resort to the better equipped and worse policed printers of the Rhineland. He began his work in Cologne, but after rumours of his enterprise reached John Cochlaeus, who was working there at the time and passed on the information to the civic authorities, Tyndale was hounded from the city. He finished his work in Worms, but by now (late 1525), Henry VIII had been warned, and the English authorities were on their guard. When the volumes finally began to arrive in 1526, they were able to suppress the edition. Archbishop Warham sent out a letter on 3 November commanding the bishops to search out and destroy any copies, and Nicholas West banned the use of the translation in Ely diocese at a synod in 1527. Tunstall preached at St Paul's beside a bonfire of confiscated copies, alleging that more than 3000 errors had been found in the translation. The campaign was so successful that no more than a few fragments of the edition survive. Although English scriptures certainly gained a wider audience during the next few years, we should not overestimate their early dissemination. Few editions of the scriptures were produced in the years before 1534, and few copies of those editions survive. Only with the break with Rome and Cromwell's rise to power was strict censorship relaxed. The result was a sharp increase in rates of publication.

The second half of the 1520s saw a rising tide of reformist propaganda pour into England from the Low Countries. The response was an attempt to impose effective censorship. The king claimed credit together with the bishops for the initial prohibition of Tyndale's New Testament, and his personal interest in censorship was further revealed by a royal proclamation of

1529 against heretical books. Henry had played a consistently prominent part in the Catholic campaign against Luther since the publication of his *Assertion of the Seven Sacraments* in 1521 had earned him the title 'Defender of the Faith'. And his transformation into the supreme head of the Church is foreshadowed in his censorship policy. Early in 1530 he sidelined Convocation with a royal commission on heretical books, manned by a combination of bishops, senior clergy, theologians from Oxford and Cambridge, and two laymen – Henry himself and his new Lord Chancellor, Thomas More. The commission compiled a catalogue of heretical and erroneous propositions drawn from influential Protestant texts: Simon Fish's *Supplication of Beggars*; the *Revelation of Antichrist*; the *Sum of Scripture*; and a number of books by Tyndale including his *New Testament*, *Wicked Mammon*, *Practice of Prelates*, and *Obedience of a Christian Man*. A summary of the commission's proceedings and conclusions was promulgated by Warham, and at the same time a royal proclamation gave it the backing of secular law. The problem of 'English books' continued to preoccupy the conservative majority of the English clergy throughout the 1530s. The conservatives dominated Convocation, and used it to petition Henry VIII to act against heretical books in December 1534 and again in June 1536.[14] But in the mid-1530s, royal concern was focussed more on papists than on Protestants. The only serious measure of censorship in these years was the banning in early 1536 of all books upholding papal authority, especially those by the recently executed Bishop Fisher. It was not until Anabaptism and Sacramentarianism reared their heads that Henry could be persuaded to take stricter measures against radical religious literature. In 1538, on the very day that he condemned the Sacramentarian John Lambert to the flames, Henry issued a proclamation banning the importation of any book printed in English – a provision intended to cut off 'English books' at a stroke. It backfired. Protestant literature continued to be produced, imported, and circulated by those who were already on the wrong side of the law. But law-abiding printers and booksellers who had for years been importing liturgical texts (which, even if Latin, often contained English rubrics or additions) into England lost one of their most lucrative lines, one which reinforced rather than subverted established religious attitudes. Francois Regnault, the Parisian publisher who had dominated this trade for forty years, incurred heavy losses on unsold stock and lost his entire English market into the bargain.[15]

The real significance of the growth of censorship under Henry VIII lay not so much in its at best limited success as in its genuine extension of the scope of royal power. Initially implemented through proclamations, in 1543 censorship was put on a statutory footing by the Act for the Advancement of True Religion, which prohibited all books which contradicted what had been published as official religious teaching since 1540, laid down suitable penalties, and empowered the king and clergy to examine religious books before they were published. On the positive side, censorship was accompanied by the deliberate use of the king's name or authority to promote literature acceptable to the regime. A dedication to the king was already an accepted method of establishing the credentials of a book, and was widely used throughout the reign. And the obtaining of simple printing and trading privileges, though primarily directed at protecting business, was also widely taken as constituting a sign of royal approval for the contents of a book – a misapprehension which had to be publicly contradicted in the 1530s. Explicit royal approval could be obtained in letters patent, such as those which were prefaced to Fisher's *Confutation* of Luther in 1523, or to Henry's own *Primer* in 1545. And the display of the royal arms in a book was often an indication of official status, or at least official sanction. The development of both negative and positive censorship was an important part of the Henrician regime's attempt to govern not just the outward behaviour but the hearts and minds of the English people.

Despite the manifest zeal of the Church of England's campaign against 'English books', there remained a deep ambivalence within the clerical establishment over the principle of making scripture available in the vernacular. There were in fact numerous individuals in positions of authority and influence who in principle recognised the value of a vernacular Bible. The best known is Thomas More, whose delicate arguments on the subject during his controversy with William Tyndale deserve to be rehearsed at this point. Tyndale had claimed that the campaign of the bishops against his translation convicted them of obscurantism, in that they wished to keep the Bible from the laity in order to forestall criticism of the clergy against the standards of the Gospels. In reply More maintained that the bishops correctly interpreted and applied Arundel's Constitution, which, he pointed out, did not forbid vernacular scripture in principle. It merely banned certain Wycliffite translations and forbade the production of new versions without episcopal licence. On the other hand, it permitted individuals to possess older translations provided that their copies were overseen by the bishop; and More claimed to know of several bishops who did indeed permit people to own the English Bible (in a version which he wrongly believed to predate Wycliffe's). The evidence for ownership of the English Bible cited earlier in this chapter suggests that his claim should receive more credit than it has commonly been accorded. Giving his own judgement on the matter, More agreed that the provision of vernacular scripture was desirable in principle. However, he denied that it was necessary for salvation, and argued that provision was therefore a matter for positive law and would depend on circumstances. In the case of contemporary England, he concluded that publishing the scriptures in the vernacular would only exacerbate the threat of doctrinal innovation, and that the bishops were therefore justified in withholding it.[16]

He was not the only prominent Catholic to think along these lines. Strong support for vernacular scripture was put into the mouth of Reginald Pole by his close friend Thomas Starkey in the *Dialogue between Pole and Lupset*, whose composition recent research now puts prior to 1530. Although caution must be exercised in equating the views of the real Pole with those of Starkey's literary creation, there is good reason to think this a true reflection of Pole's views. He was throughout his career on the reformist and 'spiritual' wing of the Catholic

Church, and even during his few years as Archbishop of Canterbury under Queen Mary he took no direct action against the by then widespread possession of the vernacular Bible. Support for vernacular scripture was also expressed by no less a pillar of orthodoxy than the Bishop of Rochester. In an unpublished treatise on the Septuagint (Greek) version of the Old Testament, Fisher laid great emphasis on the absolute necessity for the early Church of having the scriptures available in some language more readily accessible than the original Hebrew. Sounding almost like a Protestant propagandist, he took up Christ's command to scrutinise the scriptures (John 5:39) and asked, 'who can scrutinise the scriptures if they do not have them written in some language they understand?' His opinion that not only clergymen but even layfolk were obliged to make daily progress in their understanding of the scriptures is startlingly far from what historians have led us to expect of a pre-Reformation English bishop – although our surprise can be tempered by the reflection that Fisher was one of the closest English friends of Desiderius Erasmus, the humanist advocate of scripture for the people.[17] The connection with Erasmus is crucial to this new mood among English clergy and scholars. Erasmus counted much of the early Henrician episcopate among his circle of friends and patrons, including Warham, Wolsey, Ruthall, Fox, Tunstall, Fisher, and Longland. All seem to have been contented with or even enthusiastic for his *New Testament* (1516), in which he outlined his ideal of a Bible-reading laity. And several were involved in one way or another with enterprises which take their place in the rise of a vernacular religious culture. Richard Fox, for example, as Bishop of Winchester, personally produced and published a translation of the Benedictine Rule for the nuns of his diocese, who could read English but not Latin.[18] And although Tyndale was cold-shouldered by Tunstall, it is significant that Tyndale had thought it worth approaching him with the idea of a new Bible translation.

The most powerful testimony to the spread of Erasmian views on scripture among the English elite comes from Henry VIII himself. In January 1523, he wrote to the princes of Saxony, urging prompt and decisive action against Luther. In passing he advised them in particular to thwart Luther's intention of translating the Bible, adding the rider, 'Although I do not deny that it is good to read holy scripture in whatever language, nevertheless it is certainly dangerous to read from a translation whose bad faith makes faith perform all things'.[19] Well before the appearance of Tyndale's version, Henry thus entertained a favourable attitude to vernacular scripture. He retained this attitude even after Tyndale's enterprise began. In the preface to the English translation of his 1526 letter against Luther, Henry offered his subjects the vague prospect of an accurate and authorised translation if the laity would only give assurance through good behaviour that it would not do more harm than good. And in 1528, Thomas More cited this in evidence of Henry's intention to take up the matter with the bishops. Henry himself held out the same prospect once more, a little less tentatively, in his proclamation against 'English books' of May 1530. There, having declared that having 'the holy scripture in English is not necessary to Christian men' and that publishing the Bible to his people in English at that time would 'rather be to their further confusion and destruction than the edification of their souls', he nevertheless undertook to have a translation prepared for publication when circumstances became more favourable.[20] The proclamation makes distinctions between the necessity, expediency, and utility of vernacular scripture which are reminiscent of Thomas More's arguments against Tyndale, and probably reflect his influence in drafting. For the Lord Chancellor had been present with the King at the deliberations of the largely clerical committee of which this proclamation was the main product. The acceptance of such ideas in the highest circles is indicated by some of the names of the clergy on that committee. Warham, Tunstall, and Gardiner represented the bishops, while the representatives of the lower clergy and the universities included not only budding Reformers such as Hugh Latimer, Edward Crome, and William Latymer (whose support for the idea would have been entirely predictable), but conservatives such as Nicholas Wilson (the King's confessor, twice imprisoned under Henry for religious conservatism), John Watson (Master of Christ's College, Cambridge, opponent of Henry's divorce, and long-time friend of Bishop Fisher), William Mortimer (an Oxford opponent of the divorce and of Lutheranism), and Edmund Steward (Gardiner's strictly Catholic vicar-general).[21] Even before the royal supremacy had undermined the ability and inclination of the higher clergy to resist innovation, they were open to conviction on the English Bible.

There was, however, a more uncompromising wing of the English clergy which looked with equal disapproval on the endeavours of Erasmus and on the very utility, let alone the expediency, of translating the Bible. Even among the episcopate he had enemies, such as Edward Lee at York and Henry Standish at St Asaph's. Erasmus's French opponent Peter Sutor, who attacked every aspect of his scriptural programme, from the study of the original languages to the vernacular Bible, had readers in England. Among them was Tunstall's secretary Robert Ridley. We have a letter from him to Henry Gold, Warham's humanist chaplain, which cites Sutor in the course of an extensive critique of Tyndale's translation. The prior of the Cambridge Dominicans, Robert Buckenham, preaching against Hugh Latimer in 1529, was convinced of the perils inherent in giving the laity direct access to scripture. Without careful supervision, he proclaimed, they would fall into absurd literalism, and might be led to act upon such gospel injunctions as 'If thine eye offend thee, pluck it out'![22] As the English Bible became widely and legitimately available in the later 1530s, reports poured in to Cromwell about the fulminations of backwoods clergy against this newfangled custom. The curate at Enfield dismissed the English Bible as 'the book of Arthur Cobbler'. The vicar of Ticehurst in Surrey preached against those of his parishioners who paraded up and down with their New Testaments in their hands. It was the new translations of scripture in particular, and by extension the doctrines and attitudes of the Reformers in general, which were contemptuously dismissed by the traditionally minded from the late 1520s onwards as 'new learning' (a translation of the Latin description of heresy as 'nova doctrina'; 'new learning' was not used at that time to describe the revived study of classical Latin and Greek). The Duke of Norfolk himself, the very model of a crusty reactionary, was once heard to observe in a discussion of vernacular scripture and religious literature, that it had not been merry in England since this 'new learning' had sprung up.[23] There was in short every reason for the injunctions of 1538 to forbid parish priests from discouraging Bible reading, and to urge them to inform against parishioners who were hostile to the practice.

It was the patronage and encouragement of the Henrician regime after the break with Rome that gave the vernacular Bible its central place in the English church. Despite the Erasmian sympathies of the king and many clergy with the idea of an English Bible in principle, in practice nothing had been done to bring it about, and arguments about its inexpediency continued to prevail. Once Henry had detached the Church of England from the jurisdiction of the pope, however, official attitudes rapidly swung round, largely thanks to the influence of Cranmer and Cromwell – an influence which was manifestly Protestant rather than Erasmian. The first sign of this came in December 1534, when Southern Convocation, probably at Cranmer's instigation, petitioned the king not only to suppress heretical books, but at the same time to arrange for the preparation and publication of an English translation of the Bible. Cranmer divided up Tyndale's New Testament among the bishops for correction, and by June 1535 Gardiner reported to Cromwell that he had finished the task assigned to him, the gospels of Luke and John. Bishop Stokesley, however, for all his humanist attainments, refused to lift a finger for the correction of the Acts of the Apostles, and a despairing remark in a letter from Cranmer to Cromwell in August 1537 suggests that other bishops may also have been uncooperative: he thought they would not finish 'till a day after doomsday'.[24] But the new spirit was soon felt in the printing trade. Clandestine publication of the scriptures, though a heroic effort, had achieved little in material terms between 1525 and 1533. Only nine publications of parts of the Bible in English are extant for that period. Yet for 1534 alone there are ten such publications extant, mostly produced in the Low Countries. It is tempting to see in this a realisation that an official blind eye would be turned to such endeavours. George Joye, a prominent fugitive Reformer living in Antwerp, and the publisher of several scriptural texts, seems to have been in regular contact with Cromwell's chief agent in that city, Stephen Vaughan. This connection may well explain the upsurge in scriptural publication. A signal of the new policy can be seen in a prayer book published by Cromwell's client William Marshall that year: it included a plea to Henry VIII to have the Bible translated and published. Shrewd observers would have detected a similar signal in the favour Cromwell extended from 1535 to the Scottish Reformer Alexander Alesius, who had already entered the polemical lists against the Catholic Cochlaeus in defence of the vernacular Bible. Cromwell made his position crystal clear in the injunctions of 1536, which ordered every parish priest to buy an English Bible by 1 August 1537.[25] Three days after that deadline, Cranmer wrote to Cromwell seeking his good offices in securing royal approval for a new edition of the English Bible, published over the name of Thomas Matthew, and dedicated to Henry himself. Within a week or so, Cranmer was thanking Cromwell for getting that permission.[26] Cromwell's personal role in the promotion of the English Bible was crucial. In 1538 he put his own money into a project to print an English Bible on the superior presses of Paris, and it was his diplomacy which finally circumvented the efforts of the Paris Theology Faculty to suppress it. He was in close contact with the printer Richard Grafton, who proposed the policy of compulsory purchase; and in 1539 he was commissioned by Henry to supervise Biblical publication in the interests of uniformity.

Throughout the period of Cromwell's political dominance the production figures for vernacular scripture remained at their new high level, falling below ten items only in 1537 (to seven), and reaching a peak of twenty-three in 1538. This peak coincided with the promulgation of injunctions obliging parish churches to purchase a copy of the English Bible. Seventeen scriptural items were published in the year of Cromwell's fall, 1540, but thereafter there was a marked decline. In the next seven years, the rate of scriptural publications hovered around five a year, rising above ten only once, in 1545. And these figures conceal the fact that Henry's reign saw no printing of an English Bible after 1541: the stationer Anthony Marler who in 1542 was given sole rights to print the English Bible seems never to have exercised his privilege. The scriptural publications of this period were predominantly collections of liturgical readings or selections for private devotion. Comparison of printing statistics for Bibles with those for liturgical books reveals a striking negative correlation. The publication of liturgical texts (missals, Primers, ordinals, hymnals, and processionals etc) in the period 1525–33 reached unprecedented rates, averaging twelve a year (total 112). These texts were all mostly or entirely Latin. In the years of Cromwell's ascendancy, 1533–40, this rate fell to just over seven a year (total 53), an average which conceals the fact that most of these texts were English or twin-text Primers. The publication of Latin liturgical texts for the Sarum Use almost disappeared in this period, and, in the case of certain texts, for far longer: no Sarum missal was printed between 1534 and 1554. There was a degree of recovery in the 1540s. Although the average production of liturgical texts remained seven a year from 1541 to 1547 (total 49), a rather higher proportion of these were Latin. But production never returned to pre-Reformation levels, and the absence of missals is particularly telling.

The promotion of the vernacular Bible was not only an integral part of the early strategy for the enforcement of the royal supremacy, but, originally at least, an integral part of the supremacy itself. As we have already noted, from the very start the supremacy was bound up with the rhetoric of the 'word of God'. As early as November 1533 the French ambassador reported Henry's determination to make a complete break with the Holy See and have the 'holy word of God' preached throughout the realm. The association between the supremacy and the word of God was hammered home by the propaganda of 1535. The word of God was, to repeat Sampson's lapidary formulation, 'obedience to the king rather than the pope'.

The message was understood. When Lord Wentworth told Cromwell how the bailiffs of Ipswich had at his request deprived one James Crawford of a chantry and bestowed it instead on Thomas Becon, he assured Cromwell that Becon was 'a true preacher of the word of God, a great setter forth to the people of the king's most just and lawful title of supremacy, approved by God's word'. Moreover, as Sampson's dictum shows, the word of God was a weapon in the campaign for obedience. The hope plainly was that reading the Bible would inculcate the supremacy and foster obedience. Cromwell's injunctions of 1536 told parish priests to encourage people to read the Bible, 'the very word of God . . . whereby they may the better know their duties to God, to their sovereign lord the king, and their neighbour'. Miles Coverdale, seeking special powers from Cromwell to further the cause of reform in Newbury, emphasised his desire 'not only to make them more fervent towards God and his word, but also to increase their due obedience to the king's grace'. Of course, the rhetoric of the 'word of God' was neither novel nor straightforward. 'Verbum Dei' was a traditional term for the Bible, and, more loosely, 'the word of God' was what preachers were licensed to preach. But in the context of the Reformation, the phrase took on a sharper focus, often qualified as the 'pure word of God' and contrasted with human traditions and legends. And in England, the phrase becomes markedly more frequent from about 1530. Harping on 'the word of God', as on 'the Gospel', was often a sign of unorthodox sympathies – hence such pejorative terms as 'new gospellers' for evangelical Reformers. 'Scripture', 'holy scripture' or 'the scripture of God' had previously been the more common terms for the Bible. Henry VIII himself spoke only of 'scripture' in the 1520s, but began to talk of 'the word of God' in the 1530s. Yet in his case it hardly betrayed evangelical leanings. Although he took the 'word of God' as the only source for divine law, he never aligned himself with the Protestant 'scripture principle' (that scripture alone was the sole source and justification for Christian doctrine and practice), and explicitly repudiated the idea that, as king, he was bound by the word of God (i.e. divine law) to make the Bible available in the vernacular. Attempts were made to induce him to adopt these positions. The dedication to Henry of Matthew's Bible, which he was persuaded to licence in 1537, stated that the primary duty of kings was to defend, further, set out and augment the knowledge of God – implying without stating that he was obliged to publish the Bible. And in addressing a gathering of bishops and theologians in 1537, Cromwell and Cranmer claimed it to be the king's will 'that you will conclude all things by the word of God'.[27] But Henry himself never accepted these propositions.

Cromwell's fall in itself largely explains the abrupt decline in scriptural printing noticeable after 1540. But the conservative reaction that set in at that time, trading on royal fears about Anabaptism and Sacramentarianism, secured further limitations on access to the Bible. The right to read scripture privately, conceded in the injunctions of 1538 and confirmed in a proclamation of 1539, was in 1543 withdrawn by the Act for the Advancement of True Religion from all but the gentry, the clergy, and merchants, lest it promote sectarian division. The King's Book published that same year emphasised that although the study of scripture was necessary for the clergy, those who taught in the Church, it was not essential for the laity, those who were taught, but was a matter to be decided 'as the prince and policy of the realm shall think convenient'. Convocation compensated for this to some extent by instructing parish priests to read through the entire Bible to their congregations chapter by chapter at evensong on Sundays and feast days – though without any exposition of the text. Tyndale's version was banned by the act of 1543, although the official version of the so-called 'Great Bible' was explicitly permitted despite its wholesale dependence on Tyndale's work.[28] But even this authorised version had already come under attack at the Convocation of 1542. It was only by deft manoeuvring that Cranmer managed to sideline a proposal for a major and highly conservative revision of the text.[29]

The story of the English Primer is in many ways a smaller scale parallel to that of the English Bible. As we have seen, the pull of the vernacular was already exerting a marked influence on the production of Primers for the English market even before the Reformation. But in 1530 George Joye published a suitably revised and abbreviated English version of the traditional Primer. It was included on the lists of forbidden books promulgated in 1530, and was criticised by More for its omissions – most notably the Litany of the Saints and the Dirige (the office of prayers for the dead). This was perhaps the only English Primer to appear before 1534, when the project took a step towards official status. Cromwell's reformist client William Marshall published in summer that year his own version of the Primer, essentially an expanded version of Joye's work, with supplementary material drawn from Lutheran sources. This semi-official Primer ran through several editions during Cromwell's ministry, albeit with certain revisions to mollify conservative opinion, notably the restoration of the Litany and the Dirige. Its main rival was produced by Robert Redman. His twin-text Latin and English Primer according to the Sarum Use, first published in 1535, went through several editions over the ensuing decade. Apart from the elimination of indulgence rubrics, and some editorial comments in support of the royal supremacy and of the increasing official suspicion of the cult of the saints and of the dead, this Primer was traditional in content, aimed at the conservative end of the market. The growing demand for such volumes was stimulated in 1536 by the promulgation of injunctions obliging the clergy to teach their parishioners the Pater Noster, Creed, and Ten Commandments in English. These items were part and parcel of the Primers, which appeared in increasing numbers from this time, as did simple leaflets containing the enjoined prayers and commandments. From 1537, both versions of the Primer started to appear in editions which included the liturgical readings from scripture for the Sunday and feast day masses throughout the year (although the liturgical readings continued to be read in Latin until the first royal injunctions of Edward VI). Cromwell's personal interest in the Primer surfaced again in 1539, when another of his clients, John Hilsey (Bishop of Rochester), produced at his instigation and with Cranmer's approval a new Primer which drew on both the Marshall and the Redman versions. Cromwell intended this to become the uniform Primer for the kingdom, but his plans were thwarted by his fall from power in 1540. Nevertheless, Hilsey's Primer and various derivatives continued to appear throughout the early 1540s.[30]

When the dead hand of Henry VIII fell on vernacular scripture in 1543, Primers were specifically exempted from the ban. However, printers saw which way the wind was blowing, and Primers in the Marshall and Hilsey mould gave way in the market-place to Redman's Sarum version. Within a short time, the development of the Primer into an officially authorised text was completed by the publication in 1545 of King Henry's Primer. The basic structure of the hours was traditional enough, except for the Litany (where it adopted Cranmer's severely abbreviated version of 1544) and the Dirige (which was also shortened). But it eliminated all indulgence rubrics and systematically substituted scriptural readings for the more widely drawn readings of the traditional service. Moreover, its selection of occasional prayers, while including some traditional material, also drew on a variety of Reformed sources. Although there were some references to the intercession of saints, you would hardly guess from this book that Primers originated in devotions to Our Lady. And it is noteworthy that, in common with its immediate predecessors, this Primer eschewed the woodcuts of scenes from the lives of Christ, Mary, and the saints with which many of the finer pre-Reformation editions had been illustrated. However, its most significant feature was not its content, but the claims, expounded in Henry's personal introduction, that the old custom of teaching the prayers and commandments in Latin left the people with inadequate 'knowledge of their faith, duty, and obedience', and that provision of this material in the vernacular would not only supply this knowledge but also enable them to pray with greater devotion.[31] The passion for obedience which marked so many of Henry's measures of Reformation can thus be detected also in his promotion of the vernacular. If they were to render due obedience, people had to know the law. The vernacular Bible and Primers made that law known to them. Equally important in Henry's mind was the prevention of 'strife and contention' by having 'one uniform manner and course of praying throughout the realm'. Although Cranmer was to proceed in a direction which would have been anathema to Henry, his liturgical projects of the next reign were all predicated on the same principles. It was one of Cranmer's own preachers at Canterbury, John Scory (a bishop under Edward), who proclaimed in the early 1540s that prayer in anything but the vernacular was mere babbling.[32] The effective admission of the superiority of the vernacular in catechesis and prayer in the reign of Henry pre-empted intellectually credible opposition to wider use of the vernacular later on.

Despite the injunctions of the 1530s and the wide circulation of the English Primers, the impact of Henry's Reformation on private prayer in English should not be exaggerated. Resistance to the 'new Pater Noster' was noted even in Henry's reign, and under Edward VI reformers like Latimer and Hooper discovered that there were still large numbers who could recite their Latin prayers fluently enough but did not yet know them in English. The impact of Henry's Reformation on the language of public prayer was even more limited. Almost all of the traditional liturgy remained largely unreformed and entirely in Latin throughout his reign. The weekly bidding prayers were already said in English before the break with Rome, so that the regime's alterations to their substance did not involve an alteration to their language. The edition of the Sarum Breviary published at London in 1541 was amended only so far as was required by the injunctions and statutes of the 1530s, eliminating all references to the pope and omitting various abrogated feast days and legends concerning saints. The following year Convocation decreed that the Sarum Use should become the standard liturgy for Canterbury province – a move clearly in line with Henrician thinking on uniformity, and one which was followed at the 1543 Convocation by a call for a thorough revision of all Sarum service books. The only major change came in 1544, with the promulgation of an English Litany translated by Cranmer – a Litany which was imposed uniformly the following year. The main motivation for the English Litany was the state of war then prevailing. Henry wished to make the prayers for victory of his people as effective as possible firstly by having them offered in a language they could understand, and in which they could therefore pray with greater devotion, and secondly by providing a uniform text to ensure that they were all praying for the same thing. Public prayer was in effect becoming an arm of government policy. Already, in 1542, the Privy Council had instructed the Archbishops of Canterbury and York to organise prayer throughout their provinces for the success of Christian arms against the Turk. This may perhaps reflect a more direct government control of public prayer than had been known before the break with Rome. It seems as though Henry also asked Cranmer to translate the Latin Processional (or book of hymns for use in processions) into English, but no use was made in Henry's lifetime of the material Cranmer produced.[33] Nevertheless, while there was nothing intrinsically unorthodox about the use of the vernacular in the liturgy, the Henrician changes were a dramatic reversal of official English attitudes. And although the vernacular had been growing in importance even in religious contexts in the century before the break with Rome, it was the break with Rome alone which made these dramatic changes possible. The situation was not without irony. The inspiration behind many of the changes was clearly evangelical and Protestant, and yet the changes themselves were not. We must be careful not to read back the Protestantism of the Edwardian regimes into the policies of Henry.

Henrician experiments in the vernacular, like the illegal efforts of the Reformers, were building on cultural foundations already laid within the Catholic establishment of later medieval England. That ambivalence towards vernacular scripture which had arisen in the church out of the fear of Lollardy was giving way by the early sixteenth century to a more positive attitude. But when the Protestants emerged and gave the vernacular their wholehearted support, there was an immediate official reaction into strict censorship. From the appearance of Tyndale's New Testament onwards, it was the Reformers who made the running. Henceforth, Catholic use of the vernacular tended to be responsive rather than to take the initiative, which was instead taken up by the Protestant and then the Henrician Reformers. From an early stage, 'English books' became conservative code for heretical literature. Admittedly, Thomas More had been happy to meet the Reformers in controversy on their chosen vernacular ground, but he inspired few followers. Once he had been silenced, the Catholics largely abandoned the field to their opponents. Indeed, the fate of the English Catholic apologists of the 1520s was far from encouraging: More, Fisher, and Edward Powell were executed, Rastell was converted by Frith, and Henry VIII disowned his *Assertion of the Seven Sacraments*. Catholic authors like Richard Whitford confined themselves to predominantly uncontroversial works of private devotion, with at best a polemical undercurrent against religious innovation. With the exception of a minor tract against Frith in defence of the real presence, no Catholic polemic was published in English (and but one or two in Latin) until Cromwell fell from power in 1540, when John Standish published an attack on Robert Barnes. Even then there was no Catholic rush to the pen. Apart from a couple of sermons by Cuthbert Scott and William Chedsey published in 1545, no Catholic work in defence of the faith was printed in English until Stephen Gardiner, Richard Smyth, and William Peryn started to defend traditional eucharistic doctrine in 1546. Their books formed part of a shortlived printing campaign organised by Edmund Bonner, Bishop of London. But it was too little, too late. In the meantime, the Reformers had been busy at their foreign presses, and had poured considerable quantities of controversial literature into England with the enthusiastic assistance of a number of leading London stationers. As we shall see in the next chapter, the Protestant publishing campaign played an important part in fostering, during Henry's latter years, the emergence of a committed Protestant minority in a land that still remained largely Catholic. 'English books' had become the ideological monopoly of the Reformers.

Henry VIII's support for the English Bible and the English Primer, and his enthusiastic adoption of the rhetoric of the word of God, were devoid of doctrinally radical intent. Henry had no intention of promoting Protestantism, and conceded neither the Protestant 'scripture principle' nor the necessity of Bible-reading for the laity. Obedience and uniformity remained the keynotes of his Reformation, and the evangelical rhetoric of 'God's word' took on a peculiarly Henrician flavour. Nowhere is his priestly conception of his kingly office more truly captured than in the famous woodcut frontispiece to the Great Bible (partially reproduced on the cover of this book), in which he is portrayed handing down the word of God to the clerical and lay estates. This king, the Lord's anointed, is a minister of God's word of mercy as well as of God's sword of justice. He intended the Bible to increase his subjects' knowledge of and obedience to God's law, especially that part of it which concerned the overriding issue of obedience to princes. Hence the enthusiastic cheers of 'Vivat Rex' raised up by the grateful subjects depicted towards the bottom of the woodcut. Of course, it did not work out like that. His policies seemed to align his regime to some extent with the 'new learning', and this gave at least a limited encouragement to the reforming movement. The mere act of making the Tyndale and Coverdale scriptures legally available not only helped shape the long-term development of English Protestantism, but also gave it in the short-term its most potent weapon in the emerging battle for souls. Henry's Reformation had eroded too many old mental landmarks by trespassing on the ancient liberties of the church, by breaking the taboo of sacrilege that protected ecclesiastical property, and by condemning traditional pieties as idolatry and superstition. Opening the Bible to a people thus disorientated was an invitation to dissent which was readily accepted in many quarters.

# 5

## DOCTRINAL DIVISION

Whatever the doubts about the precise doctrinal affiliation of Henry VIII at different stages of his career, one thing is certain. He was as committed in 1547 as he had been in 1509 to maintaining religious uniformity within his domains. His efforts against Luther in 1521 earned him the title 'Defender of the Faith', and later, as supreme head, he assumed powers not merely to defend but in effect to define that faith. But for all his efforts, religious uniformity was never total. Nevertheless, there can be no doubt that when he came to the throne in 1509, his territories were almost entirely Catholic. By 1547 these territories were still predominantly Catholic, but to the pockets of Lollardy, the native English heresy, which were still to be found in 1509 had been added new and more appealing heresies imported from abroad – Lutheranism, Zwinglianism (or 'Sacramentarianism'), and Anabaptism. These had attracted recruits from beyond the limited social sphere of Lollardy, from the clergy, the gentry, the lawyers, the wealthy merchants, and above all the royal court. Doctrinal division was now an unavoidable fact of life, and this was reflected in the various official formulations and statements of religious belief published in England after the break with Rome. While the relationship between the native heresy and its newer rivals or allies from abroad will be debated as long as historians remain interested in the English Reformation, it is certain that both the quantity and the quality of articulate religious dissent were higher at the end of Henry's reign than at the beginning. The spread of dissent sharpened royal concern for uniformity, and thus helped to necessitate and to justify the extension of royal power into the field of religious belief.

At the beginning, the only significant body of religious dissent in England was Lollardy. Lollardy was a small and barely organised movement of English Christians whose distinctive beliefs were derived from the teachings of John Wycliffe (d. 1384) and his Oxford followers. Its main characteristics were the premium it put upon reading the Bible (especially the New Testament) in English and its rejection of the wealth, hierarchy, sacraments, theology and practice of the medieval Catholic establishment. To Wycliffe and the Lollards, the pope and the hierarchy were a corporate Antichrist, the cult of the saints was the worship of senseless images, purgatory was a mercenary imposture, and transubstantiation was nonsense. In many ways the Lollard movement was purely negative in character. Non-dogmatic, non-sacramental, non-hierarchical, practically all it kept of traditional Catholicism was its ethical system. The positive element which bolstered this was the emphasis on the moral value of Bible-reading. Literacy, or at least reading, was the distinctive element in the Lollard ethos. Even in the early sixteenth century, despite the absence of original Lollard composition for nearly a century, suspected Lollards tended to own books, although the range of titles was by now fairly limited: chiefly the New Testament, the Ten Commandments and Our Father, and *Wycliffe's Wicket.*

Lollardy was undeniably an enduring phenomenon. Although its geographical spread was limited (found predominantly along the Thames Valley and around Bristol, and also in Kent, the Midlands and East Anglia), it often struck deep local roots. Lollardy flourished in strongholds rather than outposts.[1] Individual Lollards clung to their beliefs doggedly, and many recanted in one place only to resume their dissent elsewhere. Their doctrines were spread in two ways: primarily by family connections; and also by the activities of wandering evangelists. These combined to produce a scattered movement which encompassed many shades of opinion and behaviour, from a Bible-reading conformism which at times was little more than enthusiastic lay piety, to radical heresy. For the most part, Lollards seem to have survived by blending discreetly into their surroundings. They kept on good terms with their neighbours, but could give themselves away at moments of stress. Thus Joan Baker of London pronounced at a friend's deathbed that trust should be put not in the crucifix (which was proffered to the dying for veneration) but in God above; and Alice Cowper, encouraged by her neighbours to go on pilgrimage after a serious fall during pregnancy, shocked them by condemning the very idea. Few prosecutions of Lollards charge them with absence from Sunday mass or failure to make annual confession and communion, which suggests that most conformed to avoid detection. Even Richard Hunne, who certainly was a Lollard, first got into trouble because of an argument with the parish priest over mortuary fees – firm evidence that he accepted the ministrations of the church, albeit with reservations. According to Thomas More it was accepted practice for Lollards to conform outwardly even to the cult of the saints which they inwardly abominated.[2]

Lollardy on the eve of the Reformation bore none of the hallmarks of a movement about to break through into political and popular success. It was intellectually dormant, if not dead. No new Lollard treatise can be shown to have been composed later than 1430, and even the copying of Lollard books seems to have diminished sharply after that date.[3] However, it has been maintained that Lollardy underwent a revival in the early sixteenth century. This may be true, although the evidence is patchy. Certainly the bishops embarked on a purge against Lollardy in the years following 1510. But this was not so much a reaction to a suddenly perceived and serious threat as part of a wider programme of ecclesiastical reform, inspired by the enthusiasm consequent upon the accession of a young, pious, and scholarly monarch. Moreover, the records reveal proceedings altogether less urgent and panic-stricken than those of the early fifteenth century. The king's immediate advisers were not as directly involved as they would have been had a serious threat to England's religious establishment been discerned: the central authorities had taken a much more active part in the early Lancastrian campaign against Lollardy, as they were to do again in the campaigns against heresy after 1520. In truth, the numbers of heretics turned up by the purge were paltry enough. Reasonable numbers were discovered in the dioceses of London and Canterbury, and a few in Coventry and Lichfield, but hardly any in Rochester and Norwich, while the stray Lollards who were occasionally unearthed beyond the Severn-Trent line were almost always visitors or migrants rather then representatives of an indigenous tradition. The one exception to this history of quiescence is the dramatic outbreak of Lollardy investigated by John Longland, Bishop of Lincoln, around 1520. Extracts from lost Lincoln diocesan records preserved by John Foxe indicate an outbreak around Amersham (Buckinghamshire) on a scale that had not been approached since that of Norfolk in the late 1420s. Several hundred names were taken down in the course of the protracted enquiries – proceedings which set the events around 1510 in their proper perspective. Earlier records confirm that there was indeed a Lollard tradition in this area. But a recent study of those involved in the Amersham proceedings has suggested that the accusations may well have gone beyond the boundaries of the Lollard community, or else that many of those who abjured did not subsequently return to their heretical views.[4]

There has long been dispute about the relationship between Lollardy and the reception in the sixteenth century of new Protestant or evangelical ideas. At the time, both Protestant Reformers and their Catholic opponents agreed, for different reasons, in maintaining that Lollardy was directly related to Protestantism. In the Protestant polemics of Bale and Foxe, Wycliffe and the Lollards figured partly as forerunners of the Reformation and partly as links in a fragile chain of religious truth connecting the churches of the Reformation with the primitive church across the centuries of Antichrist's reign at Rome. English Catholic writers traced elaborate genealogies of heresy starting with Arius or even Ebion and culminating with Wycliffe, Huss, and Luther. None of this, however, amounts to evidence of anything more than the preconceptions of the authors. Catholics saw all their enemies as implicated in a single diabolic conspiracy against the Church. Protestants saw their enemy's enemy as their friend. There is no more reason to take their family trees of heresy at face value than there is to credit the family trees produced at the same time for the nobility and gentry, tracing their lineage back to Charlemagne, Arthur, or Brut. Since the later nineteenth century, the relationship of Lollardy to Protestantism has been subjected to closer historical scrutiny. Although the traditional connection is still upheld by several historians, others argue that moribund Lollardy had nothing to do with the English Reformation and the triumph of Protestantism. Neither side has yet managed to produce arguments or evidence capable of convincing the other.

It is not easy to find the sort of evidence needed to test the hypothesis that Lollardy paved the way for the English Reformation. It is never easy to find out about the members and activities of dissident minorities persecuted by inefficient investigators whose patchy records have been subject to the depradations of time, crime, and neglect. The historian's task is complicated by the fact that in practice those investigators often failed to distinguish Lollardy from Protestantism. They not only saw all heretics as essentially the same, but concentrated on precise questions of what beliefs people held, and to whom they had transmitted them, rather than on general questions of self-perception and sense of identity. Many doctrinal tenets were common to both Lollardy and Protestantism. Foxe made much of this in presenting his picture of English religious history as peculiarly favoured by divine providence. And it has always been tempting for historians to follow his lead in seeing Lollardy as Protestantism *avant la lettre*. A recent and trenchant statement of the case for Lollardy as a major cause of the English Reformation proceeds on the assumption that anyone before about 1559 who expressed tenets formerly expressed by Lollards must have been either a Lollard or under Lollard influence. This may be true, but has not yet been demonstrated.[5] In fact, the resemblance of Lollard and Protestant (specifically Swiss Protestant) teachings proves nothing. Though it is at first sight plausible that Lollardy helped prepare the way for the eventual Calvinist consensus of the Elizabethan Church, the success of Calvinism in countries which had no Lollard or similar heretical tradition (France, Scotland, Switzerland, and the Netherlands) suggests that Calvinism was well able to compete with Catholicism without any preparation of the ground. The founders of the Continental Swiss-Calvinist tradition (Zwingli, Oecolampadius, Farel, Bullinger, Calvin and Beza) owed nothing to Lollardy or Hussitism. After 1525, when their ideas and writings began to circulate in England, it cannot simply be assumed that when English people expressed beliefs characteristic of both Lollardy and Protestantism they were influenced by the former rather than the latter. Nor can this be properly concluded from the fact that English investigators of heresy continued to ask the questions asked in the fifteenth century, adding only a few new ones to cope specifically with new heresies. Inertia and convenience account for this. The only surviving evidence likely to resolve the question of whether a particular suspect was under Lollard or Protestant influence is evidence showing the persons, texts, or environments in which heretical beliefs were encountered. In few cases after 1525 can suspects or known heretics be shown to have derived their beliefs from Lollard sources. There are one or two cases connecting Lollardy and Protestantism, such as that of the Essex Lollards who obtained a Tyndale New Testament from Robert Barnes in London. But where sources can be traced, they usually turn out to have been Protestant. The individuals themselves are generally of entirely, even zealously orthodox backgrounds. As was recently said of the early London Protestants, 'Everyone, or almost everyone, converted to a more radical view of the path to salvation had once been of the old faith'.[6]

This claim is of particular importance with regard to the acknowledged leaders of the English Reformation, who were drawn predominantly from the clergy and the gentry. The high social standing of many early English evangelicals contrasts markedly with the lowlier status of almost all later Lollards. While the dismissal of Lollardy as 'upland rural paganism' is too sweeping in its doctrinal, geographical, and sociological implications, the fact remains that the highest placed heretics we can find in the century between the execution of Oldcastle and the advent of Protestantism are a handful of substantial yeomen and merchants, and a few humble parish priests. Few if any graduate clergy are found after the first generation of Wycliffe's disciples, and no knights and only one or two minor gentry after Oldcastle. The early leaders of English Protestantism exhibit a very different pattern. Almost without exception they were drawn from the social, academic, or ecclesiastical elite: graduates like Frith, Cranmer and Latimer; monks and friars like Barnes, Hooper, and Bale; lawyers like John Rastell and merchants like Humphrey Monmouth; royal servants like Cromwell and Anthony Denny; gentry like Tracy; and nobles like Thomas, Lord Wentworth. In every case where we can trace the conversion or inclination of such leaders to source, that source represents the inspiration of Continental Protestantism rather than of native Lollardy. The most important feature of early English Protestantism was its ability to open doors long closed to Lollardy.

The earliest form of Protestantism to make an impact on England was Lutheranism. Although it has become a commonplace to observe that Lutheranism never gained a substantial following in England, its significance should not therefore be underestimated. The expansion of Lutheranism outside Germany was everywhere limited by linguistic considerations. Luther's commitment to the vernacular, combined with the brilliance of his vernacular style, made him and his works the expression of an emerging German national identity. But outside Germany neither he nor his supporters achieved the domination of the book-market which they established at home. This was partly because the Catholic Church's campaign to suppress his works, though too late in Germany itself, had greater success elsewhere, and partly because Luther's impact owed much to a style which lost a lot in translation.[7] It was his Latin writings which spread his teachings abroad, and in England, as in France, their impact was inevitably felt first among those academics who moved most easily in the Latin intellectual world of Renaissance Europe. Lutheran ideas began to infiltrate London and the English universities in the mid-1520s, and thus established the first bridgehead of Protestantism within the English social and political elite. Though never a large group, the English Lutherans found themselves, thanks to the break with Rome, in a position to exercise influence disproportionate to their numbers. The small group of highly placed clergymen who in the later 1530s strove to improve England's relations with the Lutheran Schmalkaldic League, to protect English evangelicals from persecution, and to make room for Reformed beliefs within the Church of England, were Lutherans to a man. The English Bible whose influence over the national religion was to be so widespread and enduring was largely the work of two Lutherans, Tyndale and Coverdale. And many of those who at first took up Lutheranism proceeded in due course to more radical doctrines. If Lutheranism succeeded only in making breaches through which other doctrines were to flood, it at least achieved more than Lollardy.

A few traces of Luther's ideas can be found in England even before 1520. Although early English Lutheranism is generally associated with Cambridge and its notorious White Horse Inn, the earliest sightings of Luther's works are in the accounts of John Dorne, an Oxford bookseller, for 1520. A dozen or so copies of Luther's Latin *Resolutions on Papal Power* were sold there – hardly significant when compared with more than 150 copies of works by Erasmus in the same set of accounts. For most of the 1520s, radical religious ideas associated with Lutheranism remained confined to London and the universities. There is no particular reason for the traditional priority given to Cambridge over Oxford in the history of English Protestantism. The myth of the White Horse, embellished by successive generations of historians upon the flimsy basis of a passing and undated reference by Foxe to gatherings of 'the godly learned in Christ' at this and other places, distorts our picture of English Lutheranism in the 1520s. With the presumable exception of Barnes himself, we know of no particular scholars who definitely attended the informal meetings of what may or may not have been a cell of proto-Protestants. Numerous historians have associated dozens of names with the White Horse, yet even when Barnes first got into trouble, by preaching a tendentious sermon at St Edward's on Christmas Eve 1525, there were only a dozen or so godly scholars (including Stafford and Bilney) to whom he felt able to turn for advice. This is not enough to substantiate the extravagant claims made for the early success of the Reformation in Cambridge. Indeed, the new doctrines made if anything a better show in Oxford, where, in 1528, a nest of Lutherans was uncovered in Cardinal Wolsey's own foundation, Cardinal's College. Although the university authorities were swift to blame the whole affair on scholars recruited from Cambridge, the key figure was in fact Thomas Garrett, who peddled Lutheran books to Oxford at the instigation of his London rector, Dr Thomas Farman of All Hallows, Honey Lane. The numbers involved were far in excess of those turned up at the same time in Cambridge, although this may reflect nothing more than the varied success of the investigators: at Cambridge Farman had got word to suspects to hide their books before the investigation commenced.[8] However, an understandable interest in the emergence of Lutheranism at the universities in the 1520s has distracted attention from the strength of Catholicism in the universities at the same time. The active opponents of the handful of Cambridge Reformers in the 1520s were remarkably numerous. More than a dozen heads of houses, besides a number of younger scholars, were active in the campaigns against Barnes and Latimer. Oxford too had a decisive Catholic majority in the 1520s and 1530s. To first generation opponents of Luther such as Drs Brinknell, de Coloribus, Kidderminster, Kington, Powell, and Roper succeeded Drs Cottisford, Crispin, Kirkham, London, Moreman, Smyth, and Tresham. The universities remained in the 1520s what they were meant to be, citadels of orthodoxy.[9]

Until the break with Rome, the official doctrine of the Church of England was unequivocally Catholic, and Henry VIII stood right behind his Church. But in the early 1530s, the leash was slipped from the necks of several academic Lutheran sympathisers in order to mobilise their talents on behalf of the divorce and the royal supremacy. This policy first became apparent in the royal protection accorded to Hugh Latimer, despite his habitually tendentious preaching. It became obvious in the campaign against the papal primacy led by Cromwell and Cranmer, which dismissed the papacy as a human tradition foisted on unwitting Christians in place of the true gospel. This kind of rhetoric lent itself, in the hands of evangelical preachers, to veiled attacks on other aspects of the Catholic faith which, in a Lutheran perspective, seemed to draw more on tradition than on scripture. Given the official sponsorship of such preachers, the doctrinal position and future of the English Church became a matter for debate and doubt. The doctrine of purgatory was especially vulnerable to evangelical attack. As stout a Catholic as John Fisher had admitted in controversy with Luther that the scriptural evidence for the doctrine was slender, and that it was barely mentioned, if that, in the first few Christian centuries.[10] Simon Fish's *Supplication of Beggars* brought doubts about purgatory before a wider popular audience in the vernacular, and, despite Thomas More's powerful riposte, the *Supplication of Souls*, these doubts spread. John Frith's pithy refutation of Fisher, More, and Rastell on purgatory did even more damage, and achieved the rare success of converting one of its targets: John Rastell, a brother-in-law of More's, was won over by it to the opposite cause.[11] The debate over purgatory rumbled on for several years. Nicholas Shaxton was persuaded by the Cambridge authorities to recant certain errors relating to purgatory and clerical celibacy in summer 1531. Edward Crome was in trouble in 1531 for undermining the doctrine, as was Hugh Latimer in 1533.[12] Yet they and others like them were to play a leading role in the preaching campaign for the royal supremacy in the years 1535–7. Their attacks went neither unnoticed nor unopposed. A controversy broke out at Doncaster in 1534 over the invocation and intercession of the saints between the respective priors of the Carmelite and Franciscan friaries, the evangelical John Bale, and the conservative Thomas Kirkham. Bale was perhaps exploiting his commission to preach the royal supremacy in order to smuggle in new ideas, while Kirkham's resentment was heightened by the fact that he was a former supporter of Catherine of Aragon.[13] John Stokesley, Bishop of London, preached at St Paul's during April 1535 in defence of prayer for the dead, and bombarded

Cromwell with complaints about how preachers appointed without his approval sniped at purgatory in their sermons. The conservative Simon Matthew, preaching at St Paul's in favour of the supremacy on 27 June 1535, pointedly dissociated himself from the attack on purgatory delivered from the same pulpit by his predecessor of the previous week.[14] The records of the later 1530s are littered with pulpit controversies over purgatory, prayer for the dead, and the intercession of the saints. Although attempts were made to forestall such controversies, they had little success.

The advance of evangelical doctrines in the mid-1530s was a matter not only of bold preachers but also of royal or at least vicegerential support. Cromwell perhaps saw some kind of Lutheranism as the best way of producing obedient subjects within the realm and of securing diplomatic support against Catholic rulers abroad. With him in charge, and with new clients eager to jump on his bandwagon, official policy as manifested in patronage and diplomacy seemed to be moving in a Lutheran direction. Episcopal nominations from 1532 to 1536 reflected a shift in royal patronage from staunch Catholics to evangelical Reformers. Out of eleven men nominated to episcopal office before the fall of Anne Boleyn, nine were Reformers: Cranmer, Hawkins (nominated, but never installed at Ely), Goodrich, Hilsey, Latimer, Shaxton, Foxe, Barlow, and Browne. Only John Salcot of Bangor (who as abbot of Hyde remained a virtual suffragan of Gardiner at Winchester) and Rowland Lee of Coventry and Lichfield can be classified as conservative.[15] When exploratory missions led by Edward Foxe and Edmund Bonner set off to Germany for negotiations with the Lutherans in summer 1535, with leading English Lutherans like Barnes and William Turner playing a prominent part, shrewd observers fancied the chances of a Lutheran settlement in England. This was certainly the interpretation which the Imperial ambassador Chapuys put upon events. When a group of prelates met at Cranmer's residence around the beginning of April 1536, he presumed that they were discussing the abrogation of purgatory and various ecclesiastical ceremonies.[16] There were even rumours that Henry would relax the obligation of clerical celibacy. And Cromwell made his intentions plain to conservatives like Dr Edmund Steward, chancellor to the bishop of Winchester. In Gardiner's absence, Steward had instituted proceedings against the prior of the Winchester Blackfriars, one James Cosyn BD, who had preached against holy water, holy bread, and auricular confession. Cromwell summoned Cosyn to London, and sent him back with his and the king's permission to preach throughout the diocese, obtaining for him shortly afterwards a dispensation from his friar's habit. John Worthiall, the chancellor at Chichester, was so nervous of the vicegerent's authority that when a parson of his diocese preached along similar lines, he wrote to ask Cromwell's advice before daring to take any action.[17] Instructions emanating from London to the diocesan bishops at this time on the subject of contentious and divisive preaching were still far more concerned about unsoundness on the royal supremacy than about deviations from doctrinal orthodoxy. Perhaps Henry, despite his innate religious conservatism, was willing to pay the price of doctrinal confusion in order to consolidate acquiescence in the royal supremacy. More probably, Cromwell was playing a complicated game, passing off to Henry as loyal preachers of the supremacy ('God's word') those whom he knew in fact to be heretically inclined. The promotion of heretical preachers without the king's knowledge and against the king's will was to be one of the main charges brought against him in his attainder in 1540.

The fall of Anne Boleyn in spring 1536 heralded a dramatic shift in policy – a shift perhaps not unconnected with the recent death of Catherine of Aragon. The elimination of the two women who posed the greatest obstacles to Anglo-Imperial friendship opened the way to a rapprochement, and Cromwell's new-found warmth towards Chapuys shows how readily he appreciated this. The shift is best illustrated once more by episcopal appointments. The strongly Catholic Richard Sampson, long a favourite of the King, played a crucial role in putting together the case for annulling Henry's marriage to Anne. His reward was the bishopric of Chichester, which he was given royal permission to hold with his full hand of archdeaconries, deaneries, and prebends. The appointment of the conservative William Rugge to the vacant see of Norwich shortly afterwards confirmed the new trend. For the rest of Henry's reign episcopal nominations were dominated by conservatives: out of 21 men nominated after Anne's fall, only Holbeach (Rochester, 1543) and Ferrar (Sodor and Man, 1545) can be regarded with any degree of confidence as evangelical Reformers, although a case might perhaps be made for Holgate (Llandaff, 1537; and York, 1545).

The conservative higher clergy took heart after Anne's fall. They were encouraged even before Convocation opened in June 1536 with the news that attention would be given to the problem of doctrinal innovation as well as to the confirmation of the recent divorce and to a reply to the pope's call for a General Council. The signals became more confused with the opening of Convocation on 9 June. Latimer preached the inaugural sermon, seizing his opportunity to propose that the moral corruption of the Church was a function of doctrinal error, and to suggest that traditional teachings were at fault. The Convocation preacher was always nominated by the Archbishop of Canterbury, and on this occasion Latimer was clearly announcing the agenda of Cranmer and Cromwell. But the effect of his sermon was probably offset by the prominent participation on 15 June of Henry himself and his new queen Jane in a grand Corpus Christi procession which included both archbishops besides a large number of lords spiritual and temporal and other worthies.[18] Once Convocation was under way, the Lower House attempted to set their own agenda, preparing a list of more than a hundred doctrinal errors, the 'Mala Dogmata', culled from heretical English books, and offering it to the bishops on 23 June for condemnation. The document was not welcome to the dominant party among the bishops, but controversy was resolved on 11 July when Foxe of Hereford produced a book of Ten Articles composed with the king's authority.[19] The Ten Articles were published by the end of the month, and their observance was made compulsory by Cromwell's injunctions shortly afterwards. Some misunderstanding of the articles has arisen from the assumption that they were meant as a comprehensive statement of the Christian faith – in which role they would be gravely inadequate. But their preface, written in the king's name, shows that their purpose was to resolve certain disputed doctrinal and ceremonial questions. Despite some scholarly claims to the contrary, the articles were, except for their reservations over purgatory and the cult of the saints, largely Catholic. Informed opinion at the time certainly regarded them as such. Although it is often asserted that the articles were among the grievances of the Pilgrimage of Grace, there is no evidence for this. On the contrary, the Pilgrims wanted the teaching of the articles enforced. Cardinal Pole, despite his hostility to the king's proceedings, found nothing to query in them except Henry's assumption of the power to define doctrine. And from the opposite perspective, the Scottish Lutheran Alesius, a client of Cromwell then lecturing at Cambridge, abandoned his post rather than seem by silence to consent to the articles, of which he sent a copy to Melanchthon in explanation of his decision.[20]

After a brief and uncontroversial exhortation to belief in the words of scripture, the three creeds (the Apostles', the Nicene, and the Athanasian), and the decrees of the first four general councils, the articles covered the sacraments of baptism, penance, and the eucharist; the nature of justification; images; the intercession of the saints; rites and ceremonies; and purgatory. The article on baptism was for the most part a polemic against Anabaptist notions. The brief paragraph on the eucharist implicitly attacked both sacramentarian rejection of the real presence and Lutheran attitudes on venerating the sacrament and on unworthy reception. The article on rites and ceremonies implicitly repudiated the Protestant polemic against human traditions while satisfying humanist critics by explaining the symbolism of various liturgical actions. There were some verbal concessions to the evangelicals, but it is wrong to read into the articles an attempt to compromise with Lutheranism or to smuggle it in through the back door. The teaching on justification, though impeccably loyal to the ideas of St Augustine (whom both Catholics and Protestants claimed as authority for their views), contained nothing that could not also be found in the writings of John Fisher. Its distance from Lutheran ideas is witnessed by its avoidance of the language of 'faith alone' and its distinctly anti-Lutheran emphasis on the necessity of good works in salvation. The definition of justification as 'remission of sins, and our acceptation or reconciliation into the grace and favour of God, that is to say, our perfect renovation in Christ' may have reflected the wording of the Lutheran Confession of Augsburg, but there was nothing unacceptable to Catholics in it, while the contention that sinners attained justification 'by contrition and faith joined with charity' constitutes an explicit repudiation of Lutheran solifidianism. The article on the real presence avoided the word 'transubstantiation', but its account of that presence was otherwise unmistakeably traditional. The article on penance affirmed the necessity of that sacrament to salvation, and divided it into the traditional three parts: contrition, confession, and 'a new obedient reconciliation unto the laws and will of God, that is to say, exterior acts in works of charity according as they be commanded of God, which be called in scripture *fructus digni poenitentia* [fruits worthy of penance]'. The avoidance of the traditional term 'satisfaction' for this catered to Reformist sensibilities, but the thing it described was affirmed in the same terms in which Fisher had defended it against Luther fifteen years before. Only in the article on purgatory was there any tangible comfort for the Reformers, but even there the word itself was retained together with the concept of an intermediate state after death which it described. Although much papal practice and popular custom regarding it was rejected, its retention in the light of the preceding controversies was regarded as a conservative triumph, and was popularly though implausibly ascribed to the Duke of Norfolk's influence with the king.[21]

The Ten Articles were intended to forestall the dire consequences which it was feared would necessarily arise from religious division. Heresy and sedition were seen as two sides of one coin in early Tudor England, as a result of the Lollard rising more than a century before. Whether the royal council was more afraid of a Protestant rising or of a Catholic backlash is unclear. What we do know is that the Ten Articles did not succeed in reassuring public opinion, at least in the northern half of England, and that the result was the most threatening revolt ever faced by a Tudor monarch, the Pilgrimage of Grace. Coming as it did on the heels of the break with Rome, at a time when England's diplomatic position was highly vulnerable, with potential focuses of discontent in the persons of Reginald Pole, the king's cousin and a conceivable Yorkist pretender abroad, and of Princess Mary, the bastardised daughter of the much-loved Catherine of Aragon at home, this rising shook Henry's regime, though briefly, to its foundations. Had the machinery of early Tudor court politics not so thoroughly implicated the high nobility with royal government, events might have taken a very different course. If one or two magnates had thrown in their lot with the people and gentry of the north, Henry's survival would have been in jeopardy.

The rising, which soon became known as the Pilgrimage, was sparked off by Thomas Kendall, the vicar of Louth (Lincolnshire), on Sunday 1 October 1536.[22] The Cromwellian visitation was due to reach the deanery of Louth the following day, and rumours were rife that this was to be the first stage in a systematic pillage of parochial churches to match the monastic dissolution already in progress. Inflamed by Kendall's Sunday sermon, the parishioners of Louth agreed to defend their church, and their defiance was spread by the sixty parish priests who came to the town the next day for the visitation. Within days, most of northern Lincolnshire was in arms, and the disturbances were spreading over the Humber into the East Riding of Yorkshire. The rebels devised an oath which they invited or compelled others, especially gentlemen to swear. Robert Aske, the lawyer who was propelled into general command of the rising, was recruited this way on 4 October. Although the rising continued to spread northwards, it was Lincolnshire that dominated the attention of the king and council in London, and the Duke of Suffolk was sent to restore the peace. Lincoln had fallen to the rebels on 6 October, but the duke was able to retake the city without bloodshed less than a fortnight later.

But while Henry was congratulating himself on the ease with which Lincolnshire had been pacified, and was even disbanding some of the troops he had mustered, the rising in Yorkshire was recruiting considerable gentry support, and was proceeding in a more organised and threatening fashion. The third week of October saw York, Hull, and Pontefract fall into rebel hands, with the rising spreading throughout Yorkshire, Durham, Northumberland, Cumberland, Westmoreland, and much of northern Lancashire. Only Carlisle, Newcastle and the castles of Skipton and Scarborough remained in royal hands by the end of the month. Royal forces under the Duke of Norfolk and the Earl of Shrewsbury secured Derbyshire and Nottinghamshire to block the rebels' route south. They were massively outnumbered by their opponents, whose numbers were at the time reckoned as high as 40,000, and whose leaders included Lords Darcy, Latimer, Lumley, and Neville, as well as major gentry such as Sir Robert Constable and Sir Thomas Percy. 'The flower of the north', as Norfolk called them, were well able to defeat the Scots (as they had shown at Flodden Field in 1513), and were no peasant rabble. Norfolk foresaw ignominious defeat if it should come to a battle, and managed to negotiate a truce by promising to support the Pilgrims' demands for the restoration of the monasteries, the suppression of heresy, and the dismissal both of heretical bishops (such as Cranmer and Latimer) and of low-born advisers (Cromwell and Rich). Both sides agreed to retire and disband – to Henry's disgust, although Norfolk's shrewd policy probably saved his throne.

Despite the truce, the north remained under the rule not of the king but of the Pilgrims, who held two great meetings at York in late November and at Pontefract in early December to hammer out their aims in detail. As with any large popular movement, the Pilgrimage was riven with differences of opinion, emphasis, and even policy. The detailed lists of grievances reflected this. The northern commons inserted a number of grievances regarding tenant right and custom, while the gentry tacked on their concerns about the Statute of Uses, common law, and parliamentary elections. There was little of common interest to these groups in social and economic matters. Yet although a case has been made for seeing the Pilgrimage more as a social than a religious rising, it is hard to see how it could have spread so far or held together as long as it did without the ideological force of religion.[23] The grievances that lent unity to the rising concerned the dissolution of the monasteries and the attack on popular religion. These were taken as evidence of the baleful influence over Henry of his upstart heretical councillors, and were thought to herald still more drastic innovation. The very title 'Pilgrimage of Grace', which was part of the rebels' oath by 17 October, has deafening religious resonances, and 'pilgrimage' had military as well as spiritual connotations. The Latin 'peregrinatio' covered what we call crusades as well as pilgrimages. To think of the 'pilgrims' under their banners of Christ's Five Wounds (first used on 12 October, and distributed as a badge in large numbers around the 22 October) and of St Cuthbert (which arrived in York from Durham on 20 October) as 'crusaders' properly captures their spirit.

In the end, the Pilgrims fell victim partly to their own good faith and partly to their own propaganda. Despite continual indications that Henry had no intention of keeping the truce, far less of making real concessions, any longer than he had to, Aske and the other gentry leaders took the king's word. Ingrained habits of loyalty and obedience combined with the myth of the 'king's evil counsellors' (with which the Pilgrims justified their action), to convince them that their wilful and vengeful ruler would gratefully accept their summons back to the straight and narrow path of religious orthodoxy.[24] In order to safeguard the concessions they thought they had won, they strove to prevent popular discontent from flaring up again in early 1537. But a renewed peasant rising in Cumberland and an attempt by the unstable Sir Francis Bigod to revive the Pilgrimage in February gave Henry the chance he wanted. Norfolk was sent north a second time to impose order. With over seventy executions in Cumberland, and a dozen or more in both Lancashire and Lincolnshire, the job was done. The gentry and clergy (including Aske, Constable, and Darcy) who had led the risings were tried and condemned in London. In total, at least 130 people (including two lords, five knights, and nine heads of religious houses) were executed in the aftermath of the Pilgrimage – considerably more than had been killed during the almost bloodless rising.

The widespread doctrinal uncertainties and anxieties which the Pilgrimage revealed called for a definitive response. A clear statement of faith was an indispensable bulwark against further unrest. Even before the ringleaders of the Pilgrimage had been brought to account, Cromwell had convoked a gathering of bishops and doctors at Westminster to debate and resolve a range of theological, ceremonial, and canonical issues. This gathering presumably paved the way for the first comprehensive account of the faith of Henry's church, the *Institution of a Christian Man*, or Bishops' Book as it came to be known. By July a draft of this work was complete – masterminded by Edward Foxe, with Latimer, Cranmer, Shaxton, Tunstall, Stokesley and Sampson playing major roles in the often tough debates. The finished article was submitted to Henry himself for approval, but he withheld his full assent, merely authorising its publication and use for a period of three years.[25] The Bishops' Book was in circulation by October, when we find the first public reactions to it. If the reaction of Thomas Cheyney, a gentleman of Kent, was typical, then it was popularly seen as a step back from the Cromwellian injunctions of the previous year. Cranmer himself wrote to reprimand him, advising him that this was by no means the case. On the other hand, informed opinion rightly saw in it more of a threat to orthodoxy. Gardiner, who first learned of the book when Cromwell sent a copy to him in France, reckoned it systematically ambiguous, and wrote promptly to Henry to dissociate himself from it.[26] Later manuscript notes on the book by the king himself show that Henry came to share Gardiner's distaste.

Unlike the Ten Articles, the Bishops' Book expressly purported to provide a full statement of belief. But while historians have customarily seen it as a conservative reaction from the allegedly Reformist tendencies of the Ten Articles, the reality is quite the reverse. The usual evidence for the traditional view is that the Bishops' Book covered all seven sacraments while the Articles mentioned only three: in Archbishop Lee's famous words, 'Those four sacraments that were omitted be found again anew'. But this remark, made in the context of Cromwell's gathering of early 1537, can hardly be taken as evidence of popular views of the Ten Articles.[27] When the text of the book is read closely, it makes far more concessions to Lutheranism than either the Ten Articles or its successor of the 1540s, the King's Book. As a whole it is clearly a compromise in which evangelical influence, though moderate, is distinct. The article on justification gives great prominence to the role of faith, though without explicitly affirming Lutheran tenets, and minimises the role of good works, though without explicitly repudiating Catholic tenets. Although the doctrine of the real presence is affirmed in no uncertain terms, there is no hint of the doctrines of transubstantiation or the sacrifice of the mass – omissions which make the book compatible with Lutheran eucharistic teaching. Tradition is put in a very subordinate role to scripture in the discussion of doctrinal authority. The exposition of the Ten Commandments is notable for its adoption of the 'Reformed' rather than the 'Catholic' enumeration: where the medieval tradition included the prohibition on graven images under the general heading of the first commandment (to worship one God alone), it now became the second commandment in its own right (the numbers were equalised at the other end, by the conflation of what were in the Catholic tradition separate prohibitions against coveting the persons and the possessions belonging to a neighbour). The purpose of this was to make an issue out of the veneration of images and the cult of the saints and thus to provide a firm theological basis for the campaign of iconoclasm which followed soon after.[28]

Official leanings towards evangelical doctrines may have been limited to minor terminological concessions to Lutheranism, but at the popular level more radical doctrines were beginning to win followers in the 1530s. Ever since John Frith had brought Swiss arguments against the real presence of Christ in the eucharist to the attention of an English public, 'Sacramentarian' doctrine had enjoyed growing popular appeal. Even as Cromwell was taking some of the most radical steps in the history of the Henrician Reformation – the welcoming of Lutheran envoys, the suppression of the friaries, the removal of relics and 'superstitious' images, and the promulgation of the English Bible – events were under way which were to provoke Henry VIII into fiercely reactionary measures. A forthright Sacramentarian named John Lambert, who had already been in trouble early in the 1530s, brought trouble upon himself in 1538 by arguing with Dr John Taylor after a sermon on the real presence. He was cited before the Archbishop of Canterbury, who tried to talk him out of his obstinacy. Proceedings dragged on, and Henry took a personal interest. Lambert wrote for him a lengthy statement of faith, which earned him a public trial before the king in person on 16 November. After Cranmer, Gardiner, Sampson, Stokesley, and Tunstall had attacked his doctrines, and Lambert had defended them, Henry, playing one of his favourite roles as theologian, delivered a powerful oration in defence of transubstantiation, and, having offered Lambert a last chance of repentance and mercy, condemned him to burn.[29] That same day a royal proclamation was issued condemning the Sacramentarians, upholding the real presence and clerical celibacy, and forbidding heretical books – the first act of censorship directed against Reformed literature since the break with Rome.[30] Around the same time, concern also arose about the Anabaptists, who outdid the Sacramentarians by rejecting the traditional understanding of baptism as well as of the eucharist. On 1 October 1538 Henry commissioned a team of bishops and theologians to seek out Anabaptists, and subsequent proclamations ordered them to recant or leave the country.[31]

It was the king's realisation of how far doctrinal deviation had gone at home together with renewed fears of foreign invasion in the wake of Pope Paul III's call for his overthrow that led to the summoning of the 1539 Parliament, whose main task was to address the religious question. Within a week of its opening on 28 April, a committee of bishops had been formed under Cromwell to produce a bill. As the religious parties were evenly balanced on this committee, it might have been deliberately chosen to achieve what it did achieve: nothing. Indeed, it was possibly a manoeuvre by Cromwell and Cranmer to stall the whole business. The ultimate passage of the Act of Six Articles was a victory for the Duke of Norfolk and for Cuthbert Tunstall (who, in Gardiner's absence abroad, was the leader of the conservative clergy).[32] On 16 May the duke personally presented six questions in the Lords, to which the articles as they finally appeared were manifestly the expected answers. The strenuous opposition of Cranmer in both Lords and Convocation availed little, though he did succeed in removing the word 'transubstantiation' from the text and in preventing the definition of auricular confession as a matter of divine law. He was less successful in his attempt to dissuade the king from defining that divine law forbade priests, once ordained, to contract marriage. Henry appeared in person to curtail discussion in the Lords – Cranmer admitted privately that his consent to the act was given only out of fear[33] – and his close interest in the bill is revealed by his annotations in surviving drafts. The Six Articles, like the Ten Articles of 1536, were intended not as a comprehensive statement of belief, but as a bulwark against the rising tide of heresy. They upheld the Catholic doctrine of transubstantiation in all but name, and defended the ecclesiastical customs of communion under one kind, the private mass, and auricular confession. In addition, they forbade priests to marry and laid down that vows of chastity freely and advisedly made were binding under divine law.

The Six Articles, however, were not merely for domestic consumption. They also had a role to play in Henry's foreign policy. They were meant to reassure the Catholic rulers of the Empire and France that Henry, despite his break with Rome, was himself fundamentally orthodox, and thus to dissuade them from heeding the pope's call for his overthrow. English ambassadors abroad were to use the articles to demonstrate Henry's commitment to Catholic tradition. The invasion scare of 1539, which led Parliament that year to vote the king an unprecedentedly large subsidy, lay behind a raft of conservative religious measures and gestures. The choice of Tunstall to preach before the king on Palm Sunday marked a move away from the more Reformist court preachers favoured since the break with Rome. His sermon, which balanced polemic against the papacy with a defence of ecclesiastical ceremonies, was carefully attuned to the needs of the moment, as was Henry's own ostentatiously devout veneration of the cross and service at mass – on which the ambassadors duly reported back to their monarchs. A further opportunity to underline his orthodox credentials was presented to the king by the death in May of Charles V's wife, Isabella of Portugal. The elaborate public obsequies held in St Paul's in her memory on the weekend after Corpus Christi involved half the bishops of England and most of the Privy Council, and were echoed in every parish church in London. The images and candles which bedecked the hearse, and the proliferation of masses and prayers and bell-ringing for the empress's soul, were an unmistakeable declaration of royal assent to the traditional Catholic apparatus of intercession for the dead. The French ambassador was prompt to report all this to his master. With the resignations of two of the more radically evangelical English bishops (Latimer and Shaxton) in protest against the Six Articles, and the death of a third (Hilsey), the Reforming party was seriously weakened. And the death of the conservative Stokesley in September gave Henry the chance to put on another display of Catholic commitment in a State funeral. If ever Henry's church was 'Catholicism without the Pope', it was so in 1539. Yet even amid the show of Catholicism, the rejection of the pope continued to be emphasised. Half a dozen maintainers of papal supremacy were executed in London a matter of days before the Six Articles came into effect; and, shortly after the obsequies of the empress, a mock naval battle was staged on the Thames in which a royal ship trounced the pope and a boatload of cardinals.[34]

While the Six Articles resolved the immediate problems, the need for a comprehensive statement of belief was also felt. In 1540, the three years which Henry had allotted to the Bishops' Book expired, and he was prompt to announce to Parliament his decision to commission a replacement from his clergy. A committee of bishops and theologians, representing a range of theological opinion (predominantly conservative), was appointed to debate a series of questions relating to the sacraments. Their answers vary from the barely veiled Lutheranism of Cranmer himself, through the humanist Catholicism of Dr Thomas Robertson and Dr John Redman, to the rigidly scholastic Catholicism of Dr Roger Edgeworth.[35] This commission was evidently the body referred to in the Act concerning True Opinions and Declarations of Christ's Religion (32 H. VIII c. 26) passed that year, which empowered the king to appoint clergy to resolve doctrinal questions and to promulgate decisions with binding force by letters patent. The relationship of the discussions of 1540 to the book eventually published in 1543 is unclear. Perhaps it was decided that such a large committee would never agree on anything, for at some point the work was delegated to a group of six: Thomas Thirlby (Bishop of Westminster), Nicholas Heath (Bishop of Rochester), George Day (made Bishop of Chichester in 1543), John Redman, Richard Cox, and Thomas Robertson. This group took the Bishops' Book, revised it heavily in a Catholic direction, and presented it to Convocation for approval in April 1543.[36] The personal involvement of Henry in the work is plain from copies of the Bishops' Book which survive bearing in his hand amendments later incorporated in the King's Book. The King's Book was in effect issued under the authority of the Act concerning True Opinions, but it soon received further statutory backing, at least implicitly, in the Act for the Advancement of True Religion (34–5 H. VIII c. 1) passed by the Parliament of 1543, which endeavoured to establish a system of censorship, restricted the right to read the Bible, and endorsed all religious doctrine published under royal authority since 1540. The series of doctrinal statutes from 1539 to 1543 mark a significant extension of the scope of parliamentary legislation, which had hitherto never encroached upon such matters. This extension was to be of the utmost importance in the religious changes of the following reigns. However, it would be a serious mistake to conclude that this represented some kind of triumph of parliamentary over royal authority. For the Act concerning True Opinions gave Henry VIII in person the power to define doctrine without any need for further statutory authority, while the Act for the Advancement of True Religion gave him the power to change any provision of that act at will. These acts therefore represented part of a tendency which had first emerged in the Act of Proclamations, to give the king powers of 'delegated legislation' – a tendency which if it had been pursued for any length of time might ultimately have led to a decline in the legislative role of Parliament itself. In fact, Henry felt no need to issue further doctrinal declarations after 1543, so these powers were a dead letter. But these statutes make an important counterpoint to the theme of the widening of parliamentary or at least statutory power that resulted from the break with Rome.

The King's Book follows the general pattern of its predecessor. The amendments and revisions are mostly matters of expression and rhetoric, but their doctrinal drift is apparent from a comparison of the two texts. In the opening section the King's Book adds to the Bishops' Book's affirmation of the infallibility and supremacy of scripture a balancing affirmation of the creed and the councils and of the need to interpret scripture in the light of patristic tradition. Where on the fifth article of the creed the earlier book speaks of Christ's will 'to redeem all those that would believe in him', the new version, anxious to exclude solifidianism, reads 'all those that believing in him ordered themselves in obeying and following his precepts and commandments'. The ascension was for the Bishops' Book a withdrawal 'of his corporal presence from the sight of the apostles'. The King's Book, anxious lest this should tell against the doctrine of the real presence, speaks of a withdrawal of 'his accustomed visible conversation'. Where the Bishops' Book affirms that Christ was more willing than any creature to mediate and intercede, the King's Book explicitly affirms the intercession of the saints. The exposition of the sacraments shows similar tendencies to reaffirm traditional beliefs. It echoes the Six Articles in its leanings towards transubstantiation: '[the] bread and wine do not remain still in their own substance, but by the virtue of Christ's word in the consecration be changed and turned to the very substance of the body and blood of our Saviour Jesus Christ'. It reaffirms and explains the place of 'satisfaction' in the sacrament of penance. The exposition of the Ten Commandments and the Lord's Prayer follows the Bishops' Book more closely, but under the second commandment trouble is taken to permit due reverence, though not divine worship, to be paid to religious images – in effect, a return to the scholastic distinction, scorned by the Reformers, between the worship of 'latria' and of 'dulia'. Articles on free will, justification, and good works take a decisively anti-Protestant line, in contrast to the studiedly ambiguous phraseology of the Bishops' Book. Only in the final section on prayer for the dead does the King's Book exhibit radical tendencies, and even here there is tension. On the one hand it adopts the classic Catholic defence of prayer for the dead on the basis of Maccabees and the ancient fathers, incidentally accepting the saying of masses for the dead; but on the other it attacks the gamut of papal teaching on purgatory, including for the first time an official repudiation of the name itself.[37]

The teachings of the Sacramentarians, unlike those of the Lutherans, never had the remotest effect upon the official doctrine of the Henrician church. However, it was these teachings that enjoyed the wider popular impact in the last decade of Henry's reign. The subtlety of Lutheranism on images and the eucharist contrasted unfavourably with the crude iconoclastic certainties of popular Sacramentarianism. The rise of Sacramentarianism was limited, but it obsessed the authorities from the time of the Six Articles. At first, they tried to win the battle by censorship and suppression rather than by debate. Forbidden books were listed for the convenience of bishops, and were hunted out where possible. In London, where early Protestantism was undoubtedly at its strongest, Bonner vigorously prosecuted suspects. But his work was not helped by the fact that so many influential London stationers were sympathetic to the new doctrines. His ability to clamp down on the trade in illicit books was decisively limited. The clandestine reissue in 1546 of Frith's influential treatise against the real presence added vigour to the Sacramentarian movement, and provoked Bonner to the first serious attempt to counter eucharistic heresy through argument. Perhaps he realised that even his relatively efficient policing was just not enough. Certainly his was the hand behind the appearance in 1546 from the same press of three robust treatises in defence of the real presence: two rather academic tracts by the Oxford doctor of divinity, Richard Smyth, and a more populist book of sermons by the former Dominican William Peryn. It is impossible at this distance to estimate the impact of this new departure in Bonner's policy. For the death of Henry VIII in January 1547, and the almost immediate steps taken by the new regime against Richard Smyth, stopped Bonner's campaign in its tracks. The few books he had managed to publish were nothing in comparison with the stream of literature imported in the early 1540s and the deluge of Protestant polemic tolerated or encouraged by Somerset's regime.

Definitive statements about popular religious beliefs and allegiances in an age which had neither the census nor the opinion-poll are always going to be beyond the scope of the historian. However, as a number of local studies have shown, a certain amount of information about popular beliefs and practices can be derived from the evidence of wills, which survive from the sixteenth century in very large numbers. Unfortunately, many studies lack sensitivity and an awareness of the limitations of the evidence, and have advanced conclusions which unwarrantably exaggerate the success of Protestantism at the popular level. This is not the place to recapitulate those studies in detail, but it is worth summarising the conclusions that can reliably be drawn from them. The evidence of wills about religious attitudes is of two kinds. The first, and less satisfactory, is the bequest of the soul. Medieval and early modern testators used to bequeath not only their worldly goods, but also their body (to be buried, often specifying the place and manner of burial) and their soul – traditionally to Almighty God and his saints and angels, in one of various available formulae. As the Reformation progressed, new formulae became fashionable. An increasing proportion of wills simply left the soul to God alone, omitting the saints, and a few introduced concepts such as the hope of salvation through the merits and passion of Christ – occasionally even affirming justification by faith alone. In Kent, almost all testators had used the traditional formula in the early 1530s, but by the late 1530s as many as a quarter were omitting the saints. In the city of London, about 85 per cent of wills in the 1530s used traditional preambles, with the proportion declining through that decade and the next, averaging about two thirds in the 1540s. More than 90 per cent of East Sussex wills remained traditional in the 1530s, a proportion which barely fell at all in the early 1540s. York was still more conservative, with a mere handful of several hundred wills omitting mention of the saints in the entire period from 1530 to Henry's death. Changes in preambles have been taken as reflecting changes in belief. The omission of the saints has been seen as a sign of doubt about the intercession of the saints, even of Protestant rejection of it. And mention of the merits and passion of Christ is widely taken as an indication of Protestant theological influence. However, omission of the saints probably reflects nothing more than an awareness of the official disfavour into which the cult of the saints fell during Henry's latter years (there was no obligation on Catholics to mention the saints in their wills). Even in Kent, where preambles began to change quite early, Cranmer in practice found the clergy and people 'very obstinate' in observing abrogated holy days in 1537. And trust in Christ's merits and passion was mainstream Catholic doctrine. Only those preambles which express the doctrine of justification by faith alone can reasonably be taken as evidence in themselves of Protestant convictions. In any case, as few testators wrote their own wills (the task was usually performed by a scribe – a curate or public notary), changes in the conventional formula for the bequest of the soul often mark the arrival of a new curate rather than the general diffusion of new ideas. Preambles tell us more about the practice of the clergy than they do about the views of testators.[38]

The more revealing kind of testamentary evidence consists of bequests for religious purposes: chiefly, before the Reformation, for masses and other intercessory prayer on behalf of the soul in purgatory. Although the intercession requested was generally of a conventional nature, its distribution and quantity reflected the views of the testator to a far greater extent than the formula bequeathing the soul. Religious bequests cost money, and would therefore vary with both the zeal and the means of the testator. Studies of bequests in late medieval wills from Bristol, Hull, Norwich, Kent, and Yorkshire indicate that Catholic practices held a prized place in the affections of the people. Evidence from the early sixteenth century confirms this picture, although unfortunately few of the published studies have explored the evidence of religious bequests. A very broad sample of wills from across most of the country has suggested that in the 1530s, two thirds of testators made some provision for prayer for their soul. Testamentary bequests in samples of wills from the archdeaconries of Lincoln, Huntingdon, and Buckingham suggest that there was some decline in traditional forms of religious giving between 1530 and 1545, but that it was only after Henry's (and Bishop Longland's) death that significant changes took place in popular religious practices. And while religious bequests tell us more about religious attitudes than do preambles, we must beware of attributing the wrong significance to fluctuations in their level. As conspicuous expenditure, religious bequests should be expected to vary with the state of the economy. The combination of high taxation and high inflation in Henry VIII's last decade may have more to do with any decline in religious bequests than a weakening of confidence in intercessory prayer for the dead.

Testamentary evidence for the diffusion and influence of Protestant doctrines would not have encouraged the first generation of Reformers. No unequivocally Protestant preambles are found in York, Leeds, Hull or Lancashire wills of Henry's reign, and only one or two among the wills of Colchester, Cornwall, Devon, the Leeds area, and East Sussex. Reformers might have derived some comfort from the spread of preambles mentioning the merits and passion of Christ, which by the end of Henry's reign were found in 5 per cent of Kent and nearly 15 per cent of London wills. It is likely that in both London and Kent these figures reflected the emergence of committed evangelical clergymen imposing the new preambles on their flocks, and perhaps even instilling new doctrines into them.

But such preambles, theologically acceptable to Catholics in any case, are often found together with bequests for masses for the soul which were anathema from an early stage to Reformers of all persuasions and degrees of commitment. To take their diffusion as an index of Protestant advance is to go beyond the evidence. Nor would the evidence of 'Protestant' religious bequests (a category difficult to identify with any confidence) have afforded much more comfort. Bequests to the poor and to civic works were no monopoly of the Reformers, although they offered an outlet for those whose beliefs prevented them from securing masses or intercessory prayer, and fluctuations in their level will again tend to reflect economic conditions. Bequests for sermons (already increasingly frequent in the first third of the century) came to take the place of bequests for masses in wills of the later sixteenth century, but never achieved the same levels of popularity. In Henry's time, they provide clear evidence of the testator's convictions only when the preacher is specified – for example by Humphrey Monmouth, who in 1537 left money for sermons by Latimer, Hilsey, and Crome among others. In short, the evidence of wills for changes in religious belief and practice in the reign of Henry VIII needs to be handled with great care. To the extent that any firm conclusions can be drawn, it seems that any changes were limited to a small minority of the people.

The evidence of wills confirms what we find from other sources, namely that while Henry's idiosyncratic and destructive Reformation was widely accepted, the Protestant Reformation made only limited headway in England in his reign. The major exception to this was the city of London, where a significant Protestant minority developed in Henry's last decade. For all the doubts that have been cast on the general value of testamentary evidence, in the case of London it is consistent with other sources. Only in London did relatively large numbers of people find themselves in trouble after the passage of the Act of Six Articles. Several hundred suspects were investigated by the zealous Bonner between 1540 and 1542. Elsewhere in the country, action against heresy remained sporadic, for the most part lighting on stray individuals rather than coherent groups. By the early 1540s, London was clearly a special case, and it is arguable that even from the 1520s London (rather than Cambridge) was the centre of the English Reformation. It was from London, after all, that Farman and Garrett ran prohibited books to the universities. It was in London that the Essex Lollards obtained from Barnes the Tyndale New Testament. Only in London were large numbers of that New Testament found and burned. And connections with London, rather than with Cambridge or the Continent, explain the early diffusion of Protestant doctrines in England. The attractions of the economic capital of the country, and of the political capital (the royal court) which orbited London through the palaces of Greenwich, Westminster, and Hampton Court, drew in most of the leading Reformers of the first generation. It was from London that they evangelised those parts of the country in which royal, episcopal, or noble patronage could find them a foothold.

Although early English Protestantism spread little beyond London, we should not be misled into assuming that it spread not at all. From the early 1530s individual Protestants are to be found in most parts of England, from Thomas Bennett in Exeter and William Tracy in Gloucestershire to John Bale in Doncaster, Sir Francis Bigod in the North Riding of Yorkshire, and Roger Dichaunte in Newcastle. In few of these places can they have been wholly without sympathisers. And in several towns it is clear that the arrival of evangelical preachers caused an immediate division in communities that had previously been united in religion. Latimer's preaching at Bristol in 1533 provoked a flurry of counter-attacks from the city's pulpits and a sharp division among the citizenry – an effect for which his preaching became notorious. Both Oxford and Cambridge saw Reforming parties emerge under the protection of powerful court patrons in the 1530s. Windsor, where the royal collegiate church was originally a bastion of conservatism, was in the later 1530s infiltrated by Reformers, led by Dr Simon Heynes. A Sacramentarian priest named Anthony Parsons introduced reformed doctrines to some of the townsfolk as well, and a cell of Protestants was flourishing there in the early 1540s to the annoyance of the predominantly conservative urban elite.[39] Cranmer's patronage of Reformist preachers is the obvious explanation of the emergence of an evangelical faction in Canterbury – though even under his nose several friars preached against him in the 1530s – and doctrinal division was institutionalised in the Six Preachers of the cathedral, three of the 'old learning' and three of the 'new learning'.[40] When Latimer, Shaxton and Barlow respectively took Reforming ideas to the dioceses of Worcester, Salisbury, and St David's, they soon aroused opposition, but also made converts. In the port of Rye it was the reactionary vicar, William Inold, whose attachment to the papacy and to the abrogated holy days divided the citizens, while Thomas Garrett and Thomas Lawney (chaplains respectively to Latimer and Cranmer) gathered the nucleus of a Reformed faction.[41] Across the Channel at Calais, Sacramentarian ideas gained easy entry from Normandy and Picardy, early centres of French Protestantism, enjoying first the uncomprehending sympathy and then the stunned incredulity of the governor, Lord Lisle. The fury with which conservative curates raged at parishioners who took up the English Bible ('new learning', 'green learning', and 'new trickery') in many parishes in the South and East during Henry's last decade shows that the king's proceedings certainly had their zealous followers, and that these people were often open to more radical ideas. Zealous conservatives were quick to associate several of Henry's reforms with Lutheranism or worse, and their reaction may have been partly accurate observation and partly self-fulfilling prophecy. Thus, although the numerical strength of late Henrician Protestantism must not be exaggerated, in many places there was a Protestant movement capable of dividing the community along religious lines.

The acceptance of doctrinal division in later Henrician England is illustrated by a change in popular attitudes to the burning of heretics. Throughout the early Tudor period and into the 1530s, there was little or no sympathy with those condemned. Recantations and burnings were religious ceremonies which took place as much for the benefit of the onlookers as for the punishment of the victims. It was customary for bishops to grant a forty days indulgence to all attending, and this made them popular occasions. John Fisher published such an indulgence at the recantation of Barnes. At the burning of one Peke in Ipswich early in the century, the Bishop of Norwich offered forty days to everyone who threw a faggot on the fire. Led by Lord Curson, Sir John Audley, and other leading gentry, the onlookers rushed to throw sticks. A similar indulgence doubtless provoked the similar rush at the burning of Thomas Bennett at Exeter in 1531. As late as 1539, Sir William Kingston (vice-chamberlain of the royal household and thus virtually a royal spokesman) offered in the Commons, in the course of the debate on the Six Articles, to bring a faggot to the pyre of Thomas Brook, the only member who dared speak against the bill. By the 1540s, however, a different attitude had begun to prevail. There was widespread disgust at the cynicism with which Henry VIII sent to their deaths in matched pairs on 30 July 1540 three papists (Thomas Abel, Edward Powell, and Richard Featherstone) and three Protestants (Robert Barnes, Thomas Garrett, and William Jerome). Bonner's persecution to the death of the boy Richard Mekins that same year likewise aroused hostility. And the reaction of the people of Ipswich in 1545 to the burning of the Sacramentarian Kirby was very different from that of their predecessors to the burning of the Lollard Peke.[42] It should not automatically be presumed that this shift reflects widespread support for Protestant teachings – though if the Protestants had remained as insignificant as the Lollards, the shift could hardly have occurred. Rather it suggests that doctrinal division was becoming a fact of life, at least in certain areas. English society was no longer religiously unified enough for the execution of heretics to be accepted without question. In other words, although Protestants were still a minority, they were no longer a small or secretive enough minority to be regarded as wholly alien and threatening to society, and thus fit for burning (as Lollards had been and as witches were to be). The Protestants of late Henrician England were an articulate, committed, and conspicuous minority. Their significance was out of all proportion to their numbers, as many of them were highly placed at court, in the church, or in the city of London.

The people of England were religiously divided at the end of Henry's reign, even if the division was unequal. In the reigns of Edward and Mary this division was to engender conflict and bitterness on a large scale. It was also to alienate many people from the religion of their forefathers without attracting them to the new doctrines and practices of the Reformers.

# CONCLUSION

If the Reformation was, in the words of Professor Dickens, 'a process of Protestantisation',[1] then how far was there really an English Reformation in the reign of Henry VIII? For by the king's death, the process of Protestantisation had barely begun, and it still lacked the official support which alone could effectively advance it. Henry himself had no intention of initiating such a process. The religious changes he introduced were often decked out in the rhetoric of 'Reformation', but they were undertaken chiefly with a view to increasing his power, swelling his coffers, and exacting stricter obedience from his subjects. Nevertheless, despite the intentions of the king, these changes contributed to the rise of English Protestantism. At almost every stage of its development, the fortunes of English Protestantism were dependent on the attitudes of the king and his close advisers. The alliance between crown and Reformers forged during the divorce controversy was decisive for the survival of the evangelical movement. Without royal protection in the early 1530s, Latimer might well have gone the way of Bilney. And with Bilney and Frith dead, and Barnes and Tyndale in exile, Latimer was the towering figure among the early Reformers, exercising a preaching ministry whose contribution to the English Reformation is incalculable. As Henry fell under the influence of Boleyn in his bed and of Cromwell in his council, a mild form of Lutheranism was able to establish itself at court and, under court patronage, elsewhere. Latimer himself was invited to deliver the Lenten sermons at court in 1534, and though he doubtless moderated his tone in the presence of the Defender of the Faith, it is inconceivable that his eloquence failed to imbue some listeners with Reforming sympathies. Episcopal appointments during the brief reign of Anne Boleyn were predominantly of evangelical Reformers. Cromwell too was deeply involved in the patronage and protection of evangelical preachers. His efforts remained consistent in their aim – to promote the royal supremacy by undermining much of the more obviously papal aspects of Catholicism. His injunctions of 1536, which responded to Convocation's complaints about 'English books' by instructing curates to provide an English Bible in their churches, made his position clear, even as the Ten Articles they accompanied and interpreted reflected the king's conservative inclinations. The orientation of Cromwell's foreign policy towards an understanding with the Lutheran powers of Germany was the natural counterpart to his ecclesiastical policy, and may indeed have been the driving force behind it. It was the simultaneous collapse of the talks with the Lutherans and of the anti-imperial policy in 1538, together with the king's rising anxiety about the papal axis abroad and heresy at home, that put an end to court patronage for Reformers and threatened Cromwell's security.[2] After his fall in 1540, the Reformers lost their main defence. However, there remained a number of men around the king whose Reformist sympathies were as strong, though not as effective. Personal connections with the king, rather than high political office, were now the strength of the evangelical faction.

It must not be imagined, however, that the evangelical faction was unopposed. Religious conservatives also played the game, often to great effect, as in the toppling of Boleyn and Cromwell. Henry's doctrinal conservatism gave them a head start, although his often intense but rarely enduring personal loyalties prevented them from ever making a clean sweep of their opponents. This can be seen in the boldest coup of the Catholic clergy after the break with Rome: the attempt in 1543 to turn the king against his beloved Archbishop of Canterbury by revealing the extent to which Cranmer had tolerated and encouraged heresy within his diocese. Gardiner had apparently been keeping his eye on Canterbury for some time. Now that the King's Book had decisively repudiated Protestant doctrines, he and certain theological allies – notably Dr John London, the Warden of New College and a former client of Cromwell – thought it a good moment to blow the whistle. Information against several of Cranmer's clerical protégés was laid before the Privy Council (which took a close interest in religious affairs throughout the 1540s), and a thorough investigation was launched. However, Henry decided from an early stage that he was not going to destroy Cranmer, and ultimately put him in charge of the investigation, turning the threat into a warning.[3] Despite Cranmer's survival, the King's Book and the Prebendaries' Plot created an essentially conservative atmosphere. A number of former Catholic fugitives returned to England at this time, while the number of Protestants seeking refuge abroad increased. Protestant polemic against the chief demon, Gardiner, became both strident and impotent. A series of notable recantations and the burning of Anne Askew in 1546 seemed to herald a new age for English Catholicism, an impression strengthened by the narrow escape of Catherine Parr and the opening of a major polemical offensive under Bonner's auspices.

However, the conservative dominance was to prove illusory. It was covertly undermined by the commitment of the education of Prince Edward and Princess Elizabeth to tutors of evangelical sympathies. And it was to be dramatically reversed by a court coup in the last weeks of Henry's reign. Both Edward's education and the coup reflected the growing influence with the king of Sir Anthony Denny, the premier Gentleman of the Privy Chamber, a man of distinct Reformist sympathies.[4] It was his influence which secured as tutors for Edward and Elizabeth alongside Richard Cox (who already enjoyed Henry's favour), the services of John Cheke, William Grindal, and Roger Ascham (all fellows of Denny's old college of St John's, Cambridge, the foremost centre of humanist studies in England). Although it has been argued that Henry must have been aware of the religious views of these men and thus have had some sympathy with them, there is no evidence for this. Their academic credentials and their connections with Denny account for their appointment. It is unlikely either that their views were especially radical at this stage or that they made them public during the Henrician reaction. Only Cox, who presided over Edward's education, had shown any Reformist sympathies before this time. And despite his later prominence as a Marian exile and Elizabethan bishop, his record under Henry was at best cautious. Though implicated in the scandal at Cardinal's College back in the 1520s, he subsequently kept well out of trouble as chaplain to Goodrich and then Cranmer. And while the opinions he gave on the seven sacraments in 1540 were not traditional, they were guardedly expressed and gave nothing away. In the 1540s he helped compile the conservative King's Book, which remained the standard of orthodoxy from 1543 until Henry's death. And in 1546 he took a prominent part in urging the Reformer Edward Crome to recant. It is unlikely in the extreme that Henry would have suspected this man, much less his son's other tutors, of daring to depart from his orthodoxy in schooling his son. This is not to deny that they probably did so – merely to doubt that Henry would have foreseen or expected it.

Whatever the importance ascribed to Edward's tutors, there can be no doubting the importance of the coup preceding Henry's death, or of Denny's place in it. The factions of Henry's declining years were indeed aligned on religious grounds. Denny was firmly in the Seymour faction, which favoured further ecclesiastical reform: it was Denny who put Cranmer's scheme for a pruning of ecclesiastical ceremonies before Henry VIII in 1546. The wars with France and Scotland in the 1540s had benefited both the Seymours, who had done well in Scotland, and their chief rivals the Howards, who had served with some distinction in France. But at the close of the reign the Seymours managed to implicate the Earl of Surrey, heir to the Duchy of Norfolk, in a charge of treason. He and his father were gaoled in December 1546, and Gardiner was left without his chief political ally on the Privy Council. Then Henry died. The Seymour faction successfully disposed of Surrey, toyed with and abandoned the idea of executing Norfolk, and, crucially, excluded both Norfolk and Gardiner from the council for Edward's minority established under Henry's will – over the composition of which they exercised a decisive influence. Henry's own disinclination for further reform is evident from the conservative character of his will's religious provisions (presumably arranged rather more in advance than the political provisions) which included a large number of masses for his soul. Nevertheless, he had left his son, already perhaps predisposed to Protestantism by his teachers, in the hands of a faction committed to further reform out of mixture of zeal and greed. The religious direction of the new regime was swiftly revealed in 1547, although at that point even the leaders probably had little idea how far they would go. The agenda was set by Cranmer's emotive sermon at Edward's coronation, presenting him as the new Josiah who would complete the overthrow of the idols. The new departure in policy was marked within weeks of Edward's accession by the successful demand for the leading Catholic theologian Dr Richard Smyth to recant several of his opinions. The doomed rearguard action of Gardiner against the religious policies of Cranmer and Somerset represented the death throes of the Henrician Settlement. The conservative King's Book was soon supplanted by the evangelical Book of Homilies, which aligned the Church of England with the doctrine of justification by faith alone, and thus took it clearly into the Reformed camp. This Protestant denouement was far from inevitable, and the religious conservatism of the English people, though perhaps not as profound as it seemed, remained largely unshaken. But the foundations of Protestant England had been laid. The doctrinal divisions and confusions which Henry's policies engendered had created a situation in which the religious future of England could be called into question and manipulated by a well placed court faction. The royal supremacy was the tool they needed.

If there was any coherence in the Henrician church that so soon became a thing of the past, it is not to be found in such slick labels as 'Catholicism without the Pope', 'via media', or 'Protestantism'. 'Catholicism without the Pope' it certainly was not. The exclusive nationalism which rejected the papacy in theory and the general council in practice contrasts sharply with that universalism inherent in the very name 'Catholic'. Henry VIII himself felt the tension, admitting to Chapuys during a discussion of Paul III's projected general council in 1537 that if he alone among the Christian princes held aloof, it would look as though he was separating from the 'whole corps of Christendom'.[5] Official Henrician doctrine always maintained that the Church of England remained in communion with the universal Church – although the English schism was an obvious fact from the other side of the Channel. In the strictest sense, Catholicism in England might be said to have died with Thomas More, whose stand against the royal supremacy was based on his commitment to the universality of the Church. Given the extraordinary nature of Henry's supremacy, one might almost describe his settlement as 'the papacy without Catholicism'. But to call it Protestant would be even less helpful. The consistent affirmation of free will, denial of justification by faith alone, and defence of Catholic eucharistic doctrine run counter to the teachings of all the major evangelical Reformers. The predominantly conservative doctrinal stance of Henry's church can hardly be doubted. The appellation 'via media' has something to be said for it, in that Henry and his supporters at times presented his church as steering between the blind traditions of the papists and the wanton innovations of the Protestants. According to Cromwell, 'the king leaned neither to the right nor to the left hand', and Henry himself observed to Parliament in 1545 that 'some be too stiff in their old Mumpsimus, others too busy and curious in their new Sumpsimus'.[6] But the definition of a middle way depends on the selection of extremes, and in an intellectual culture founded on Aristotelian ethics, the 'golden mean' was an ideal to which all laid claim. To call Henry's church a 'via media' does not tell us why it stood where it did. That church was an idiosyncratic creation. Its official teachings reflected the conscience of a king who was himself the conscience of his church. His conscience had been formed, and largely remained, within the Catholic tradition – hence its enduring commitment to such doctrines and practices as the real presence and auricular confession. However, it was capable of a certain flexibility. It could be re-formed, especially where reform served the king's interests. There can be no doubting the reality of Henry's scruples about his first marriage. And the consistency which he subsequently brought to maintaining his own supremacy within the Church of England and to eliminating the worship of images betrays the characteristic self-righteousness of what, for want of a better word, we must call his 'mature' conscience.

If there was any consistency to the various policies which Henry imposed on his church, it is to be found in the image of kingship which he adopted together with the royal supremacy. Once his kingship was recast by the supremacy propaganda into the image of the Old Testament monarchs, he sought to play the part. Like an Old Testament king, he tried to enforce the law and word of God in his kingdom lest the wrath of God fall upon it. His own experience over his first marriage had convinced him of the reality of the divine penalties threatened under the law of Moses. Here surely lies the explanation for that most curious feature of the legislative programme of 1534, the enactment of a statute against sodomy which made the offence punishable by death (in accordance with Lev 20:13). The absence of a law against it in England was a perilous lacuna which a king convinced of his duty to execute the law of God could hardly leave unfilled. Did not Jehosaphat purge the land of sodomites (1 Kings 22:46)? The dissolution of the monasteries, which the royal visitation had 'revealed' to be dens of vice, was a natural concomitant of this moralistic policy. And had not Jehoash taken back from the priests 'all the hallowed things that Jehosaphat, and Jehoram, and Ahaziah, his fathers, kings of Judah, had dedicated, and his own hallowed things, and all the gold that was found in the treasures of the house of the Lord?' (2 Kings 12:18)? The destruction of venerated images makes sense not in terms of Catholicism (which accepted the practice) nor of Lutheranism (which merely abandoned it) nor of radical Protestantism (which regarded all images as inherently idolatrous). But it was a strict interpretation of what in Henry's church became the second commandment.

And the elimination of the worship of images, of idolatry in the strict sense, was the paradigmatic act of the Old Testament kings, for example Jehu (2 Kings 10:26), Hezekiah (2 Kings 18:4), and Asa (2 Chronicles 14:3). The royal supremacy itself, with its power to order the church, could be paralleled from Solomon's establishment of the Temple (2 Chronicles 6). And it was as Solomon in judgement that contemporaries saw the white-clothed Henry preside at the trial of Lambert in 1538. The closest model for Henry himself, as his contemporaries realised, was Josiah, the king who was thunderstruck when the high priest read to him from the books of the Law, and set about enforcing it. Josiah's suppression of idolatrous priests, the houses of sodomites, the vessels of idolatry, idolatrous relics, and images (2 Kings 23:25) almost forms a programme for the campaigns of the later 1530s against monasticism and the cult of saints. Henry's decision to promulgate the English Bible and to inculcate a thorough knowledge of the Ten Commandments and the creed looks remarkably like Josiah's promulgation of the law to his people. Of course, Henry did not adopt his policies *just* because the Old Testament kings had acted in this or that fashion. Necessity, expedience, and pragmatic realism remained crucial elements of political decision-making. But as, after his formative experiences in the divorce controversy, he became convinced both of the normative status of the Mosaic law and of the direct correlation between divine favour and the fulfilment of that law, the histories of the Old Testament kings became not only propaganda – the flatterers of kings had long compared them to the worthies of the Old Testament – but also political programmes. In the pithy words of Cuthbert Tunstall, Henry as supreme head merely acted 'as the chief and best of the kings of Israel did, and as all good Christian kings ought to do'. Nor was it the least among the attractions of this political and theological programme that it strengthened the monarchy both in theory and in practice. Perhaps the last words might suitably be left to that tireless Henrician propagandist, Richard Morison, for whom Henry was as David, Jehosaphat, Amaziah, Josiah, and Hezekiah rolled into one: 'Where before he was called king, and yet had against all right and equity a ruler above him, which ever enforced himself to keep his highness and all the rest of his subjects in servitude, error, and idolatry; God has made him, as all his noble progenitors of right ought to have been, a full king, that is, a ruler, and not ruled in his own kingdom as others were'.[7]

# NOTES

LP is short for *Letters and Papers* (see bibliography under 'Documents'), and references to it are given by volume, part, and document number.

## INTRODUCTION

1. Morison, *An Invective ayenste . . . treason*, sig. D4v.
2. See e.g. Dickens, *English Reformation*; Elton, *Reform and Reformation*; and Scarisbrick, *Henry VIII*.
3. Powicke, The *Reformation in England*, p. 1.
4. I do not propose to get bogged down in terminological agonising, but should make it clear at this point that I use 'evangelical' and 'Protestant' interchangeably and in a general sense. No affiliation to any specific theological school (e.g. Lutheranism or Zwinglianism) is implied, simply a measure of sympathy with the doctrines of justification by faith alone and of the sufficient authority of scripture in doctrinal disputes, combined with a degree of hostility to the structures and traditions of the late medieval Church. The very slight anachronism in using the term 'Protestant' (first found in English in 1539) *avant la lettre* is justified by convenience, by modern usage, and by the fact that once it had appeared in English, it was used to describe those otherwise known as 'evangelicals'. I describe as 'Catholic' or 'conservative' those who remained sympathetic to traditional doctrines and practices, and who did not accept the sole sufficiency of faith for justification or of scripture for doctrinal authority.

## 1  DIVORCE AND SUPREMACY

1. Ives, *Anne Boleyn*, is the best biography, offering at pp. 99–110 the most plausible account of her early relationship with the king.

2. For a fuller account of the roles of Fisher and Wakefield in the divorce controversy, see Rex, *Theology of John Fisher*, ch. 10.

3. Murphy's introduction to Surtz and Murphy, *Divorce Tracts*, elucidates the development of the king's case for the divorce.

4. Kelly, *Matrimonial Trials*, pp. 75–131, gives the fullest account of the legatine court, but needs to be supplemented by Surtz and Murphy, *Divorce Tracts*. See Scarisbrick, *Henry VIII*, p. 214, for Campeggio's hopes of consigning Catherine to a convent.

5. Ives, 'The Fall of Wolsey', is the fullest and ultimately most convincing account of this hotly debated episode, but see Gwyn, *King's Cardinal*, pp. 549–98, for a view which disputes the importance of court faction in the cardinal's fall.

6. Gwyn, *King's Cardinal*, pp. 587–98. This insight is perfectly compatible with the factional explanation advanced by Ives, and helps explain what both Ives and Gwyn emphasise, namely Henry's reluctance to proceed with the final destruction of his former minister.

7. *I Diarii di Marino Sanuto*, vol. 54, p. 162, transcribes a report dated 22 Nov 1530 by the Mantuan envoy at Augsburg to the effect that he has seen a letter from England reporting their arrest. In a later letter from Brussels (25 February 1531), the same man, this time reporting the Pardon of the Clergy, again alludes to their arrest. Any arrest must have been brief. Fisher's episcopal register shows him at Rochester in October, and again in December (Bradshaw and Duffy, *Humanism, Reform and Reformation*, p. 246).

8. Scarisbrick, *Henry VIII*, pp. 255–8, and Bedouelle and Le Gal, *Le 'Divorce'*, *passim*, are the best published accounts of these affairs.

9. Scarisbrick, *Henry VIII*, pp. 267–8 and 290. The Duke of Norfolk took up Suffolk's refrain in Jan 1531 (p. 272). By June 1531, Henry was blustering about refusing papal jurisdiction in his case, and scorning the risk of excommunication (p. 290).

10. Nicholson, 'Act of Appeals', pp. 19–23.

11. Guy has explored the works of St German in a number of important works, especially chs. 5 and 7 of Fox and Guy, *Henrician Age*, where further references will be found.

12. For detailed analysis and some controversy over the praemunire, the submission, and the pardon, see Scarisbrick, 'Pardon of the Clergy'; Kelly, 'Submission of the Clergy'; Guy, 'Praemunire Manoeuvres'; and Bernard, 'Pardon of the Clergy'.

13. For this controversy, see Guy, 'Thomas More and Christopher St German', ch. 5 of Fox and Guy (eds), *Henrician Age*.

14. Elton, *Reform and Reformation*, ch. 6, especially pp. 130–8;

Scarisbrick, *Henry VIII*, ch. 9, especially pp. 261–73; Guy, *Tudor England*, ch. 5, especially pp. 124–32, and 'Thomas Cromwell and the Henrician Revolution', ch. 7 of Fox and Guy, *Henrician Age*.

15. Scarisbrick, *Henry VIII*, pp. 287–95, argues that Henry was already committed to some sort of break with Rome from late 1530. Elton associates the firm decision for a break with the beginning of Cromwell's ascendancy early in 1532 (*Reform and Reformation*, p. 175). More recently and more convincingly scholars have emphasised Henry's indecision and hesitation until Anne's pregnancy: see Ives, *Anne Boleyn*, p. 209; Guy, *Tudor England*, pp. 130–2; and Redworth, *Church Catholic*, pp. 35–48.

16. If mistake it was. Redworth, *Church Catholic*, pp. 36–7 and 41–4, argues that Gardiner was taking a calculated risk in opposing the king's wishes over a matter of the deepest concern to the episcopal order to which he now belonged.

17. For a full account of this girl see Neame, *Holy Maid*, for want of anything better.

18. And for that matter with that of Professor Elton. For Cromwell and statute, see e.g. *Reform and Reformation*, pp. 196–200.

19. Lockwood, 'Marsilius of Padua', pp. 90–1, 94, 97–9, and 108–10 ('Parliament was not, however, a check on the king's will, but an emanation of it').

20. Gardiner, *Letters*, p. 56.

21. Foxe, *Acts and Monuments*, vi, p. 594, during the trial of John Rogers in 1555. It is not entirely clear which statute Gardiner had in mind.

22. Elton, *Policy and Police*, pp. 282–3.

23. His tract 'Si Sedes illa' is printed in Janelle, *Obedience*, pp. 22–65. See also pp. lii–liv.

24. The propaganda campaign of Cromwell's regime has been definitively explored in Elton, *Policy and Police*.

25. Nicholson, 'Act of Appeals', pp. 25–6.

26. As reported by Chapuys, *LP* 10. 283. William Marshall also made the identification, in his adulterated translation of the *Defender of the Peace*, published in 1535 probably under Cromwell's auspices (Lockwood, 'Marsilius of Padua', p. 92). The doctrine that the pope was Antichrist was never official doctrine under Henry as it certainly was under Edward VI and Elizabeth, but it surfaced occasionally without rebuke, sometimes even on the royal lips (as reported by Marillac, *LP* 15. 848, 6 July 1540).

27. Strype, *Ecclesiastical Memorials* I ii p. 175.

28. Sarcerius, *Loci Aliquot Communes*, fol. 6v; Morison, *Lamentation*, sig. A3r and C3v.

29. Aston, 'Lollardy and the Reformation', p. 165.
30. McKisack, *Medieval History*, ch. 5; and Levin, 'A Good Prince'.
31. Ullmann, 'This Realm of England is an Empire', pp. 176–80 and 184–5.
32. Elton, *Reform and Reformation*, p. 177.
33. Paynell, *Conspiracy of Catiline*, sig. A2v; Elyot, *Dictionary*, sig. A2r.
34. Haas, 'Divine Right Kingship', has some useful comments on this, but his dating of documents relevant to this theme as early as 1531 is insecure.
35. *LP* 8. 406–7. The preacher is identified in these papers only as 'Mr Wakefield', curate of St Peter's parish and chaplain to Cranmer. Probably Robert Wakefield, it might perhaps have been his brother Thomas. Both were in Cranmer's service (Cranmer, *Works*, ii, p. 349; and *LP* 13 ii 1223).
36. *LP* 8. 600, 839, 854, 915, 921, 963, 968, 1082; Gardiner, *Letters*, p. 66; Bowker, *Henrician Reformation*, p. 143.
37. Chambers, *Faculty Office Register*, p. 39; *LP* 12 i 757.
38. Brigden, *London*, pp. 233–5, on Paul's Cross. *LP* 10. 284, on Catherine's funeral.
39. Chambers, *Cardinal Bainbridge*, pp. 1–13.
40. The best account is Lehmberg, 'Parliamentary Attainder'.
41. *LP* 13. ii. 986, item 13.
42. Redworth interprets Gardiner's attitudes to the papacy under Henry rather differently (*Church Catholic*, e.g. pp. 56–7, 144, 153–4), but not to my mind convincingly.
43. Brigden, London, pp. 242, 258, and 279; and Elton, *Policy and Police*, pp. 19–20.
44. Wright, *Suppression*, pp. 37–8 and 49; *LP* 10. 346 and 462, and 14 i 1074; Brigden, *London*, p. 243.

## 2  CHURCH AND CROWN

1. Heal, *Prelates and Princes*, p. 54.
2. Houlbrooke, *Church Courts*, p. 37.
3. Heal, *Prelates and Princes*, appendix III.
4. Thompson, 'The Bishop in his Diocese', on Fisher; and 'Appendix 3: statistics of episcopal residence', in Bradshaw and Duffy (eds), *Humanism, Reform and Reformation*, p. 250; Lander, 'Chichester' (on Sherbourne); Bowker, *Henrician Reformation*, on Longland; Heal, 'Ely' (West).
5. William Warham junior, Archdeacon of Canterbury, may perhaps have been the Archbishop's illegitimate son. However, though known suspiciously enough as a 'nephew', he may have been nothing more than that. James Stanley, Bishop of Ely (1505–14), a scion of the Stanley Earls of Derby,

appointed under Henry VII thanks to the influence of his stepmother Lady Margaret Beaufort, had at least two sons and a daughter by the woman who lived with him at his palace of Somersham.

6. Jones, *Church in Chester*, pp. 28–9; Clark, *Provincial Society*, p. 27 finds that about a fifth of Canterbury clergy were graduates under Archbishop Bourchier (1454–86), while Zell, 'Clergy in Kent', pp. 525–6, finds about two fifths under Warham (1503–32), a proportion which then declined, despite Cranmer's personal efforts, until Elizabeth's reign; Brigden, *London*, p. 58; Bowker, *Secular Clergy*, pp. 44–6 and 78–80.

7. See Orme, *English Schooling*, and Moran, *Growth of English Schooling*.

8. Williams, *Recovery, Reorientation and Reformation*, pp. 282–3 (Wales); Haigh, *Reformation and Resistance*, pp. 40–51 (Lancashire).

9. Heath, *Parish Clergy*, pp. 49–69; Bowker, *Secular Clergy*, pp. 104–5; Haigh, *Reformation and Resistance*, pp. 36–40.

10. Leach, *Southwell Minster*; Jones, *The Church in Chester*, p. 35; Bowker, *Henrician Reformation*, pp. 34–7; Lehmberg, *Reformation of Cathedrals*, pp. 218–23 and 264–5.

11. These figures were kindly provided by Dr Peter Cunich of Magdalene College, Cambridge, and are based chiefly on the records of the Court of Augmentations. Absolute certainty about the allocation of some houses to particular orders is precluded by the paucity of information. In addition to those listed in the text, there were 16 hospitals which may perhaps have belonged to religious orders, and a further 6 monastic colleges in Oxford and Cambridge.

12. Heal, *Hospitality*, pp. 228–46, presents a balanced yet largely favourable view of monastic hospitality. See also Haigh, *Lancashire Monasteries*, pp. 53–6. Although certain monasteries (e.g. Winchcombe and Bury St Edmund's) remained major centres of learning, their educational vitality was increasingly dependent on contact with the universities.

13. Gwyn, *King's Cardinal*, p. 466; Haigh, *Lancashire Monasteries*, p. 5.

14. For the anticlerical thesis see Dickens, *English Reformation*, especially ch. 6, and Cross, *Church and People*, *passim*. Scarisbrick, *Reformation*, chs 1–3; and Haigh, 'Anticlericalism' are powerful attacks; and Dickens, 'Shape of Anticlericalism', offers a vigorous defence.

15. Gleason, *Colet*, especially pp. 199–200 and 211–13. For the Pseudo-Dionysius and 'hierarchy' see Ullmann, *History of the Papacy*, pp. 35–6.

16. Jones and Underwood, *King's Mother*, p. 173.

17. Barlow, *A proper dialogue*, sig. B3v. The speaker contests this claim.

18. Crofts, 'Books, Reform and the Reformation'; Schutte, 'Printing, Piety, and the People in Italy'.

19. Ogle argues that Hunne's case was crucial in transmuting cant criticism of the clergy and hierarchy into politically significant anticlericalism, especially in the city of London: *Lollards' Tower*, p. 47.

20. Brigden, 'Tithe controversy', especially pp. 288 and 294; Haigh, *Reformation and Resistance*, pp. 58–62.

21. Marshall, 'Priests and Priesthood', especially conclusion, pp. 307–10.

22. *Faculty Office Register*, pp. xvii–xviii and xxxvii. Papal figures derived from *Calendar of Papal Registers*, vol. 18.

23. Wilkins, *Concilia*, iii, p. 803.

24. Chambers, *Faculty Office Register*, introduction, pp. xx–xxxi. Elton, *Policy and Police*, pp. 247–8, makes some important observations on Cromwell's vicegerency. A comprehensive account of Cromwell's ecclesiastical patronage and intervention would be a valuable addition to our understanding of the later 1530s.

25. Logan, 'Henrician Canons'.

26. Houlbrooke, *Church Courts*, pp. 11–15, 37, and 49–50.

27. Scarisbrick, 'Clerical Taxation'.

28. Youings, *Dissolution*, p. 36–7.

29. Gasquet's *Henry VIII and the English Monasteries* was the first scholarly attempt at this subject. The classic account remains that of Knowles, *Religious Orders*, vol. III; see also Youings, *Dissolution*, for excellent analysis and discussion of the main issues and documents. There are many valuable local studies.

30. Pole, *Epistolarum*, i, pp. 178–9; but see Elton, *Tudor Revolution*, pp. 71–6 and *Reform and Reformation*, p. 136. Van Ortroy, 'Vie de Fisher', x, pp. 342-4.

31. *LP* 9. 321, referring to Cromwell's words during a visit to Winchcombe Abbey by the royal court in late July.

32. See for example the report of Chapuys to Charles V, *LP* 9. 434, 25 Sept 1535.

33. Bradshaw, *Dissolution in Ireland*, p. 47.

34. Knowles, *Religious Orders*, iii, pp. 268–90.

35. Knowles, *Religious Orders*, iii, pp. 315–16. Latimer, *Works*, i, p. 123.

36. Cross, 'Religious life of women'; Woodward, 'Yorkshire Priories', pp. 396–401; Kitch, 'The Reformation in Sussex', pp. 88–9.

37. Wright, *Suppression*, p. 197.

38. *LP* 7. 1607, a report on the Observants dating from 1534, lists about 140 friars: 40 in prison; 30 in exile; 36 'exempt'; and 31 dead.
39. *LP* 7. 805 and 8. 1151; Elton, *Policy and Police*, pp. 18–19 [*LP* 10. 594].
40. Wriothesley's *Chronicle*, p. 81; Knowles, *Religious Orders*, iii, p. 350–3.
41. The other two monastic cathedrals, Bath and Coventry, were not refounded, because their bishops already had secular cathedrals at Wells and Lichfield.
42. Scarisbrick, 'Secular Colleges', p. 64; Heal, *Prelates and Princes*, pp. 116–17; Lehmberg, *Reformation of Cathedrals*, pp. 84–94.
43. Heal, *Prelates and Princes*, ch. 5 and appendices I and II.
44. Lehmberg, *Reformation of Cathedrals*, p. 94; Wright, *Suppression*, pp. 206–10; Scarisbrick, 'Secular colleges', pp. 56–60.
45. Logan, 'Visitation of the Universities'.
46. More, *Utopia*, p. 238.

### 3  POPULAR RELIGION

1. Burgess, 'A fond thing', provides an excellent account of the place of purgatory in late medieval English religious life.
2. Haines, *Ecclesia Anglicana*, p. 135. It may also have been included in Wolsey's lost legatine constitutions of 1519 (Gwyn, *King's Cardinal*, p. 267–70).
3. Brigden, *London*, pp. 273–4.
4. Galpern, *Religions of the People*, p. 20.
5. Eisenstein, *Printing Press*, i, p. 375.
6. Jones and Underwood, *King's Mother*, p. 175.
7. Latimer, *Works*, ii, p. 364; Wright, *Suppression*, pp. 190–1; Foxe, *Acts and Monuments*, v, p. 467.
8. *LP* 13 i 634.
9. Clark, *Provincial Society*, p. 26; *LP* 5. 273.
10. Nash, *Worcestershire*, i, pp. 519–20 and ii, app. pp. xi. Somers and O'Brien, *Halesowen Churchwardens' Accounts*, pp. 7 and 78. Halesowen abbey (Premonstratensian) surrendered on 9 June 1538 (*LP* 13 i 1155). The abbey held the rectory of Halesowen and provided the chaplain for the shrine at Kenelmstowe.
11. Foxe, *Acts and Monuments*, iv. 177. As a Lollard, she scorned their advice.
12. Wright, *Suppression*, p. 58; Jones, *Church in Chester*, p. 115 [ *LP* 10, p. 141].
13. Bradshaw, *Saynt Werburge*, book 2, ch. 8, pp. 164–5.
14. 'Documenta de S. Wenefreda', *passim*; Fraser, *Mary Queen of Scots*, pp. 437–9.

15. Wright, *Suppression*, p. 234; Foxe, *Acts and Monuments*, v, p. 467; *LP* 13 ii 1243.
16. Lambarde, *Perambulation of Kent*, pp. 183–4 (Rood of Grace); Thomas, *The Pilgrim*, pp. 38–9; Latimer, *Works*, ii, p. 364; Foxe, *Acts and Monuments*, v, p. 406.
17. Johnston, 'Cult of St Bridget', pp. 88–93, commenting that the cult was highly literary.
18. Rogers, 'Cult of Prince Edward', pp. 187–9; Tanner, *Norwich*, pp. 231–3; *Testamenta Cantiana II*, pp. xix and 312; Bale, *Catalogus*, i, p. 632; Whiting, *Blind Devotion*, pp. 56 and 58–9.
19. Tanner, *Norwich*, pp. 58–63; More, *Dialogue Concerning Heresies*, i, pp. 87–8; MacCulloch, *Suffolk*, pp. 143–5; Neame, *Holy Maid*, pp. 141–7.
20. See Finucane, *Miracles and Beliefs*, pp. 195–6, for the growth of Marian and Christocentric devotions in the later middle ages.
21. Bond, *Chapter Acts of Windsor*, p. 10.
22. Haigh, *Lancashire Monasteries*, p. 5.
23. Rubin, *Corpus Christi*, gives a comprehensive account of the cult of the eucharist in the later middle ages, with especial reference to England, and draws out both its social dimension (pp. 213–87) and its connection with other Christocentric images and devotions (pp. 302–16).
24. Weever, *Funerall Monuments*, p. 569. Whiting, 'Abominable Idols', p. 32, notes the proliferation of Passion images.
25. Scribner, 'Ritual and Popular Religion', especially p. 52 and pp. 64–5; Pfaff, *Liturgical Feasts*, pp. 62–83 and 84–91.
26. Hughes and Larkin, no. 161, pp. 236–7.
27. *LP* 10. 1125 and 1140.
28. Bale, *Catalogus*, i, p. 648.
29. *LP* 9. 42; Wright, *Suppression*, p. 85.
30. Frere and Kennedy, ii, pp. 12–18.
31. *LP* 10. 246, no. 16.
32. *LP* 13 ii 409; Latimer, *Works*, ii, pp. 406–9; Wriothesley, *Chronicle*, i, pp. 75–6 and 90; Cranmer, *Works*, ii, p. 378.
33. Whiting, 'Abominable Idols', p. 41.
34. Frere and Kennedy, ii, pp. 59–60; Hughes and Larkin, pp. 301–2; Wriothesley, *Chronicle*, p. 152 (the bleeding host – after an investigation in Star Chamber, the priest was compelled to do public penance at Paul's Cross); Dickens, *Lollards and Protestants*, p. 81; Brigden, *London*, p. 427 (Houghton's arm).
35. Wilkins, *Concilia*, iii, 701–2 and 803.
36. Hughes and Larkin, pp. 301–2, and 341–2.
37. *LP* 14 i 295.
38. Latimer, *Works*, ii, p. 403.

39. MacCulloch, *Suffolk and the Tudors*, pp. 154–5.
40. Kitch, 'Reformation in Sussex', pp. 97–8.
41. *LP* 12 ii 587, 592, and 703.
42. Wriothesley, *Chronicle*, pp. 75, 77, 80; *LP* 13 ii 256, 259, 328, 345, 596; Wright, *Suppression*, p. 224.
43. *LP* 13 i 192; ii 674 and 1103.
44. *LP* 15. 772.
45. Cranmer, *Works*, ii, p. 490.
46. Hughes and Larkin, pp. 274 and 278–80.
47. Cobb, *Rationale*, pp. xlvi and xlix. The six bishops were Clerk of Bath, Goodrich of Ely, Salcot of Salisbury, Sampson of Chichester, Bell of Worcester, and Holgate of Llandaff.
48. The text has been edited from the two extant manuscripts in Cobb, *Rationale*. Cobb dates it convincingly between 1540 and 1543, but no further precision is possible. The fact that the manuscripts survive respectively in the Cottonian collection (British Library Cottonian MS Cleo E v fols. 268–93) and in Lambeth Palace Library (MS 1107, fols 167–202) suggests that Henry and Cranmer were the recipients of the completed text. Cobb dismisses the conjecture that Cranmer somehow managed to forestall publication (pp. liv–lv), chiefly on the basis of his anachronistic and optimistic vision of Cranmer as a High Anglican.
49. Cranmer, *Works*, ii, pp. 414–16; Foxe, *Acts and Monuments*, v, pp. 562–3. As Gardiner was abroad at the time, and none of his many surviving letters allude to the matter, Henry may have been masking his own disinclination to carry out Cranmer's wishes.
50. Scarisbrick, *Reformation*, ch. 1.
51. Hutton, 'Local Impact', pp. 116–19.
52. Dickens, 'The Reformation in England', in *Reformation Studies*, at p. 449.
53. McConica, *English Humanists*, p. 199. Strype, *Ecclesiastical Memorials*, I ii 388 – undated, it is perhaps a protest against Cromwell's injunctions of 1536.
54. For an extensive discussion of this issue, with particular reference to the Ten Commandments, see Aston, *England's Iconoclasts*, pp. 371–92 and 408–30.

#### 4 VERNACULAR RELIGIOUS CULTURE

1. Chillingworth, *Religion of Protestants*, p. 375.
2. Legge, *Anglo-Norman Literature*, pp. 5–8 and 176–9.
3. Deanesley, *Lollard Bible*, pp. 252–67, puts the Lollard origin of the 'Lollard Bible' beyond doubt.
4. Hudson, *Premature Reformation*, pp. 231–8.

5. Fines, 'Heresy Trials', p. 160; More, *Dialogue*, p. 330. Hunne had bought his copy from his apparently orthodox fellow parishioner Thomas Downes; Brigden, *London*, p. 107. Ogle's conjecture that the copy exhibited as Hunne's was Blythe's, exhibited by the clergy in bad faith, is bold and implausible (*Lollards' Tower*, pp. 118–27).

6. Blunt, *The Myroure of Oure Ladye*, p. 71; Green, *Pecock*, pp. 201–2; Ker, *Medieval Manuscripts*, iii, pp. 404–5; Luxton, 'Lichfield Court Book, p. 124.

7. Green, *Pecock*, pp. 193–7.

8. Hudson, *Premature Reformation*, pp. 267–8 and 437–40.

9. McFarlane, *Lancastrian Kings and Lollard Knights*, p. 209; Furnivall, *Fifty Earliest English Wills*; Heath, 'Urban Piety', p. 212.

10. Rex, 'Monumental Brasses'.

11. These statistics are derived from the list compiled by Bennett in *English Books and Readers*, pp. 239–76. Figures for other printers are based on the recent index volume to the revised *Short Title Catalogue*. For Continental patterns see Crofts, 'Books, Reform and the Reformation'; and Schutte, 'Printing, Piety, and the People in Italy'.

12. Summer, *Kalender of Shepherdes*, iii, p. 169. As we have seen, the English Bible was available, but only on a limited basis.

13. Birch, *Early Reformation English Polemics* explores the significance of this controversy for the development of English.

14. Wilkins, *Concilia*, iii, pp. 727–37, 776, and 804–7; Hughes and Larkin, pp. 181–6 and 193–7.

15. Hughes and Larkin, pp. 270–6; Redworth, 'Six Articles', p. 46; *LP* 13 ii 336.

16. More, *Dialogue*, pp. 331–44.

17. Starkey, *Dialogue between Pole and Lupset*, pp. x–xii and 90–1; Rex, *Theology of Fisher*, pp. 158–61.

18. Greatrex, 'Certayne Devoute and Religiouse Women', pp. 224–33.

19. Henry's letter to the Saxon dukes, in *Assertio Septem Sacramentorum*, sig. b2v.

20. Henry VIII, *A copy of the letters* (London, n.d.), sig. A8; Hughes and Larkin, p. 196.

21. Wilkins, *Concilia*, iii, p. 737.

22. Rex, *Theology of Fisher*, pp. 152–3; Foxe, *Acts and Moùments*, vii, pp. 449–50.

23. Rex, 'New Learning', forthcoming; *LP* 13. i. 1199 and 16. 101.

24. Gardiner, Letters, p. 66; Cranmer, *Works*, ii, pp. 344–6.

25. Frere and Kennedy, ii, p. 9. The authenticity of the provision relating to the English Bible has been impugned, but its

inclusion in the original printed copy of the injunctions (Cambridge University Library Sel. 3. 196, p. 1) is decisive.

26. Cranmer, *Works*, ii, pp. 344–6.

27. Thomas, *The Pilgrim*, p. 99; *LP* 13 ii 1063 and 14 i 245; Foxe, *Acts and Monuments*, v, p. 379–80. Becon seems not in fact to have obtained the Ipswich chantry (Bailey, *Becon*, pp. 13–14).

28. Hughes and Larkin, pp. 285–6. The Act for Uniformity in Religion of 1543 curtailed the right to read it privately.

29. Redworth, *Church Catholic*, pp. 160–4.

30. This paragraph follows Butterworth, *English Primers* and White, *Private Devotion*.

31. *The Primer, set foorth by the Kynges maiestie*, sig. ***i.

32. Redworth, *Church Catholic*, p. 185.

33. Lehmberg, *Later Parliaments*, pp. 165 and 184; Wriothesley, *Chronicle*, pp. 148 and 161; Cranmer, *Works*, ii, pp. 412 and 494–5.

## 5  DOCTRINAL DIVISION

1. Davies, 'Lollardy and Locality', gives a balanced and sympathetic account of later Lollardy which is largely but not entirely endorsed here. His own evidence for the strict geographical limitations of the later Lollard communities undermines his argument against their relative isolation.

2. Foxe, *Acts and Monuments*, iv, pp. 175 and 177; More, *Dialogue*, i, p. 191.

3. Hudson, *Premature Reformation*, is a thorough investigation of the intellectual history of Lollardy down to the Reformation, although its evidence does not support the conclusions its author draws about the vitality of Lollardy after 1430. As Davies concludes ('Lollardy and Locality', p. 212) 'If Wyclifitism was what you knew, Lollardy was whom you knew'.

4. Foxe, *Acts and Monuments*, iv. pp. 211–43; Plumb, 'Rural Lollardy' (the suggestions above are raised by the article rather than the author). Davies ('Lollardy and Locality', p. 208) judges that the attacks of Smith, Fitzjames, and Longland did serious damage to Buckinghamshire Lollardy.

5. Davis, 'Lollardy and the Reformation'; 'Joan of Kent'; and *Heresy and Reformation*. These valuable and informative pieces are flawed by the presupposition in the argument of what the argument should seek to prove. It is probable that many cases do reflect Lollard rather than Protestant influence. Unfortunately, unless specific evidence relating to the source of heretical doctrines survives, it is difficult to decide. Still more damaging to Davis's case is the fact that even if all cases which cannot be explicitly put down to Protestantism should

be put down to Lollardy, it remains difficult to identify any link between the two.

6. Brigden, *London*, p. 108.
7. Moeller, 'Luther in Europe', pp. 236 and 239–41.
8. Foxe, *Acts and Monuments*, v, pp. 415–16 and 421–7.
9. Rex, 'English Campaign', pp. 87–95.
10. Kreider, *English Chantries*, ch. 4, for the early attack on purgatory. Rex, *Theology of Fisher*, pp. 98–9.
11. Axton, *Three Rastell Plays*, pp. 9–10.
12. *LP* 5. 297; Latimer, *Works*, ii, pp. 225–39, especially 236–8; Brigden, *London*, p. 187.
13. Dickens, *Lollards and Protestants*, pp. 140–3.
14. For Stokesley see Elton, *Policy and Police*, p. 214; Brigden, *London*, p. 234; and *LP* 13 ii 695, item 2. For Matthew on purgatory, *Policy and Police*, p. 188, n. 1.
15. Ives, *Anne Boleyn*, p. 303. I differ in viewing Salcot – and later Skip – as conservative.
16. *LP* 10. 601.
17. *LP* 10. 357, 512–13, 588, and 723, and Chambers, *Faculty Office Register*, p. 59, for Cosyn, February to June 1536; *LP* 10. 277, Worthiall to Cromwell, 9 February 1536.
18. Latimer, *Works*, i, pp. 33–57; *LP* 10. 1147.
19. Wilkins, *Concilia*, iii, pp. 803 (diary of Convocation) and 804–7, 'Mala dogmata'.
20. *LP* 11. 1182, 'that the book of articles lately commanded by the advice of the Catholic bishops and doctors be taught'. Pole, *Epistolarum Collectio I*, pp. 481–2; Wiedermann, 'Alesius on the Psalms', pp. 18–19. The fullest attempt to demonstrate that the Ten Articles provoked conservative criticism is Kreider, *English Chantries*, p. 130. Of the four documents cited, *LP* 12 i 256 (2) does not mention them; *LP* 11. 954 is a vague comment about the 'untowardness' of some curates in declaring them; *LP* 11. 1110 is Henry VIII's proclamation against the Pilgrims, which orders the sincere declaration of the articles in an obvious response to the Pilgrims' wish to have them enforced; and *LP* 12 i 830 is a letter from Bishop Barlow testifying to popular discontent at his way of preaching the articles – which was probably not what the king meant by 'sincere'. *LP* 11. 1393 (2) shows a parson reading them and then inveighing against 'English books' – but he is probably using the articles against such books. In any case, the Pilgrims' endorsement of the articles is probably a better indication of their reception.
21. The Ten Articles are reprinted in Burnet's *History of the Reformation*, iv, pp. 272–85. For the rumour about the Duke, see *LP* 12 i 778.

22. This summary is based on Dodds and Dodds, *Pilgrimage of Grace*.

23. There is a considerable literature on the Pilgrimage. Dickens, 'Secular and Religious Motivation', minimises the importance of religion; James, 'Obedience and Dissent', though also too dismissive of religious motivation, explores the Lincolnshire rising in terms of prevailing ideologies and imageries of obedience and deference; Elton, 'Politics and the Pilgrimage', usefully connects the rising with the 'Aragonese' faction, but is too ready to minimise the role of popular religious sentiment; Davies, 'Pilgrimage Reconsidered' and 'Popular Religion', convincingly reaffirms the role of religion; Bush, 'Up for the Commonweal', emphasises the role of fiscal grievances in the risings, but together with rather than instead of religious grievances. Like any large popular movement, the Pilgrimage was a coalition of diverse interests. But by common consent, religion was not only the efficient cause of the rising, but also provided its rhetoric, its imagery, and most of its agenda.

24. James, 'Obedience and Dissent', pp. 260–9, brings out the importance of the ideology of obedience in restraining the leaders of the Pilgrimage from decisive action against the king

25. Kreider, *English Chantries*, pp. 130–3.

26. Cranmer, *Works*, ii, pp. 349–56; Gardiner, *Letters*, pp. 350–1.

27. *LP* 12 i 789, p. 346. No official doctrinal statement of Henry's reign ever cast doubt on the seven sacraments. To that extent, Henrician orthodoxy was always Catholic. The fact that the Ten Articles included only three sacraments under the heading of items 'necessary to salvation' means nothing. Not all things necessary to salvation were in fact treated under this heading, nor would most theologians have ventured to assert that any of the other four sacraments were necessary to salvation: though matrimony and ordination were held to be necessary for the growth of the Church, no individual was obliged to receive either for the sake of salvation. Lee's comment has been taken as indicative of wider public opinion, yet the Pilgrims of 1536 – predominantly from his own diocese – called for the enforcement of the articles (see above, p. 106, n. 20).

28. The Bishops' Book is most easily consulted in the original or in the facsimile reprint of 1976.

29. Foxe, *Acts and Monuments*, v, pp. 229–34; Leland, 'Antiphilarchia', pp. 336–9.

30. Hughes and Larkin, pp. 270–6.

31. *LP* 13 ii 498. The commissioners were the Reformers Cranmer, Barnes, and Crome; the definitely conservative Stokesley,

Sampson, and Gwent; and the probably conservative Heath, Skip, and Thirlby.

32.    Redworth, 'Six Articles', supersedes all previous accounts of this statute.

33.    Alesius, letter to Queen Elizabeth, 1 Sept 1559, PRO SP70/7, item 1, fol. 9v. Alesius himself promptly followed Cranmer's advice to flee the country.

34.    *LP* 14 i 585 and 967; Wriothesley, *Chronicle*, pp. 97–101, 104, and 106–7.

35.    Burnet, *History of the Reformation*, iv. pp. 443–96.

36.    Kreider, *English Chantries*, pp. 150–2. The 6 had all been among the 20 in 1540.

37.    The King's Book is most easily consulted either in the original or in Lacey's 1932 reprint.

38.    Refer to the bibliography under local studies for the books and articles on which this and the next two paragraphs are based. See Alsop, 'Religious Preambles', for an excessively harsh view of the unreliability of testamentary evidence.

39.    Foxe, *Acts and Monuments*, v, p. 464–97.

40.    *LP* 18 ii 546, pp. 334 and 345.

41.    Elton, *Policy and Police*, pp. 86–90.

42.    Foxe, *Acts and Monuments*, v, pp. 26, 254, 442, 505, and 532. His date of 1537 for Peke's burning is corrected to around 1515 by MacCulloch, *Suffolk under the Tudors*, p. 148, n. 62.

## CONCLUSION

1.    Dickens, *Reformation Studies*, p. 443.

2.    Redworth, 'Six Articles', pp. 46.

3.    Redworth, *Church Catholic*, pp. 176–200.

4.    This account is based on Dowling, 'Gospel and Court', pp. 60–7, but adopts a more cautious view of the Reformist sympathies of the princely tutors.

5.    Sawada, 'General Council', p. 213, citing *LP* 13 i 756.

6.    Lehmberg, *Later Parliaments*, pp. 90 and 231.

7.    Tunstall, *A letter . . . to Reginald Pole, sig. D4–5; Morison, An Invective ayenste . . . treason, sig. D5r.*

# BIBLIOGRAPHY

All the books, articles, and unpublished dissertations mentioned in the footnotes are included in this bibliography. Under 'General Accounts', 'Background', 'Local Studies', and 'Biographies' are included some works not specifically cited at any point but nevertheless indispensable for a general understanding of this period and subject.

### GENERAL ACCOUNTS

C. Cross, *Church and People 1450–1660* (London, 1976).
A. G. Dickens, *The English Reformation* (2nd edn, London, 1989).
A. G. Dickens, *Reformation Studies* (London, 1982).
G. R. Elton, *Reform and Reformation* (London, 1977).
P. Hughes, *The Reformation in England*, vol. I (London, 1954).
S. E. Lehmberg, *The Reformation Parliament 1529–1536* (Cambridge, 1970).
S. E. Lehmberg, *The Later Parliaments of Henry VIII 1536–1547* (Cambridge, 1977)
J. K. McConica, *English Humanists and Reformation Politics* (Oxford, 1965).
M. McKisack, *Medieval History in the Tudor Age* (Oxford, 1971).
F. M. Powicke, *The Reformation in England* (Oxford, 1941).
J. J. Scarisbrick, *The Reformation and the English People* (Oxford, 1984).

### DIVORCE

E. Surtz and V. Murphy (eds) *The Divorce Tracts of Henry VIII* (Angers, 1988).
G. Bedouelle and P. Le Gal (eds) *Le 'Divorce' du Roi Henry VIII* (Travaux d'Humanisme et Renaissance 231, Geneva, 1987).
H. A. Kelly, *The Matrimonial Trials of Henry VIII* (Stanford, 1976).

# Bibliography

## ROYAL SUPREMACY

G. W. Bernard, 'The Pardon of the Clergy Reconsidered', *Journal of Ecclesiastical History* 37 (1986), pp. 258–82.

G. R. Elton, *Policy and Police* (Cambridge, 1972).

A. Fox and J. A. Guy, *Reassessing the Henrician Age: Humanism, Politics and Reform 1500–1550* (Oxford, 1986).

J. A. Guy, 'Henry VIII and the Praemunire Manoeuvres of 1530–1531', *English Historical Review* 97 (1982), pp. 481–503.

S. W. Haas, 'Martin Luther's "Divine Right" Kingship and the Royal Supremacy: Two Tracts from the 1531 Parliament and Convocation of the Clergy', *Journal of Ecclesiastical History* 31 (1980), pp. 317–25.

M. J. Kelly, 'The Submission of the Clergy', *Transactions of the Royal Historical Society* 5th ser. 15 (1965), pp. 97–119.

S. E. Lehmberg, 'Parliamentary Attainder in the Reign of Henry VIII', *Historical Journal* 18 (1975), pp. 675–702.

C. Levin, 'A Good Prince: King John and Early Tudor Propaganda', *Sixteenth Century Journal* 11 (1980), pp. 23–32.

S. Lockwood, 'Marsilius of Padua and the Case for the Royal Ecclesiastical Supremacy', *Transactions of the Royal Historical Society* 6th ser., 1 (1991), pp. 89–119.

G. Nicholson, 'The Act of Appeals and the English Reformation', in C. Cross, D. Loades, and J. J. Scarisbrick (eds), *Law and Government under the Tudors* (Cambridge, 1988), pp. 19–30.

P. A. Sawada, 'Two Anonymous Tudor Treatises on the General Council', *Journal of Ecclesiastical History* 12 (1961), pp. 197–214.

J. J. Scarisbrick, 'The Pardon of the Clergy, 1531', *Historical Journal* 12 (1956), pp. 22–39.

W. Ullmann, 'This Realm of England is an Empire', *Journal of Ecclesiastical History* 30 (1979), pp. 175–203.

## BACKGROUND

E. Cameron, *The European Reformation* (Oxford, 1991).

E. Eisenstein, *The Printing Press as an Agent of Change*, 2 vols (Cambridge, 1979).

G. R. Elton, *The Tudor Revolution in Government* (Cambridge, 1953).

D. Fenlon, 'Encore Une Question: Lucien Febvre, the Reformation and the School of Annales', *Historical Studies* 9 (1974), pp. 65–81.

A. N. Galpern, *The Religions of the People in Sixteenth-Century Champagne* (Harvard, 1976).

J. A. Guy, *Tudor England* (Oxford, 1988).

R. M. Haines, *Ecclesia Anglicana: studies in the English Church of the later middle ages* (Toronto, 1989).

E. -M. Jung, 'On the Nature of Evangelism in Sixteenth Century Italy', *Journal of the History of Ideas* 14 (1953), pp. 511–27.

B. Moeller, 'Luther in Europe: his works in translation 1517–46', in E. I. Kouri and T. Scott (eds), *Politics and Society in Reformation Europe* (London, 1987).

R. N. Swanson, *Church and Society in Late Medieval England* (Oxford, 1989).

W. Ullmann, *A Short History of the Papacy in the Middle Ages* (London, 1972).

### THE CHURCH AND THE MONASTERIES

M. Bowker, *The Secular Clergy in the Diocese of Lincoln, 1495–1520* (Cambridge, 1968).

B. I. Bradshaw, *The Dissolution of the Religious Orders in Ireland under Henry VIII* (Cambridge, 1974).

S. Brigden, 'Tithe Controversy in Reformation London', *Journal of Ecclesiastical History* 32 (1981), pp. 285–301.

C. Cross, 'The religious life of women in sixteenth-century Yorkshire', in W. J. Sheils and D. Wood (eds), *Women in the Church, Studies in Church History* 27 (1990), pp. 307–24.

A. G. Dickens, 'The Shape of Anticlericalism and the English Reformation', in E. I. Kouri and T. Scott (eds), *Politics and Society in Reformation Europe* (London, 1987), pp. 379–410.

F. A. Gasquet, *Henry VIII and the Dissolution of the Monasteries*, 2 vols 4th edn. (London, 1889).

J. Greatrex, 'On Ministering to "Certayne Devoute and Religiouse Women": Bishop Fox and the Benedictine Nuns of Winchester Diocese on the Eve of the Reformation', in W. J. Sheils and D. Wood (eds), *Women in the Church, Studies in Church History*, 27 (1990), pp. 223–35.

C. Haigh, *The Last Days of the Lancashire Monasteries and the Pilgrimage of Grace*, Chetham Soc. 3rd ser., 17 (1969).

C. Haigh, 'Anticlericalism and the English Reformation', *History* 68 (1983), pp. 391–407.

C. Harper-Bill, 'Dean Colet's Convocation Sermon and the Pre-Reformation Church in England', *History* 73 (1988), pp. 191–210.

F. Heal, *Of Prelates and Princes: a study of the economic and social position of the Tudor episcopate* (Cambridge, 1980).

F. Heal, *Hospitality in Early Modern England* (Oxford, 1990).

P. Heath, *The English Parish Clergy on the Eve of the Reformation* (London, 1969).

R. Houlbrooke, *Church Courts and People during the English Reformation, 1520–1570* (Oxford, 1979).

D. Knowles, *The Religious Orders in England*, 3 vols (Cambridge, 1948–59).

S. E. Lehmberg, *The Reformation of Cathedrals* (Princeton, 1988).

F. D. Logan, 'The Henrician Canons', *Bulletin of the Institute of Historical Research* 47 (1974), pp. 99–103.

F. D. Logan, 'The First Royal Visitation of the English Universities', *English Historical Review* 106 (1991), pp. 861–88.

J. A. H. Moran, *The Growth of English Schooling 1340–1548* (Princeton 1985).

N. Orme, *English Schooling in the Middle Ages* (London, 1973).

J. J. Scarisbrick, 'Clerical Taxation in England, 1485–1547', *Journal of Ecclesiastical History* 11 (1960), pp. 41–54.

J. J. Scarisbrick, 'Henry VIII and the Dissolution of the Secular Colleges', in C. Cross, D. Loades, and J. J. Scarisbrick (eds), *Law and Government under the Tudors* (Cambridge, 1988), pp. 51–66.

G. W. O. Woodward, 'The Exemption from Suppression of Certain Yorkshire Priories', *English Historical Review* 76 (1961), pp. 385–401.

J. Youings, *The Dissolution of the Monasteries* (London, 1971).

M. L. Zell, 'The Personnel of the Clergy in Kent in the Reformation Period', *English Historical Review* 89 (1974), pp. 513–33.

POPULAR RELIGION

M. Aston, *England's Iconoclasts: laws against images* (Oxford, 1988).

C. Burgess, '"A fond thing vainly invented": an essay on purgatory and pious motive in later medieval England', in S. J. Wright (ed), *Parish, Church and People: local studies in lay religion 1350–1750* (London, 1988), pp. 56–84.

R. C. Finucane, *Miracles and Beliefs: popular beliefs in medieval England* (London, 1977).

R. Hutton, 'The Local Impact of the Tudor Reformations', in C. Haigh (ed), *The English Reformation Revised* (Cambridge, 1987), pp. 114–38.

F. R. Johnston, 'The English Cult of St Bridget of Sweden', *Analecta Bollandiana* 103 (1985), pp. 75–93.

R. W. Pfaff, *New Liturgical Feasts in Late Medieval England* (Oxford, 1970).

N. J. Rogers, 'The Cult of Prince Edward at Tewkesbury', *Transactions of the Bristol and Gloucester Archaeological Soc.* 101 (1983), pp. 187–9.

M. Rubin, *Corpus Christi: the eucharist in late medieval culture* (Cambridge, 1991).

R. Scribner, 'Ritual and Popular Religion in Catholic Germany at the Time of the Reformation', *Journal of Ecclesiastical History* 35 (1984), pp. 47–77.

R. Whiting, 'Abominable Idols: images and image-breaking under Henry VIII', *Journal of Ecclesiastical History* 33 (1982), pp. 30–47.

### VERNACULAR CULTURE

H. S. Bennett, *English Books and Readers 1475–1557* (Cambridge, 1952).

D. Birch, *Early Reformation English Polemics* (Salzburg, 1983).

C. C. Butterworth, *The English Primers (1529–1545): their publication and connection with the English Bible and the Reformation in England* (Philadelphia, 1953).

R. Crofts, 'Books, Reform and the Reformation', *Archiv für Reformationsgeschichte* 71 (1980), pp. 21–35.

M. Deanesley, *The Lollard Bible and Other Medieval Biblical Versions* (Cambridge, 1920).

M. D. Legge, *Anglo-Norman Literature and its Background* (Oxford, 1963).

R. A. W. Rex, 'New Learning', *Journal of Ecclesiastical History*, forthcoming, 1993.

R. A. W. Rex, 'Monumental Brasses and the Reformation', *Transactions of the Monumental Brass Society*, forthcoming

A. J. Schutte, 'Printing, Piety, and the People in Italy: the first thirty years', *Archiv für Reformationsgeschichte* 71 (1980), pp. 519.

H. C. White, *The Tudor Books of Private Devotion* (Wisconsin, 1951).


### OFFICIAL DOCTRINE

M. Dowling, 'The Gospel and the Court: Reformation under Henry VIII', in P. Lake and M. Dowling (eds), *Protestantism and the National Church in Sixteenth Century England* (London, 1987), pp. 36–77.

A. Kreider, *English Chantries: the road to dissolution* (Harvard, 1979).

G. Redworth, 'A Study in the Formulation of Policy: the genesis and evolution of the Act of Six Articles', *Journal of Ecclesiastical History* 37 (1986), pp. 42–67.

R. A. W. Rex, 'The English Campaign against Luther in the 1520s', *Transactions of the Royal Historical Society* 5th ser., 39 (1989), pp. 85–106.

G. Wiedermann, 'Alexander Alesius' Lectures on the Psalms at Cambridge, 1536', *Journal of Ecclesiastical History* 37 (1986), pp. 15–41.


### LOLLARDY

M. Aston, 'Lollardy and the Reformation: survival or revival?', *Journal of Ecclesiastical History* 49 (1964), pp. 149–70.

R. G. Davies, 'Lollardy and Locality', *Transactions of the Royal Historical Society* 6th ser., 1 (1991), pp. 191–212.

J. F. Davis, 'Lollardy and the Reformation in England', *Archiv für Reformationsgeschichte* 73 (1982), pp. 217–36.

J. F. Davis, 'Joan of Kent, Lollardy and the English Reformation', *Journal of Ecclesiastical History* 33 (1982), pp. 225–33.

J. Fines, 'Heresy Trials in the Diocese of Coventry and Lichfield, 1511–12', *Journal of Ecclesiastical History* 14 (1963), pp. 160–74.

A. Hope, 'Lollardy: the stone the builders rejected?', in P. Lake and M. Dowling (eds), *Protestantism and the National Church in Sixteenth Century England* (London, 1987), pp. 135.

A. Hudson, *The Premature Reformation: Wycliffite texts and Lollard history* (Oxford, 1988).

I. Luxton, 'The Lichfield Court Book: a postscript', *Bulletin of the Institute of Historical Research* 44 (1971), pp. 120–5.

K. B. McFarlane, *Lancastrian Kings and Lollard Knights* (Oxford, 1972).

A. Ogle, *The Tragedy of the Lollards' Tower* (Oxford, 1949).

D. Plumb, 'The Social and Economic Spread of Rural Lollardy: a reappraisal', *Studies in Church History* 23 (1986), pp. 111–30.

J. A. F. Thomson, *The Later Lollards, 1414–1520* (Oxford, 1965).

## PILGRIMAGE OF GRACE

M. L. Bush, '"Up the Commonweal": the Significance of Tax Grievances in the English Rebellions of 1536', *English Historical Review*, 106 (1991), pp. 299–318.

C. S. L. Davies, 'The Pilgrimage of Grace Reconsidered', *Past and Present* 41 (1968), pp. 54–76.

C. S. L. Davies, 'Popular Religion and the Pilgrimage of Grace', in A. Fletcher and J. Stevenson (eds), *Order and Disorder in Early Modern England* (Cambridge, 1985), pp. 58–91.

A. G. Dickens, 'Secular and Religious Motivation in the Pilgrimage of Grace', in his *Reformation Studies*, pp. 57–82.

M. H. Dodds and R. Dodds, *The Pilgrimage of Grace, 1536–1537, and the Exeter Conspiracy, 1538*, 2 vols (Cambridge, 1915).

G. R. Elton, 'Politics and the Pilgrimage of Grace', in B. Malament (ed), *After the Reformation* (University of Pennsylvania Press, 1980), pp. 25–56.

M. E. James, 'Obedience and Dissent in Henrician England: the Lincolnshire Rebellion, 1536', in his *Society, Politics and Culture: studies in early modern England* (Cambridge, 1986), pp. 188–269.

## LOCAL STUDIES

J. D. Alsop, 'Religious Preambles in Early Modern English Wills as Formulae', *Journal of Ecclesiastical History* 40 (1989), pp. 19–27.

M. Bowker, *The Henrician Reformation: the diocese of Lincoln under John Longland, 1521–1547* (Cambridge, 1981).

S. Brigden, *London and the Reformation* (Oxford, 1990).

C. Burgess, '"By Quick and by Dead": wills and pious provision in late medieval Bristol', *English Historical Review* 102 (1987), pp. 837–58.

P. Clark, *English Provincial Society from the Reformation to the Revolution: Religion, Politics and Society in Kent 1500–1640* (Hassocks, 1977).

C. Cross, 'The Development of Protestantism in Leeds and Hull, 1520–1640: the evidence from wills', *Northern History* 18 (1982), pp. 230–8.

J. F. Davis, *Heresy and Reformation in the South-East of England, 1520–1559*, Royal Historical Soc. Studies in History 34 (London, 1983).

A. G. Dickens, *Lollards and Protestants in the Diocese of York 1509–1558* (Oxford, 1959).

A. G. Dickens, 'The Early Expansion of Protestantism in England 1520–1558', *Archiv für Reformationsgeschichte* 78 (1987), pp. 187–221.

C. Haigh, *Reformation and Resistance in Tudor Lancashire* (Cambridge, 1975).

P. Heath, 'Urban Piety in the Later Middle Ages', in B. Dobson (ed), *Politics and Patronage in the Fifteenth Century* (Gloucester, 1984), pp. 209–34.

D. Jones, *The Church in Chester 1300–1540*, Chetham Soc. 3rd ser., 7 (1957).

M. J. Kitch, 'The Reformation in Sussex', in M. J. Kitch (ed), *Studies in Sussex Church History* (London, 1981), pp. 77–98.

D. MacCulloch, *Suffolk and the Tudors* (Oxford, 1986).

G. Mayhew, 'The Progress of the Reformation in East Sussex 1530–1559: the evidence from wills', *Southern History* 5 (1983), pp. 38–67.

J. E. Oxley, *The Reformation in Essex* (Manchester, 1965).

D. Palliser, *Tudor York* (Oxford, 1979).

H. C. Porter, *Reformation and Reaction in Tudor Cambridge* (Cambridge, 1958).

E. M. Sheppard, 'The Reformation and the Citizens of Norwich', *Norfolk Archaeology* 38 (1983), pp. 44–58.

N. P. Tanner, *The Church in Late Medieval Norwich 1370–1532* (Toronto, 1984).

J. C. Ward, 'The Reformation in Colchester, 1528–1558', *Essex Archaeology and History* 15 (1983), pp. 84–95.

R. Whiting, *The Blind Devotion of the People: Popular Religion and the English Reformation* (Cambridge, 1989).

G. Williams, *Recovery, Reorientation and Reformation: Wales, c. 1415–1642* (Oxford, 1987).

## BIOGRAPHIES AND STUDIES OF INDIVIDUALS

D. S. Bailey, *Thomas Becon and the Reformation of the Church in England*

(Edinbugh, 1952).

B. Bradshaw and E. Duffy (eds), *Humanism, Reform and the Reformation* (Cambridge, 1989).

D. S. Chambers, *Cardinal Bainbridge in the Court of Rome 1509 to 1514* (Oxford, 1965)

L. P. Fairfield, *John Bale: Mythmaker for the English Reformation* (West Lafayette, 1976).

D. Fenlon, *Heresy and Obedience in Tridentine Italy: Cardinal Pole and the Counter Reformation* (Cambridge, 1972).

A. Fox, *Thomas More: history and providence* (Oxford, 1982)

A. Fraser, *Mary Queen of Scots* (London, 1969).

J. Gleason, *John Colet* (Berkeley and Los Angeles, 1989).

V. H. H. Green, *Bishop Reginald Pecock: a study in ecclesiastical history and thought* (Cambridge, 1945).

S. J. Gunn, *Charles Brandon, Duke of Suffolk, c. 1484–1545* (Oxford, 1988).

S. J. Gunn and P. G. Lindley (eds), *Cardinal Wolsey: church, state and art* (Cambridge, 1991).

P. Gwyn, *The King's Cardinal: the rise and fall of Thomas Wolsey* (London, 1990).

D. Hay, *Polydore Vergil* (Oxford, 1952).

E. W. Ives, *Anne Boleyn* (Oxford, 1986).

E. W. Ives, 'The Fall of Wolsey', in Gunn and Lindley (eds), *Cardinal Wolsey*, pp. 286–315.

M. K. Jones and M. G. Underwood, *The King's Mother: Lady Margaret Beaufort, Countess of Richmond and Derby* (Cambridge, 1992).

T. F. Mayer, *Thomas Starkey and the Commonweal* (Cambridge, 1989).

A. Neame, *The Holy Maid of Kent: the life of Elizabeth Barton, 1506–1534* (London, 1971).

A. F. Pollard, *Wolsey* (London, 1929; but best in the 1965 reprint by Fontana Books, with G. R. Elton's introduction).

G. Redworth, *In Defence of the Church Catholic: the life of Stephen Gardiner* (Oxford, 1990).

R. A. W. Rex, *The Theology of John Fisher* (Cambridge, 1991).

J. J. Scarisbrick, *Henry VIII* (London, 1968).

C. Sturge, *Cuthbert Tunstal* (London, 1938).


UNPUBLISHED DISSERTATIONS

F. J. Heal, 'The bishops of Ely and their diocese during the Reformation period: ca. 1510–1600' (Cambridge, Ph.D., 1971).

S. J. Lander, 'The diocese of Chichester, 1508–58' (Cambridge, Ph.D., 1974).

P. Marshall, 'Attitudes of the English people to Priests and Priesthood, 1500–1553' (Oxford, D. Phil., 1990).

## DOCUMENTS

A. Alesius, letter to Queen Elizabeth, Public Record Office SP70/7, fols. 1r–10r.

R. Axton (ed), *Three Rastell Plays* (Cambridge, 1979).

J. Bale, *Scriptorum Illustrium Maioris Brytanniae Catalogus*, 2 vols (Basel, 1557).

W. Barlow, *A proper dialogue between a gentelman and a husbandman* (no place or date).

Bishops' Book. *The Institution of a Christen Man* (London, 1537; or facsimile reprint Amsterdam, 1976).

J. H. Blunt (ed), *The Myroure of Oure Ladye*, Early English Text Soc., extra series 19 (1873).

S. Bond (ed), *The Chapter Acts of the Dean and Canons of Windsor, 1430, 1523–1672* (Windsor, 1966).

H. Bradshaw, *The holy lyfe and history of Saynt Werburge*, ed. E. Hawkins, Chetham Soc., 15 (1848).

G. Burnet, *The History of the Reformation of the Church of England*, ed. N. Pocock, 7 vols (Oxford, 1865).

*Calendar of Papal Registers*, vol. 18 (Dublin, 1989).

D. S. Chambers (ed), *Faculty Office Registers 1534–1549* (Oxford, 1966).

W. Chillingworth, *The Religion of Protestants* (London, 1638).

C. S. Cobb (ed), *The Rationale of Ceremonial 1540–1543*, Alcuin Club Collections 15 (London, 1910).

T. Cranmer, *Works*, ed. J. E. Cox. Parker Society. 2 vols (Cambridge, 1844–6).

'Documenta de S. Wenefreda', *Analecta Bollandiana* 6 (1887), pp. 305–52.

T. Elyot, *The Dictionary* (London, 1538).

J. Foxe, *Acts and Monuments*, ed. G. Townsend. 8 vols (London, 1843–9).

W. H. Frere and W. M. Kennedy (eds), *Visitation Articles and Injunctions of the Period of the Reformation*, Volume II: 1536–1559, Alcuin Club Collections 15 (London, 1910).

F. J. Furnivall (ed), *The Fifty Earliest English Wills in the Court of Probate*, London, Early English Text Soc. 78 (1872).

S. Gardiner, *The Letters of Stephen Gardiner*, ed. J. A. Muller (Cambridge, 1933).

Henry VIII, *Assertio Septem Sacramentorum* (London, 1523) STC 13083.

Henry VIII, *A copy of the letters / wherin . . . Henry the eight . . . made answere unto a certayne letter of Martyn Luther* (London, no date).

[Henry VIII]. *The King's Book, or, A Necessary Doctrine and Erudition for any Christian Man*, ed. T. A. Lacey (London, 1932).

[Henry VIII]. *The Primer, set foorth by the Kynges maiestie* (London, 1545).

P. L. Hughes and J. F. Larkin (eds), *Tudor Royal Proclamations*, vol. 1 (Yale, 1964).

A. Hussey (ed), *Testamenta Cantiana II* (London, 1907).

P. Janelle (ed), *Obedience in Church and State* (Cambridge, 1930).

N. R. Ker, *Medieval Manuscripts in British Libraries*, 3 vols (Oxford, 1969–83).

W. Lambarde, *Perambulation of Kent* (London, 1576).

A. F. Leach (ed), *Visitations and Memorials of Southwell Minster*, Camden Society new ser. 48 (1891).

J. Leland, 'Antiphilarchia', Cambridge University Library MS Ee. 5. 14.

*Letters and Papers, Foreign and Domestic, of the Reign of Henry VIII*, ed. J. S. Brewer, J. Gairdner, and R. H. Brodie (London, 1862–1932).

H. Latimer, *Works*, ed. G. E. Corrie. Parker Society. 2 vols (Cambridge, 1845).

T. More, *Utopia*, ed. E. Surtz and J. H. Hexter, The Complete Works of St Thomas More 4 (Yale, 1965).

T. More, *A Dialogue Concerning Heresies*, ed. T. M. C. Lawler, G. Marc'hadour, and R. C. Marius, The Complete Works of St Thomas More 6 (Yale, 1981).

R. Morison, *A Lamentation in whiche is shewed what ruyne and destruction cometh of seditious rebellyon* (London, 1536).

R. Morison, *An Invective ayenste the great and detestable vice, treason* (London, 1539)

T. R. Nash, *Collections for the History of Worcestershire*, 2 vols (London, 1781–2).

T. Paynell (tr.), *The Conspiracy of Lucius Catiline* (London, 1541).

R. Pole, *Epistolarum Reginaldi Poli*, 5 vols (Brixiae, 1744–57; facsimile edn. Farnborough, 1967).

M. Sanuto, *I Diarii di Marino Sanuto*, ed. F. Stefani, G. Berchet and N. Barrozzi. 58 vols (Venice, 1879–1903).

E. Sarcerius, *Loci Aliquot Communes et Theologici* (Frankfurt no date).

*A Short-Title Catalogue of Books Printed in England, Scotland, and Ireland, and of English Books Printed Abroad 1475–1640*, ed. A. W. Pollard and G. R. Redgrave, 2nd edn. ed. W. A. Jackson, F. S. Ferguson, and K. F. Pantzer. 3 vols (London, 1976–91).

F. Somers and M. O'Brien (eds), *Halesowen Churchwardens' Accounts (1487–1582)*, Worcestershire Hist. Soc. (1957).

T. Starkey, *A Dialogue between Pole and Lupset*, ed. T. F. Mayer, Camden Soc. 4th ser. 37 (1989).

J. Strype, *Ecclesiastical Memorials*, 3 vols (Oxford, 1822).

H. O. Summer (ed), *The Kalender of Shepherdes*, 3 vols (London, 1892).

*Testamenta Cantiana II: East Kent,* ed. A. Hussey (London, 1907).

W. Thomas, *The Pilgrim: a dialogue on the life and actions of King Henry the Eighth,* ed. J. A. Froude (London, 1861).

C. Tunstall, *A Sermon of Cuthbert Bysshop of Duresme, made upon Palme Sondaye laste past* (London, 1539).

C. Tunstall and J. Stokesley, *A Letter to . . . Reginald Pole* (London, 1560).

*Valor Ecclesiasticus,* ed. J. Caley and J. Hunter. 6 vols (London, 1810–34).

F. van Ortroy (ed), 'Vie du Bienheureux Martyr Jean Fisher', *Analecta Bollandiana* 10 (1891), pp. 121–365, and 12 (1893), pp. 97–287.

J. Weever, *Ancient Funerall Monuments* (London, 1631).

D. Wilkins, *Concilia Magnae Britanniae et Hiberniae,* 4 vols (London, 1737).

C. Wriothesley, *A Chronicle of England during the Reigns of the Tudors,* ed. W. D. Hamilton, vol. 1, Camden Society (1875).

# INDEX

201